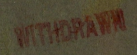

The Shaping of FRANCE

HISTORIES BY ISAAC ASIMOV

The Shaping of
FRANCE

BY ISAAC ASIMOV

HOUGHTON MIFFLIN COMPANY BOSTON
1972

To Ruth and Stan,
who have helped

CONTENTS

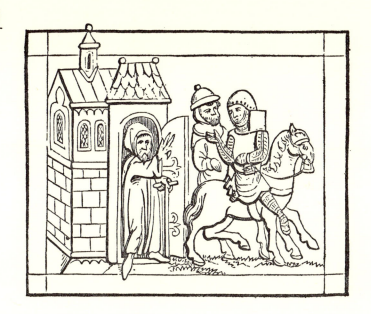

THE NEW LINE

THE LAST CAROLINGIAN

In the month of May of the year 987, a young man fell from his horse during an exhilarating hunt in what is now north-eastern France. He injured himself severely and bled from nose and throat. On the 21st of May, he died.

The young man had very little importance in himself. His name was Louis and he was a king, but that was about all one could say about him. He was twenty years old, he had been reigning only a year, and his only real concern was to enjoy himself. He goes down in history as Louis V, the Do-Nothing.

In one respect, though, there was a melancholy significance to his death. He was the great-great-great-great-great-grand-son of Charlemagne, the most powerful monarch of the Middle Ages. That made him a "Carolingian," and Louis the Do-Nothing was the last Carolingian ever to be called king.

Charlemagne had, in 800, ruled firmly over a Frankish Empire, vast for its time, an Empire that stretched over the nations we now call France, the Netherlands, Belgium, Switzerland, Austria, West Germany and the northern half of Italy.* After he died, in 814, the Empire fell apart.

The decay was partly because of squabbling among his descendants, partly because of destructive raids by Norse pirates (the Vikings) on all its coasts, and partly out of the sheer difficulty of holding together so large a domain under the primitive conditions of transportation and communication of those days. Charlemagne's ability, force and personality could do it, just barely, but none of his descendants was more than a shadow of himself. They could not manage.

By 911, the eastern half of the Empire saw its last Carolingian ruler die. Rulers of other families succeeded. The region was no longer Frankish in the old sense and could be more accurately described in modern terms as Germany, though it still thought of itself as an Empire, and of its rulers as successors to Charlemagne, even if not his descendants.

The western half of Charlemagne's realm retained rulers of the Carolingian line for three quarters of a century more. It was still Frankish in that sense and could be referred to in Latinized fashion as "Francia." A form of the name remains to this day, for from that western half of Charlemagne's Empire there descended the modern nation of France.

But the whole Empire, whether the king was Carolingian or not, was in fragments. Under the terrible onslaught of the Vikings it was a case of every man for himself. The people huddled together for defense under any strong local leader who was willing to fight and paid little heed to the distant king, who was, in any case, helpless. The king lacked a central army and there was no way in which he could travel rapidly from end to end of the great areas that were theoretically under his control.

* The story of Charlemagne, his predecessors and his successors, is told in my book *The Dark Ages* (Houghton Mifflin, 1968).

Certainly one of the reasons why Louis V was a "Do-Nothing" was that there was nothing much he could do. By the time the last Carolingian died, the name of king was just about worthless in his realm. The king had social prestige and people bowed low before him and addressed him in high-flown terms, but he had no power, and every nobleman was a law to himself.

The prosperity of the realm had shrunk as the king's power had. Trade and commerce had dwindled to almost nothing and every estate had to support itself in bare and tattered fashion. Towns had sunk to villages, the population was far below what it had been in Roman times, and only a few priests could still make out their letters well enough to read the few religious books that remained.

Yet a turning point had been reached. The ingenuity of man had not died. A new kind of plow had been invented which was particularly well adapted to the heavy, damp soil of northern Europe. Horse-collars and horseshoes came into use and made it easier for the horse to be a drudge. The collar eased the pull of harness on his throat and made it possible for the horse to tug with five times the force that earlier harnesses had allowed. The iron shoes nailed to his hoofs protected them and made him less vulnerable to injury. When horses replaced the slow, dull oxen as the prime work-animal on the farms, the food supply began to increase. This, in combination with the new plow, made the regions bordering on the English Channel a major agricultural area for the first time.

With the food supply beginning to increase, the population of the area began to increase slowly for the first time since the Roman Empire had fallen. Men still died like flies from disease, but death from famine, though by no means wiped out, began to decrease.

The water mill also started to come into widespread use. This was a system whereby the current of a rapidly moving stream turned a wheel that caused a heavy millstone to turn. This could be used to grind grain or power such simple devices as saws and hammers. Flour and lumber became more readily available.

The water mill was an invention of Roman times, actually, but it was only now, as the Carolingian line faded out, that it was coming into its own. Where there had been dozens in Roman times, hundreds were springing up — and soon, thousands.

The brawling streams of northern Europe were better suited to the purpose than the quiet, shallow rivulets of the Mediterranean area. Besides that, the general shortage of labor (worse in the primitive France of the Dark Ages than in the comfortable Roman Empire of eight centuries before) placed greater pressure on the search for a nonliving source of power.

The water mill was the first important "prime mover" (any device to turn natural energy into useful work) other than living muscle, either human or animal. Those servicing and constructing mills ("millwrights") were the first modern mechanics. The water mill was, in fact, to remain unsurpassed as a prime mover for eight more centuries — till the coming of the steam engine.

Yet this turning point, this gradual lifting of darkness, while clear to us, a thousand years later, as we look back on it, could not possibly have been visible to the people of the time. They could not have guessed that the bottom had been safely passed, that material progress would now slowly, slowly, raise the land again, after the long decline — up into improving economy, gathering wealth, increasing population, intensifying learning and culture.

Quite the contrary! In 987, the people looked forward to the future with pessimism. The very year itself seemed threatening.

In the mystic Biblical Book of Revelation, the 20th chapter speaks of a period of a thousand years after which there would be a final reckoning with the forces of evil, a final judgment, and the end of the old Earth. There were some who believed that the thousand years must surely be counted from the birth of Jesus and, in that case, would not the year 1000 mark the end of the world? And was that not a bare thirteen years into the future?

It was possible to argue that all the calamities that had fallen upon the land since the fall of the Roman Empire were part of the long slide toward that end. And now, within reach of the mystic year 1000, came the end of the line of Charlemagne, the only ruler under whom it looked — for just a moment — as though the glories of Rome might somehow revive. Surely that was the last sign.

We don't know how many people thoroughly believed in the doom of 1000; perhaps only a few mystics. But surely even those who did not really believe must have been uneasy and downhearted.

But whatever the gloom and depression, life (even if only for the moment) had to go on. *Someone* had to be king, and it would fall to the great nobles, the lords of the realm, to choose that someone.

To be sure, Carolingians still existed. The dead Louis V had an uncle, Charles of Lorraine. That uncle, however, acknowledged the German monarch as overlord of his own land of Lorraine. The French lords would not dream of having as king the underling of some foreigner and besides Charles was unpopular for other reasons. The lords would have none of him.

But if not Charles, then who? The German lords had set the precedent of selecting one of themselves to be ruler when their last Carolingian had died, and it seemed as though the French lords would now have no choice but to follow suit.

THE FIRST CAPETIAN

The most forceful of the lords of northern France was Hugh Capet (kuh-pay'). Capet is not a family name but a nickname derived from a particular cape he was accustomed to wear when fulfilling certain functions as an abbot. The nickname gained all the force of a family name, however, and Hugh and his descendants are generally known as "Capetians."

The lands of Hugh Capet centered about Paris, the most important city in France even then, and extended eight miles northeast to Laon (lahn) and eighty miles southwest to Orléans (awr-lay-ahn'). He also owned scraps of land here and there outside the main body of his dominions. It was not a compact realm but it included areas that were, by the standards of the time, populous and rich.

He was powerful enough to have seized the throne by force from either of the last couple of Carolingians, and so had his father been before him. In fact, his grandfather Robert had actually made the attempt and had ruled as King Robert I for a year or so, more than half a century before. That rule had been an unhappy one, however, and had been spent entirely in trying, and failing, to get himself accepted by the other lords.

Hugh and his father thought it better to be the power behind the throne. There was less status to such a position and it might be annoying to see some incapable Carolingian wear the crown and robes and have the title, but it was also quieter.

Nor did it mean the permanent giving over of ambition. The time might come when conditions would make kingship possible for some non-Carolingian and when that happened Hugh and his father meant to be ready.

Hugh's father died before the moment arrived, but Hugh Capet continued to wait and to plan. His cleverest move was to ally himself with Adalbero, the Archbishop of Reims and the highest prelate in France. Together, the greatest lord and the greatest bishop of the realm worked quietly to bind together a party favorable to themselves, and waited. When Louis the Do-Nothing died, without sons and with only an unpopular uncle to carry on the name, the chance came.

When the Carolingian, Charles of Lorraine, claimed the

throne to be his by right as descendant of the great Charlemagne, Adalbero shook his head firmly. It was Adalbero who, as Archbishop of Reims, had the task of crowning the king. If he refused to do so, Charles of Lorraine could not become king — at least, not unless and until he disposed of a force large enough and fearless enough to impose his will on the Church.

Charles was willing to try but it took time, and while the Carolingian was scrabbling about for ways and means to seize the throne, Adalbero declared that the lords of France had the right to choose whom they wished for king, Carolingian or not, and then moved heaven and earth to persuade them to choose Hugh Capet. In this, he was greatly helped by his secretary, Gerbert (zher-behr′), who prepared the necessary learned arguments to show that a king might be elected and that Hugh should be the man.

Hugh was indeed the man. The lords gathered in midsummer of 987 and prepared to deliberate. It didn't take long. Thanks to Hugh's careful political preparations and to the sheer lack of any alternative candidate on whom they could agree, he was elected unanimously.

Hugh was somewhat better off materially than the Carolingians that had preceded him had been. The Carolingians had ruled directly over little or no land, but had merely held the title of king, together with the social prestige of being considered of higher rank than other noblemen. This meant they had no income and no soldiers except what was granted them by some lord who did have land and income and who chose to be on the king's side for his own purposes.

Hugh Capet, on the other hand, had considerable land of his own and could therefore lay his hands on soldiers and money without going to anyone else. He was not, however, the only landowner in northern France. West of his own royal domain centered about Paris, there was the County of Blois (blwah), for instance, and to its northwest the Duchy of Normandy.

South of Normandy were the County of Maine and the County of Anjou (ahn-zhoo′) while to its west was the County of Brittany. Eastward were the County of Champagne and the Duchy of Burgundy. To the southwest was the County of Poitou (pwah-too′) and so on.*

These counties and duchies were an important stumbling block to Hugh. The disintegration of the realm since Charlemagne's time had resulted in a patchwork system, arranged in pyramid form, which governed the economy, law and politics of France. By it the king's realm was divided among the rule of several great "vassals" (from an old Celtic word meaning "servant"), who owed the king allegiance as their "liege." Each vassal's land was divided among smaller vassals, who each divided his among still smaller vassals, until the bottom of the pyramid — the landless peasants — was reached.

In theory, every vassal had a single liege to whom he owed certain clearly specified duties and from whom he received certain specified privileges. If this "feudal" system (from an old Teutonic word meaning "property," since it was based on land ownership) had fit the theory, it might have worked well, but it didn't.

The duties a vassal owed his liege were usually paid only when superior force was clearly on the side of the liege —

---

* In this book, I will give the pronunciation of proper names in French, when they are not familiar in English. The English spelling of such names is often different from the French. For instance, Brittany is Bretagne in French, and Burgundy is Bourgogne. It would be folly, though, to insist on using the French form to English-speaking readers when the English form is so familiar. Again, some words that are spelled the same in English and French are familiar in English pronunciation and I will not try to force French pronunciation on the reader in that case. Thus, Paris is pronounced puh-ree by Frenchmen and Charles is pronounced Shahrl, but to us it might just as well stay pa′ris and chahrlz. Sometimes there are uncertain cases such as Orleans, which in French is awr-lay-ahn, with an accent, and in English is awr-lee′unz or awr-leenz, without an accent. In such cases, I will have to use my own judgment.

ENGLAND

London

Hastings

ENGLISH CHANNEL

FLANDERS

EMPIRE

Rouen   Laon

Bayeux   Reims

Les Andelys

NORMANDY   Paris   CHAMPAGNE

BRITTANY

MAINE   Troyes   Clairvaux

BLOIS

ANJOU   Dijon

BURGUNDY

POITOU   Cluny

AQUITAINE

ANGOULÉME

GASCONY

TOULOUSE

SPAIN

MAP I

France in Time of Hugh Capet ─ 1000

which it sometimes wasn't. Owing to the accidents of birth and war, a vassal might own more land and have more power than his liege; he might have several lieges over the various portions of his territory.

The counts and dukes fought endlessly among themselves in consequence and with their vassals; and if they ever united, it was only in stubborn resistance to the king.

To be sure, the lords had voted Hugh into the kingship, but that was all, as far as they were concerned. They were not particularly interested in letting him have more than the title. They went their own way, behaving, in practice, as independent sovereigns. Hugh had to hang on to his kingship, therefore, once he had gained it, without much help.

For instance, there was still Charles of Lorraine to contend with. Charles had by no means accepted the decision of Adalbero and the assembled lords. He was a Carolingian and he meant to be king. He gathered an army and managed to seize the important cities of Laon and Reims, on the very borders of Hugh's territories. The people tended to rally about Charles for the sake of his ancestry and Hugh was in a ticklish position.

According to feudal theory, Hugh might have called on his vassals to rally around him against Charles, but they all had other interests. Hugh therefore worked through the clergy. He persuaded the Archbishop of Laon to organize a conspiracy against Charles. The Carolingian was seized in his bed and handed over to Hugh. Without a leader, Charles' forces promptly faded away.

Hugh put him in prison, and since in those days prisoners did not usually live long (particularly if their lives were inconvenient to their jailers), Charles was dead by 992.

Again, according to feudal theory, Hugh had the right to judge disputes between his vassals and to prevent warfare in that way. In actual fact, the powerful lords of France scorned to seek Hugh's judgment and preferred to settle the matter by trial of force. Sometimes, in striving to keep his powerful vassals in line, Hugh found no other way than to choose the side of one against the other.

Thus, Blois and Anjou were constantly fighting, with each of them equally wrong and equally hostile to Hugh. Nevertheless, it was Blois who directly adjoined Hugh's own territory. It was Blois therefore that was the more immediate danger and Hugh fought on the side of Anjou.

Occasionally, Hugh was exasperated at having to fight his own vassals when these were, in theory, subject to him. There is a tale that, at one point, he cried out to the Count of Angoulême (ahn-zhoo-lem'), a territory in southwestern France that was opposing him on the battlefield, "Who made thee Count?"

By feudal theory, of course, the vassals owed their titles to the king, for it was a king that had (in theory) conferred it upon them. That was not how the Count of Angoulême looked at it at all, however. Haughtily, he replied, "The same right that made thee King."

And, of course, that was Hugh's weak point. He had been elected; he had not inherited his rule. It was not he who had made counts after all, but all the counts together who had elected him king.

For himself that could not be helped, but he was bound to worry about the succession and he began to do so as soon as he became king.

Would his son become king in his place? Or would there be another election? Family pride made him want the royal title to continue in his family and for himself to become the founder of a new line of kings. Concern for the nation would have made him wish the same. If an election followed the death of every king, there would be nothing but civil wars filling the annals of the land.

His solution was to go through the motions of crowning his son Robert as king while Hugh himself was still alive. Within half a year of his own accession, Hugh had Robert crowned by the Archbishop of Reims and consecrated in full religious ceremony in the presence of the lords of the realm who, perforce, swore allegiance in the most solemn fashion.

That made Robert king along with his father, though in a subordinate role, of course. Then, when Hugh's time came to die, France would already have a king, completely crowned and consecrated, and the lords could do nothing about it for they had already sworn allegiance. Nor could they argue its legality for there was ample precedent for this sort of thing in past history. Charlemagne himself had had his son crowned in his own lifetime.

The Capetians continued this practice of crowning the son in the father's lifetime for two centuries. In Hugh Capet's time, few people may have thought it at all likely that the new line would long continue, but this practice, combined with the fortunate fact that each king happened to have a son who could be crowned and who then survived his father, kept the line going.

Other factors that helped the Capetians was that each king in the line carried on a smooth and not too ostentatious struggle to increase his own holdings and make his position stronger in that way. Then, too, they were all careful to follow Hugh Capet's policy of working hand-in-glove with the clergy. They continued to encourage a profoundly religious flavor to the coronation and deferred to the great archbishops. In return, the clergy exerted their always powerful effect on public opinion. Even a hostile lord, careless of the Church and of churchmen, had to be careful how he attacked someone on whose side God was proclaimed to be. If they themselves were impervious to such things, their soldiers might not be.

And so it came about that Hugh Capet, whose own hold on the throne throughout his life was as fragile as a spiderweb, gave rise to a long and renowned line of kings. For eight centuries, from 987 to 1792, France was ruled without a break by this line, which included thirty-two kings altogether. Three more Capetians reigned from 1815 to 1848. And under those

Capetians, France experienced periods when she was the military and, even more important, the cultural leader of Europe.

CROWN AND CLERGY

Hugh Capet died in 996 and his son became king as Robert II. He was a gentle ruler and a well-educated one, having been placed as a youth under the charge of the scholar Gerbert, who had been so useful to Hugh in his drive to the throne.

Robert was pious, too, and, indeed, goes down in history as "Robert the Pious." He enjoyed, as one of his pleasures, the composing and singing of hymns, and even donated a hymn of his own composition to a monastery during a pilgrimage to Rome. (The story is that he left it in a sealed packet, and the monks, who had expected a generous donation of money, were very humanly disappointed to find nothing inside but the praise of God.)

Robert's piety led him to support reform within the Church.

There is, apparently, a sort of rhythm in the history of monasticism. Monasteries would be founded according to strict and virtuous rules, but as the generations passed conditions would grow relaxed and abuses would creep in. There would then be a reforming movement in which new rules would be set up and another period of rigid virtue would be initiated — which would, in turn, gradually relax and require new reforms.

In the dark days of the ninth century, when Viking raids had reduced France to chaos, the monasteries, too, were laden with decay and corruption. In 911, however, at Cluny (a town in the Duchy of Burgundy some 200 miles southeast of Paris) a reform-monastery was established. Under a series of able abbots, it flourished and its reputation spread. In the time of Robert II, the third abbot, Odilo, was in charge and, under his leadership and with Robert's help, other monasteries following the same rules were established. These "Cluniac" monasteries spread throughout France and Germany and gave new life to the monastic movement.

Robert and the Church combined forces in supporting another reform, too, one that was passionately desired by both.

Improving economic conditions were making it possible for lords to support more men and horses than they needed for actual food production. They could also afford more and better armor. In that time of cultural dearth, when few men outside of the Church could read and write, there was little a lord could do to amuse himself but hunt — animals if he had to, but men if he could. With more men, horses and armor at his disposal, a lord would grow more sensitive to slight and more bellicose in response.

The endless private warfare that grew worse as times grew better placed the Church in constant peril. In theory, churchmen believed in peace, and in practice, too, for the fury of battle did not spare churches and monasteries, and clerics could be hurt, or even killed.

In 990, various gatherings of bishops in southern France tried to set up a "Truce of God," a subjection of warfare to rules. The chief rule was to convert all ecclesiastical property and persons into a kind of neutral territory that was not to be touched. Eventually, this was extended to a total prohibition of warfare from Wednesday evening to Monday morning of each week, and on numerous fast and feast days as well. In the end, as much as three fourths of the year was put off limits to fighting.

Naturally, the power of the Church was insufficient to enforce the Truce of God fully, but there were always lords who felt inhibited about doing something that was solemnly forbidden by the priesthood, so that the Truce did some good.

It was to the benefit of the king to keep his lords from fighting, so first Hugh Capet and then Robert the Pious strongly backed the Truce of God. That made it further desirable for the clergy to push for a strong central government to keep the quarrelsome lords in order. The common danger of brawling armies kept crown and clergy together, and this, too, helped strengthen the Capetian line.

Robert's piety did not prevent him from having some personal trouble with the Church (which did not, however, fortunately for himself and his line, affect the general alliance of crown and clergy).

He had made a love match with the widow of a neighboring lord of Blois, but she was a cousin. This, in itself, was a rather common situation since lords might only marry in their own social class; and since all the noble families of France were interrelated, it was hard to marry anyone but a cousin.

In theory, though, such matches were forbidden by the Church and special dispensations had to be received before they could take place. In general, these dispensations were not hard to get. Sometimes, though, politics might intervene. If a particular marriage would lead to a joining of territory and a strengthening of the groom, a competing lord might try to influence the Church not to grant the dispensation. Then, again, the Church itself chose to withhold dispensation, on occasion, as a device to bring a troublesome enemy to heel or merely in order to demonstrate its power over secular rulers. In Robert's case, the Church objected.

Often, rulers fought back, especially when they felt strong affection for their betrotheds, as, in this case, Robert did. He held out for four or five years, even withstanding excommunication (by which he was forbidden to take part in religious rites — a terrible fate for a pious king). Finally, he gave in and dismissed his wife in September, 1001.

By that time, his old teacher, Gerbert, was Pope, reigning as Sylvester II, and one can't help but wonder if Robert might not have gotten a sympathetic papal ear. But then, his beloved wife had borne him no children and that was even more serious than excommunication. A king had to have an heir.

Robert married again, with a sigh, and found that his second wife, Constance of Toulouse, was a fearsome shrew. He hid from her whenever he could, but during those intervals when he did not, he managed to father four sons and a daughter.

Robert's greatest enemy was Eudes (yood) of Blois. Eudes ruled over Blois, immediately to the west of the royal territory, and over Champagne, immediately to the east. Robert had the humiliation of seeing his own land nearly surrounded by a man who was nominally a vassal but who was actually a more powerful ruler than himself.

Robert had to seek allies and found a powerful one in Normandy. That duchy had been established in 912 by Rollo the Ganger, a Viking, who had forced the weak Carolingian king then on the throne to cede him the rich territory at the mouth of the Seine.* His descendants had become thoroughly assimilated to the French language and customs and had established a strong, centralized government. The Norman dukes managed to keep their own vassals in pretty good order.

The dangerous enemies of the Norman dukes were the lords of the lands adjoining them on the south, the Count of Anjou and the Count of Blois. Since Blois was the common enemy of both Normandy and the king, the latter two drew together. With Normandy's help, King Robert was able to hold off Blois.

Robert had one piece of territorial good fortune. The Duke of Burgundy died in 1002 and left no heir. Under such circumstances, the king automatically inherited the land, *if* he could keep it. (That was one of the advantages of being king.) Naturally, though, there was a claimant, and he managed to seize the duchy. Robert had to fight him for a dozen years before finally making good his own claim, but make it good he eventually did.

* For detail on the history of Normandy, see my book *The Shaping of England* (Houghton Mifflin, 1969).

When Robert's oldest son, Hugh, died, the king lost no time in having his next son, Henry, crowned. Thus, when Robert died in 1031, after a thirty-five-year reign which saw him preserve the royal power with steadiness if not with brilliance, and saw further the safe passing of the mystic year 1000, there was still a king in France — Henry I.

Or there should have been. His mother, that fearsome shrew, Constance of Toulouse, favored a younger son, Robert. (Mothers have their favorites, after all.) She might have triumphed, too, but Henry, in the civil war that followed, had a helper in the Duke of Normandy.

By that time, the alliance between the Norman duke and the French king was almost a matter of tradition. Besides, the Norman duke at the time was Robert the Devil (so-called for his harsh cruelty and his readiness to anger) and he needed a favor.

Robert the Devil had no legitimate son of his own, but he had an illegitimate son by a low-born girl, and it was in his mind that this young boy (who was only four when King Robert II had died) might succeed him. Royal support would go a long way toward making such a succession legal. It was to Robert the Devil's advantage, then, to find some way of placing King Henry under an obligation.

The duke therefore came strongly to Henry's help and by 1032 Henry's seat on the throne was made firm. Henry's younger brother Robert was given a consolation prize in the form of the Duchy of Burgundy and that duchy remained in the brother's family for over three centuries.

This is an example of another of the difficulties of the time. Even when a lord managed to enlarge his domain, it was all too easy to break it up again for family reasons — to keep a brother quiet or to reward a younger son. This kept the map of western Europe a complicated checkerboard of lands throughout the Middle Ages.

KING AND DUKE

Robert the Devil turned out to have done well in investing in King Henry's goodwill. Robert went off on a pilgrimage to the Holy Land and died in 1035 on his way back, leaving his illegitimate son, William, as the only heir to Normandy.

To be sure, before leaving on his pilgrimage, Robert had made all his vassals swear allegiance to William, in the usual way, on holy relics. To break such an oath meant damnation, but a surprising number of lords were willing to take such a risk when increased power and broader acres beckoned. After all, they could always do penance later on.

For years, then, young William was kept in virtual hiding, lest some of his rebel lords take him and put him out of the way. If King Henry had not done his best to support the young boy, the lords might have succeeded, too. Fortunately for himself, William turned out to have a strong personality and considerable military skill. By the time he was in his middle teens he was taking the field against his unruly lords and in this he continued to have the faithful help of King Henry.

By 1047, William was firmly ensconced as duke and he set about strengthening his duchy further. Though his lords swore allegiance, William knew what *that* was worth by hard experience and he kept after them harshly, punishing the slightest infraction by the prompt application of fire and slaughter. Normandy quickly reached a peak of power under Duke William the Bastard (as he was widely known, though probably not to his face).

As the years went by, King Henry regretted having helped William, for a too strong Normandy was entirely too close a neighbor. The king's capital, Paris, and the duke's capital, Rouen (roo-on'), were both on the Seine River, Rouen being some eighty miles downstream from Paris.

Henry, though king, was far weaker than the duke, however, both militarily and economically. He could oppose Normandy only indirectly and one way of doing so was to ally himself with Anjou, Normandy's southern neighbor and its perennial enemy.

Henry made an interesting second marriage, after his first wife gave him no son. Remembering his father's problems, he was determined to take no chance on marrying a cousin or any kind of relative. He turned therefore to the other end of Europe to search for a wife who could not possibly be related to him, however distantly. In his day, the vast plains of southern Russia were governed by a powerful prince, Yaroslav I, whose capital was in Kiev. He had a daughter named Anne, and it was she whom Henry married.

By her, Henry had three sons. Since all subsequent kings of France were descended from the marriage of Henry and Anne, it follows that they all had a far distant Russian descent.

Henry I naturally supported the Truce of God movement but he was rather cool toward the Cluniac reform. The reform had by now spread and become powerful and its idealistic views, while all right as long as they hampered the unscrupulous behavior of the lords and vassals of France, became annoying when they were directed against the king.

But it was too late to do anything about that. The Cluniac reform, like the Duke of Normandy, had been supported by the king when it was weak, and had then grown dangerous so quickly that there was no time to stop it before it became too strong to stop. Reform had by now become an international force and the great power of the papacy was solidly placed behind it.

The real power behind the new papal attitude was a brilliant and forceful monk named Hildebrand, who preferred to remain in the background but who dominated every Pope over a nearly thirty-year period. When Pope Leo IX was elected in 1049, Hildebrand had him hold solemn councils in three different places, one in Germany, one in France and one in Italy, in order to push reform.

There was reason in this. During the tenth century, the papacy had gone through a low point. It had become the sport of the petty Roman nobility and the Popes were, in some cases, men of no worth whatever, and, in other cases, even children. The papacy had managed to emerge from the morass but it needed to re-establish its prestige, and how better to do that than to take over the leadership of the monastic reform movement and to make its thunderous voice heard on the side of virtue?

King Henry, for his part, was content to deal with his own clergy and did not want a strong papacy since that would represent an outside force that would contest with him control of the French church. He did his best to quash that section of the council which was held in Reims in his own territory. He failed, though, and that was a remarkable sign of the rapidity with which the papacy was regaining its strength.

Though Henry had allowed himself to be outmatched by Normandy and by the papacy, his greatest failure was not really his fault. He died too soon. His death came in 1060, when he had reigned twenty-nine years, yet that death created a problem in the succession.

A year before, he had followed the Capetian practice of having his oldest son, Philip, crowned so that he might succeed as Philip I, but Henry hadn't lived long enough to allow Philip to reach adulthood. For the first time in Capetian history, the crown had fallen to a child, for Philip I was only eight years old when he succeeded.

Naturally, an eight-year-old can't really rule, so while he is king in title, some adult must make the necessary decisions for him, and must serve as "regent." In this case the regent was Count Baldwin V of Flanders.

While a capable regent can keep a land from falling into anarchy, he is rarely able to do as much as a capable king might. The regent lacks the royal title and the prestige that goes with it. His tenure is limited, for soon the king will achieve adulthood, and the lords would intrigue against him in delaying actions, waiting for that day.

It followed that where the earlier Capetians had little enough power, Philip I and his regent had less still. This was a bad blow for France, as it turned out, for this period of less than normal power came at a time when Duke William of Normandy was making soaring plans — and there was no one to counter him or interfere with him.

Duke William aspired to nothing else than the conquest of England, which, at the time, was under Edward the Confessor, who was weak and pro-Norman. (He had had a Norman mother and had been brought up in Normandy.) What's more, the land was distracted by the strong rivalries of its own lords.

Even so, the task was hard for William and it could have been countered easily enough if a French king even as vigorous as the dead Henry had opposed it resolutely. But in 1066, when the invasion was being prepared, the French king was still only fourteen, and as for the regent, Baldwin, he was nothing less than William's father-in-law. He actually accompanied William on his invasion, leaving young Philip to take care of the royal duties by himself.

By the time Philip could really take hold of the kingship, William had succeeded in winning a dramatic battle at Hastings, on the southern coast of England, and in conquering all the land, changing the name by which history knows him from William the Bastard to William the Conqueror.

William had followed the ducal policy of keeping his vassals under control, so that Normandy, with its new English colony, was easily the most efficiently, if harshly, ruled portion of western Europe. The Normans, furthermore, advanced the art of warfare — in which they excelled — by the development of the castle.

Castles had come into existence during the period of the

Viking raids. Rulers of vulnerable territories fortified their homes so that in case of need they, together with the surrounding population, might retreat there until the Viking fury passed. The Normans now extended and improved the concept.

They placed the castle on a height that was difficult for assaulters to scale, surrounded it with a stockade and a water-filled ditch, or moat. The moat could be crossed but only by means of a drawbridge, one that could be drawn up when access was to be denied. There was a central stronghold, which could serve as a last-ditch defense, stores of arms and foods, places for animals to be kept and for the peasantry to remain.

It was by means of strategically placed castles under loyal retainers that a small group of Normans could keep firm hold over the broad English territory. It was by means of strategically placed castles in Normandy itself that William made himself invulnerable to assault. In the end, William had nothing to fear from France; indeed, it was France which, for centuries, was to be endangered by William and his successors.

Philip I recognized the danger, of course, and did what he could to counter Normandy. Though he grew fat with age, he had the Capetian toughness. He developed the technique of encouraging his vassals to fight among themselves under conditions whereby they weakened each other while leaving the king to pick up the pieces. When two brothers, both claiming the overlordship of Anjou, came to blows, Philip did nothing to stop them. He maintained a careful neutrality and as a reward for that ended with a piece of Anjou territory that rounded out his own domains.

Similarly, he encouraged William's grown son, Robert Curthose ("Short-pants," so called because of his short legs), to rebel against his father, then supported him when he did. William defeated his son but the fight kept him busy and gave him that much less chance to push against the king.

Like his father, Philip I supported the Truce of God but opposed Church reform. Indeed, the growing strength of the papacy was beginning to endanger his economic welfare. The king's narrow lands could not properly support the expenses of his policy and his position, and he had to get money where he could. Whenever a new bishop succeeded to a post, it was necessary for the king to approve the selection, which had been made, in theory, by the Pope. As a matter of course, the king would charge a healthy fee for the approval.

This meant a steady flow of money from the Church to the State and, whenever the papacy was strong, it opposed this practice forcefully. Indeed, under Hildebrand and those who followed, the papacy opened a movement against the practice which was to fill the twelfth century with drama not only in France, but in England and Germany as well, as secular and religious rulers fought over which were to control the investiture of bishops.

Philip's insistence on making money out of investiture helped make him unpopular with the clergy, and such unpopularity was, in those times, a serious thing. In a religious age, when the priests have the ear of the people, they fulfill some of the functions of newspapers of our day. If the priests say a king is wicked, the people are bound to believe it, and the king gets the equivalent of a "bad press."

In fact, the bad press continues past death, for medieval chronicles were kept by priests and if they disapproved of someone, they said so, describing his wickedness (or supposed wickedness) in full. Often that is the only detailed information we have of a king's private life and it may be exaggerated.

So we might wonder how far we can trust the account of Philip's most notorious private action. The story, as we hear it, is that, in 1092, he fell in love with the wife of Count Fulk IV of Anjou. Philip was married and had been for twenty years. He had two children by that marriage and one of them was his son Louis, whom he had had crowned and who was his heir.

Nevertheless, Philip had no intention of keeping the new love a platonic affair. He abducted the count's wife and managed to find some bishops who agreed to give them both annulments from their respective spouses on some pretext, leaving them free to marry.

This, however, was adultery to most people — adultery in flagrant disregard of the laws of God and man; and Pope Urban II excommunicated Philip in 1094.

That, then, was the situation in France as the eleventh century drew to a close. The four kings of the Capetian line had ruled France for a little over a century and had managed to hold their own. That wasn't entirely satisfactory; the lords still went their way, essentially uncontrolled, and the Church went its way. France continued to be a crazy quilt without any real central power anywhere.

Yet the Capetians *had* held their own. They were no weaker at least and they had kept the royal power in being long enough to give their line the sanction of tradition. And they were strong enough now to hold France together at a time when it was to be shaken to its core by news from the east; from the dim east concerning which it knew practically nothing but what had been learned, after a fashion, from the Bible.

Let us turn to the east ourselves, then, and see what was happening.

2

WAR IN THE FAR EAST

THE FIRST CRUSADE

The strongest Christian power in eastern Europe in the time of the early Capetians was the still-standing remnant of the old Roman Empire, with its capital at Constantinople. We refer to this eastern remnant of Roman dominion as the "Byzantine Empire," from Byzantium, the ancient name of Constantinople. To the west Europeans of the time, however, the Empire was referred to simply as "the Greeks." This was fair enough, in a way, since the language of its people was indeed Greek.

At the time Hugh Capet had gained the French throne in 987 and taken over the rule of a barbarous patchwork whose lords could defy him with impunity, the Byzantine Empire was a centralized monarchy with fifteen centuries of unbroken civilization behind it.*

* For the long and active history of the Byzantine Empire, see my book *Constantinople* (Houghton Mifflin, 1970).

The distance between France and the westernmost limits of the Byzantine Empire was only about 600 miles or so, not much by modern standards, but astronomical in the eleventh century.

To the French, and to western Christians generally, the "Greeks" were not merely a far distant people but a wicked one. They refused to accept the supremacy of the Roman Pope, but insisted on maintaining that of the Patriarch of Constantinople instead. What's more, they differed on various points of doctrine in ways that seemed important to the theologians of the day and that served to whip up bitter ideological hatred between the Christians of the west and the east. By 1054, in the last years of Henry I of France, there was a final schism, or break, between the two halves of the Christian world, one that has never been healed to this day.

About that time, too, the Byzantine Empire found itself facing a new and dangerous enemy in the east, the Seljuk Turks. The Empire was weakened by internal political turmoil and in 1071, when Byzantine and Turk met in a large-scale battle at Manzikert in eastern Asia Minor, the Turkish army won a complete victory.

The Turks swept over the interior of Asia Minor and, simultaneously, western armies from Italy (led by Norman adventurers from northern France) were invading Byzantine dominions from the west. It seemed the Byzantine Empire might be wiped out, and so, indeed, it might have been but for the exertions of a capable Byzantine general, Alexius Comnenus (kom-nee'nus), who seized the throne and began to rule as Alexius I, in 1081.

For a decade, Alexius carefully and tirelessly fought the enemies of the Empire on every border and within. Always, he needed more soldiers and it occurred to him that he might raise a band of mercenaries in the west by suggesting action against the common Moslem foe and by holding out the possibility of healing the split between eastern and western Christianity.

The western Christians could not, of course, have cared less

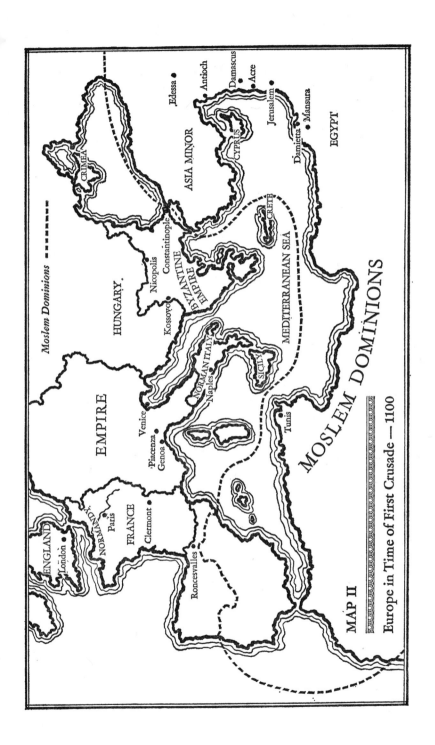

MAP II

Europe in Time of First Crusade — 1100

for the Byzantine Empire and would cheerfully have seen it destroyed. They were, however, concerned over the fact that the Seljuk Turks had gained control of Jerusalem. With the religious enthusiasm of relatively new converts, the Turks sharply limited Christian pilgrimages to the land of Jesus' birth and soon horror tales were sweeping the west concerning Turkish atrocities against humble Christian pilgrims.

What's more, Pope Urban II had reasons of his own to listen to the pleas of the Emperor Alexius. At that time, the papacy was in a struggle for power with the German Emperor, Henry IV, who supported an "anti-Pope" (one who was not recognized as legitimate by later papal doctrine). Indeed, it was the anti-Pope who ruled in Rome while Urban II was forced to remain in those areas where the German Emperor's armies were not in control.

In 1095, the year after Urban had shown his strength by excommunicating Philip I of France, he called a council in the north Italian city of Piacenza, forty miles south of Milan. There he placed Alexius' call for mercenaries on the agenda.

As a strong Pope and as an ardent proponent of Cluniac reform, he felt a sincere desire to strengthen Christianity by defeating the Turks and retaking the Holy Land. If, in so doing, the eastern Christians could be brought back into the fold and made to accept papal supremacy, so much the better. Furthermore, it would give the endlessly quarreling barons a common enemy to fight and would further peace at home by sending them far away.

The council at Piacenza came to no conclusion about Alexius' appeal, however. The troubles with the German Emperor occupied too much of its collective mind. Urban therefore called a second council in November of that same year, 1095, at Clermont, in south central France. Here, further from Emperor Henry, the problem of Emperor Alexius might be seen in clearer perspective.

In Clermont, Urban had an audience made to order for himself. He was after all a Frenchman, and the French clergy had been on his side in his struggle against the Emperor and his anti-Pope. The best and most belligerent knights, to whom he hoped to appeal, were French, too.

Urban began by stressing reform, by renewing the Truce of God, and by pleading for peace among the nobility. Then came the real purpose of the assembly.

Urban arose to address the huge crowds of the faithful who had come to hear him. He was a skillful orator and, in moving and emotion-filled terms, he described the city of Jerusalem, so long in chains under its infidel rulers. He described the sufferings of the pilgrims. He urged the knights of Europe to take up arms against the infidel, to strike on behalf of pious Christians, to take back the land of Jesus.

The atmosphere was that of a revivalist camp. The listeners were moved to an almost maniacal frenzy. "God wills it!" they screamed over and over again. "God wills it! God wills it!"

Great numbers pledged themselves to go eastward to fight and in token of that pledge they pinned a cross to their clothing, ripping some garment, if necessary, to obtain the material for it. The war was to be fought for the honor of the Cross and the cross was to be the emblem of its warriors. The movement was therefore called "Crusade" from the Latin word for "cross."

What Urban began at Clermont was a struggle that was to continue for two hundred years and more, and the flow of knights, eastward, was to continue, more or less, for all that time. There were, however, particularly dense flows under particularly eminent leaders, now and again — eight of them according to the most usual counts. For this reason, historians usually speak of the Crusades, in the plural, and what was about to take place after the Council of Clermont was the "First Crusade."

The First Crusade was not a movement of monarchs, and, indeed, Urban didn't want it to be. The two most important monarchs in Europe, Henry IV of Germany and Philip I of France, were hostile to him and, in fact, both were excommunicated. Urban wanted the movement to be under papal leadership, and it was to the smaller nobles and to the people that he appealed, not to those who would dispute his leadership.

The armies marched eastward, ignorant of the lands they were to pass through and reach, ignorant of their Byzantine allies, ignorant of their Moslem enemies, reeking fanaticism and filled with desire for blood and loot. Yet though they suffered great losses, they won astonishing victories and, on July 15, 1099, actually took Jerusalem.

It is tempting to follow that rather unbelievable story in detail, but, in this book, our attention remains on France. What happened in France while the French knighthood was winning glory in the Holy Land?

To Philip I, the First Crusade was all to the good. He got rid of many of his more turbulent subjects and he had less to fear in his continuing fight with the Pope. (Philip, you see, couldn't bring himself to give up his adulterous marriage, and the excommunication which was lifted when he promised to be good was reimposed when he backslid — several times.)

William the Conqueror had died in 1087 and his son, Robert Curthose, who succeeded him in Normandy, was far less capable than his father, and besides went off on the crusade. Robert's younger brother ruled in England as William II, and, though he controlled Normandy while Robert Curthose was off crusading, he was not minded for anything more than limited French adventures.

Robert returned in 1100, but by that time William II had been assassinated and Robert was occupied in fighting for England with another brother, Henry.

It might have seemed that between the Crusades and the troubles of the Norman sons of William the Conqueror, it was a good time for France to grow more united, but such union was a very difficult thing to bring about.

Nowadays, as we look back on the France of early Capetian days, we think of it as "France," but there was no such feeling among the people of the time. Each province had its own dialect, distinctive and different, sometimes even quite different; and to each group of provincials men speaking other dialects were foreigners to be despised, feared, hated or all three.

To be sure, the dialect of the Parisian area, called "Francien," had a certain prestige because it was the language of the court, but by 1100 this was still far from enough to give it the status of a common language.

And yet there was a change coming. The spirit and mood of the crusading era helped give rise to a new and more national feeling among the people. However different the people of this or that province felt themselves to be, they were all Christians and all fighting the distant Moslems.

The First Crusade also gave rise to the first great literary product that swept all the provinces with its popularity, appealed to all as a common heritage, and gave all a common pride.

This was the *Chanson de Roland* (*Song of Roland*), which was put into its final form about 1100. Its plot took advantage of the anti-Moslem feeling generated among Frenchmen by the First Crusade. It had as its historical basis an incident that had taken place over three centuries earlier, when a monarch whom the French considered the greatest in their history — Charlemagne — had fought gloriously against the Moslems in Spain. During that campaign the rear guard of one of Charlemagne's armies, under the command of Roland, was cut to pieces by Christian Basques in the defiles of the Pyrenees.

The poem, however, has virtually no breath of the real event. Where Charlemagne in actual fact conquered only that strip of Spain directly south of the Pyrenees, he is pictured in the poem as having conquered all of Spain but one city. The rear guard is pictured as being attacked by a vast Moslem army, instead of by Christian guerrillas, and the whole is drawn in the impossibly heroic colors of medieval chivalry. Every Christian is a match for a thousand Moslems, except Roland who is a match for ten thousand. Even the final defeat of Roland is so glorious it is a victory.

No Frenchman could help but be proud of being French, whatever his province, when he read this epic, which was not only the first but the greatest of its type in medieval literature.

The *Chanson de Roland* spawned a great imitative literature of "chanson de gestes" ("songs of knightly exploits"), of which some eighty have survived and still exist today. Most were fantasies dealing with the legendary knights of Charlemagne's court. One of them, *Huon de Bordeaux,* introduced Oberon, a king of the fairies, and Shakespeare borrowed him four centuries later, as a character in his play *A Midsummer Night's Dream.*

The chansons de gestes, generally, together with the First Crusade, produced the first great impetus toward French nationalism.

LOUIS THE WIDE-AWAKE

Philip I had followed the usual Capetian practice of assuring the succession by having his son Louis crowned and associated with himself in his rule. When, in 1108, Philip died, his son succeeded peacefully and ruled as Louis VI.

Louis was the first Capetian to possess a name associated with the older Carolingian line. (Louis V was the last Carolingian.) It is a measure of the success of the Capetians that they no longer feared to invoke the memory of Charlemagne.

Louis VI, like his father before him, was fat. Indeed, his overweight is frozen in history for he is known by the name of "Louis the Fat." If he was fat-bodied, he was not, however, fat-headed. In fact, he was the first of the Capetians who did more than merely strive to hold his own and who stepped boldly out in the direction of centralization.

He recognized that it was the unruly lords who were his greatest danger and that his strength, such as it was, came from the peace and prosperity of the royal lands about Paris. Indeed, another one of his names, and a much more suitable one, is "Louis the Wide-Awake."

Eschewing distant wars as far as he could, he settled down to the unglamorous but enormously important task of beating down the proud lordlings who held their strongholds within sight of Paris itself and who looted merchants and peasants when it suited them to do so. He spent a quarter of a century at the task but by the time Louis was done, the menace of the robber baron was gone from his directly ruled dominions.

As a result, his own subjects loved him and made of him the first really popular Capetian. As for those who were ruled by lords beyond Louis's reach, they earnestly wished for the victory of the king over their own feudal rulers. Louis thus began the process of centralizing the monarchy and the nation that was to continue for five centuries after his time. The move toward centralization had a tendency to feed on itself. For instance, the greater the royal power and the more extended the royal domain, the greater the prestige of the court dialect of Francien and the closer France came to a national language which could in turn enforce nationalist feelings.

Louis did not work toward centralization by feats of arms alone. Deliberately, he supported those social classes who could be counted on to work against the lords. He continued the Capetian habit of supporting the clergy, for instance, and abandoned the policies of his father and grandfather by returning to a program of supporting reform. He felt — rightly — that, in the long run, there was more to gain from this.

He also used the royal influence to establish towns in the

lands of his troublesome vassals (not in his own) and to ac-
cord them special privileges that he knew would be inconvenient for the lords. The townsmen would naturally find the
lords of the surrounding lands to be enemies and would seek
protection for themselves and their privileges from the king.
As the towns grew prosperous and wealthy, it meant that a
source of money (needed to pay soldiers and buy arms) would
always be available to the king for use against the nobles.

Louis was even far-sighted enough to avoid using his most
important vassals in administration, realizing that they would
be hard to control and that the power he gave them could
easily be used against him. He picked his advisers from the
lower nobility, from the clergy and from the townsmen. These
advisers, having no great power of their own, would depend
for their welfare on the king alone, and could be relied on,
out of sheer self-interest, to be loyal to him.

The most important of Louis's counselors was the abbot
Suger (syoo-zhair), an ecclesiastic of lower-class origins. Suger
was about the same age as Louis and had been the royal tutor
when both were in their twenties. Suger strongly encouraged
his monarch in his enlightened policies against the lords, and
his influence was to extend beyond Louis's lifetime. Suger
lived to be seventy and to be adviser to Louis's son and successor. Not only that, but he was the best historian of his
times and he wrote highly favorable accounts of both kings.

Suger was also responsible for an important advance in architecture.

Lacking modern materials, the Roman architects had found
it impossible to build large structures without thick walls.
When stone came to be used for the roof, the weight was all
the heavier and the walls had to become enormously thick.
Nor could there be more than few and narrow windows if
fatal weaknesses were not to be introduced. The result was
that "Romanesque" churches of the early Middle Ages bore a

predominant atmosphere of squat gloom, relieved by candle-lit interiors and colorful artwork.

In the twelfth century, however, the notion arose of designing large structures so as to concentrate the weight of the roof in certain areas where outside buttresses of masonry could be built. For further strength, buttresses, standing well away from the building, could be connected to the key points needing support by diagonal structures. These latter were "flying buttresses."

Since the buttresses carried the weight, those sections of the walls not directly involved in support could be left thin and could be pierced with numerous windows. These windows were filled with stained glass, so that the interior of the structure was drenched with colored light in a beautiful and impressive manner. What's more, the cathedrals could be built to unprecedented heights of hundreds of feet; heights that were not to be surpassed, indeed, until the nineteenth century introduced the age of steel.

The new style appeared unobtrusively here and there, and then in 1137, Suger began renovation of the abbey of St. Denis, not far north of Paris, where he served as abbot. He used the new style in a bold and wholesale manner and helped establish its popularity.

To the men of more southerly regions, particularly Italy, where the Romanesque style, and its evocation of old Roman days, had the prestige of antiquity, the new architecture was considered to be barbaric in its stress on height and size, and in the overflowing vigor of its buttresses and ornamentation. It was called "Gothic" in derision.

The name stuck but the insult vanished. The style grew ever more popular and cathedrals were built all over Europe during the next few centuries and with greater and greater elaboration. Gothic architecture became one of the artistic glories of the Middle Ages.

THE SONS OF THE CONQUEROR

The external problem that chiefly complicated Louis's reign was the matter of Normandy. He had to face the sons of William the Conqueror. One of the two surviving sons, Henry I of England, the younger, had beaten Robert Curthose, and now ruled in Normandy as well.

Louis did not care much who ruled England, but Normandy was, of course, another matter. It occupied the lowermost reaches of the Seine River and its border was only about sixty miles downstream from Paris. To have it belong to England made it possible for the English king to be as important in France as the French king was, and Louis made it his business to see that, at the very worst, if Normandy could not be controlled by himself, it should at least not be controlled by England.

He had therefore supported Robert Curthose, who now lay imprisoned by his brother; and he next supported Robert's son, William Clito (kligh'toe), who was still at liberty. Thus began a duel between France and England over Normandy that was not to be decided for over three centuries.

In 1119, Louis, accompanied by William Clito, led a force of armed men down the Seine. There was probably no intention to do more than reconnoiter and win a psychological victory over Henry. Henry, however, who was in Normandy at the time, was leading a troop of men up the Seine with the same purpose in mind. The two armies met quite unexpectedly near Les Andelys (lay-zahn-dlee), a town on the Norman border.

Battle could not be avoided and the two bands of horsemen came together with much clanging and shouting. By this time, armor had come to enclose the entire body and much of the horse as well, and the knights were living tanks.

Armor might be heavy to wear and devilishly hot in the summer (the battle was fought on August 20); it might make it impossible to wipe sweat from the eyes, or to scratch where the body lice itched; but it did hold off the flailing of swords and clubs.

Of the nine hundred knights at the battle, on both sides, only three were killed and that was probably by accident. Even when a knight managed to be banged off his horse and captured, he was generally held for ransom, which was much more profitable than killing him would be.

It all boiled down, then, to which side wearied of the noise and heat first, and decided it had had enough. They would then turn their horses and trundle away, while the other side would trot after halfheartedly, shouting insults. It was the French who turned away in this case and Henry I had a clear, if nonbloody, victory.

This battle of Les Andelys was typical, by the way, of early medieval battles. They were generally tedious draws and there was little point in fighting them. Instead, as the Norman castle spread out into regions beyond Normandy, it was the siege that became characteristic of the warfare of the times. As a result, castles were built with greater and greater attention to strength. After 1100, castles, which had till then been built of wood, began to be constructed of stone.

The year after Les Andelys, a stroke of fortune played into Louis's hands and gave him infinitely more than he lost at the battle. The English king was returning to England and his only son, William, on another ship, drowned in the channel. There was left only a daughter, Matilda, to inherit the Anglo-Norman crown. It was not very difficult for Louis the Wide-Awake to see that this meant that there would be turmoil in England once Henry died. He concentrated, from then on, in doing his best to make sure this turmoil would indeed take place.

The death of the prince meant opportunity, also, for Henry V, the German Emperor and son of that old papal enemy, Henry IV.

In 1114, Henry V had married Matilda of England and now it seemed to him that he stood a good chance of inheriting the rule of England and Normandy through his wife. He could not resist attempting to hasten and assure the day by invading France in 1124 and accomplishing some feat against the French enemy that would make him popular with his future subjects.

The increasing sense of nationality in France, and Louis's personal popularity, now stood the king in good stead. The great lords and the people alike rallied around Louis, and the Emperor, finding he had stirred up a hornet's nest, decided he had business elsewhere and returned to Germany.

Henry V died in 1125, leaving Matilda a widow. Henry I, in agony, tried to assure the succession by forcing the English and Norman lords to swear loyalty to her. He also looked about for some way of arranging a second marriage that would supply his daughter with a husband capable of defending her.

His eye fell on Anjou, whose counts controlled an area of France just as large as Normandy. There had been steady enmity between Normandy and Anjou (its southern neighbor) for over half a century, but circumstances had now changed. The Count of Anjou, Fulk V, was about to go eastward to head the Christian forces still fighting in the Holy Land, and he was going to leave his son Geoffrey as his successor.

Geoffrey was young, only in his early teens, and was good-looking enough to be called "Geoffrey the Handsome." He also derived a nickname from a sprig of broom ("planta genêt") which he wore in his helmet for some reason, so that he was Geoffrey Plantagenet.

If he could be induced to marry Matilda, he would be a

young, vigorous husband who would, according to Henry's calculation, defend his daughter's crown when the time came. In the end, he would pass on to his sons the rule not only of England and Normandy, but of Anjou as well, founding an "Angevin dynasty" (the adjective derived from Anjou) that would be more powerful than the Norman dynasty of which Henry I seemed doomed to be the last male representative.

In 1128, the marriage took place, and the next year Fulk V departed eastward. Geoffrey was Count of Anjou and husband of the heiress to the throne of England and Normandy.

Louis VI could do nothing to stop this involved plan for the future (except to hope that it wouldn't work), but he prepared an involved plan of his own that might serve as a neutralizing factor. Northeast of the royal dominions was Flanders, a region that is now chiefly included in western Belgium, and Louis's eyes came to rest there.

Flanders had a very advantageous position just across the channel from southeastern England, and was a midway house between Germany and France. The low-lying land was marshy and when the marshes were drained, the result was not suitable for agriculture. Instead, sheep were raised for the land was good for pasture. The Flemish people used the wool to make cloth and export it southward in exchange for Mediterranean luxuries. Not surprisingly, then, the towns growing in Flanders were the most prosperous outside Italy.

When, in 1127, the Count of Flanders was assassinated, Louis VI quickly intervened and, by sheer pressure, forced the Flemish to accept William Clito as their count. The intention was clear. William Clito, nephew of Henry I and son of Henry's *older* brother, had a legitimate claim on the English throne. He could be counted on, it seemed to Louis, to start a civil war in England at some convenient time, a war in which he would have behind him the wealth of Flanders.

Louis's plan didn't work. William Clito remained unacceptable to the Flemish people. He was constantly embroiled with them and, in 1128, died in battle so that Louis's influence in that direction vanished.

Louis VI, gritting his teeth, was forced to make final peace with Henry I in 1129, and wait. In 1134, Robert Curthose died at the age of eighty, removing another possible source of dynastic trouble and then, in 1135, Henry I died.

Now what would happen?

Louis VI had not long to wait in suspense. Matilda tried to have herself accepted as queen, but all the Anglo-Norman lords who had sworn to accept her shied away after all from petticoat rule and backtracked in favor of a charming cousin, Stephen of Blois. What followed was twenty years of civil war and anarchy, during which England remained under Stephen and Normandy under Matilda — to the benefit of France.

Louis VI could not relax, however. He was in his fifties, which was quite old at this period of history, and he had to settle his own succession. In Capetian fashion, he had had his son, another Louis, crowned in 1131 and the two now ruled together. But Louis wanted to do more. He wanted to make an advantageous marriage for him that would counter Matilda's advantageous marriage.

Fortunately, he had his chance. Almost all of what is now southwestern France was controlled by the Dukes of Aquitaine. Aquitaine was fair and fertile, with mild weather and a culture gentler and farther advanced than that of northern France, for it lay nearer Italy where there still breathed the memory of Rome, and nearer Spain where the Moslem culture was far more advanced than anything in Christian Europe.

Aquitaine was, in fact, all but a foreign country. Although feudally it acknowledged the ruler in Paris as overlord, there were virtually no ties of sympathy between north and south. Even the languages were different. Aquitaine spoke "Provençal," a language more closely related to some of the Spanish dialects than to Francien.

Yet Louis had his chance. In 1137, William X, Duke of Aquitaine, died, leaving no male heirs. His only child was a young daughter, Eleanor of Aquitaine, only fifteen at the time of her father's death. She was the richest heiress in Europe and she badly needed a husband to protect her lands. What better husband could she have than the next King of France, himself only sixteen? Their heirs would then directly rule over all of eastern and southern France, surrounding the Norman hold on the northwest in a great semicircle. Then, even if the Anglo-Norman civil war resolved itself, France would be in a favorable position to renew the struggle.

The marriage was carried through in July, 1137, and then Louis, having done all he possibly could, wearily let go of life, dying on August 1.

THE SECOND CRUSADE

The new king succeeded as Louis VII, and was known at the time as "Louis the Young" for he was still a teen-ager.

The new reign, through Eleanor's influence, brought the culture of the south northward and made it powerful. The south of France was the home of the "troubadours" or, as they were known in the south, "trouvères" (from a local word for "poet"), who wrote in Provençal.

The troubadours sang of love, something which through most of Europe was unknown. Marriages were made for economic or political reasons with no consideration of personal taste or feelings at all. As for sexual connection, that usually had little to do with anything but sex.

The troubadours thought of love, however, as being aside from either sex or marriage; and of the subjection of the lover to his love almost in the fashion of a vassal to his lord. The origins of the notion could be traced back to Roman writings by the poet Ovid, and to Moslem notions from Spain.

William IX of Aquitaine, Eleanor's grandfather, was himself the first of the important troubadours, and Eleanor patronized them generously. The vogue of "courtly love" arose in which men were supposed to pine for women they might not attain (usually because they were married to someone else).

The fashion was stylized and trivial, but it helped improve the status of women, something badly needed at the time. Women, in general, were vilified by the nonmarrying priesthood and they received little consideration as human beings prior to the troubadours. They were considered primarily as baby machines, often married at an age as early as twelve* and had, on the average, three times as many children as do European and American women of today. There was, however, a high death rate for infants, which prevented the population from increasing rapidly, and few women escaped death in childbearing sooner or later. The life expectancy for women was considerably less than that for men because of this (and stayed so till the last century when the dangers of childbearing were finally brought under control).

Eleanor held court for troubadours and poets and discoursed on the esoteric problems of courtly love. She gave judgment in such matters after hearing evidence on both sides, just as her husband would do in more serious matters. Eleanor decided, for instance, that love and marriage were incompatible; something she had probably already found out in her own case through personal experience, though she dutifully bore her husband two daughters.

(It may seem that the troubadour movement favored infidelity and immorality on the part of high-born married women, but actually most of it was just talk. Living conditions were

---

* This continued in Europe for centuries. In *Romeo and Juliet*, written by Shakespeare at the end of the sixteenth century, Juliet is described as not quite fourteen. When her father worries that she may be too young for marirage, he is told, "Younger than she are happy mothers made."

so crowded in the great homes, which were so full of servants and retainers, that ladies could scarcely find the privacy to make love to their husbands, let alone to others.)

While Eleanor dealt with problems of courtly love, Louis had to wrestle with more prosaic ones. There was the question of Anglo-Normandy, for instance. Stephen and Matilda wrangled and fought for the united crown of England and Normandy (with Anjou now added), and Louis had to keep a sharp eye on them, and interfere in such a way as to allow neither side to win. This was precisely what came about. Neither Stephen nor Matilda was truly capable and each threw away several chances to win all.

Matilda, after a short stay in London in 1141, was driven out and was forced to retire to France for good. Stephen, while ruling England in rather feckless manner, was unable to establish himself on the continent. There, Geoffrey Plantagenet managed to bring Normandy into line for Matilda, and was recognized as Duke of Normandy (in addition to his inherited title of Count of Anjou) in 1144.

Louis VII was naturally delighted with this arrangement, for not only was the dangerous heritage of William the Conqueror broken in two but both parts were sure to remain at prime enmity with each other, leaving it to the French crown to gain at the expense of each and eventually (who knows?) to swallow all.

Had Louis VII been as prudent and as far-sighted as his father, he might have advanced far in this direction. Unfortunately, for himself, he had serious misfortunes which began out of religious problems. To start with, he made the mistake of trying to pressure the appointment of one of his chaplains to an archbishopric against the wishes of Church officials.

Louis VII saw this as his feudal right, but the Church did not, and stiffened against him. The papacy was, at that time, steadily growing in power, and it was less and less minded to allow kings to interfere unduly in ecclesiastical appointments.

Pope Innocent II even threatened to place an "interdict" (a complete stop to all churchly functions) on the royal domains and might have done so had he not died, soon after, in 1143.

The king strongly maintained what he believed to be his rights, but was pious enough to be badly upset by finding himself in the bad graces of the Church. What's more, in 1142, while fighting the Count of Champagne, Louis VII's troops stormed a castle about ninety miles east of Paris and set fire to it. The flames spread to a nearby church, in which 1300 people had fled for refuge. All died. The atrocity had not been intended; it was an accidental concomitant of the supreme atrocity of war; but Louis VII's conscience was weighted down by the horrid sight of the burned bodies.

All this served as background for the news arriving from the east. Nearly half a century had passed since the Crusaders had taken Jerusalem. A "Latin kingdom," under the control of Frenchmen, had been carved out along the entire eastern shore of the Mediterranean.

But that had been when the Moslem world had been badly divided, and it had been that division which had been the chief factor in permitting the Christian success. Now the Moslems were recovering. Strong leaders made their appearance and, in 1144, one of them retook the town of Edessa, the northeasternmost bastion of the Crusaders' kingdom. When the tale of Moslem resurgence and the loss of Edessa reached the west, there came the beginning of a renewal of crusading fervor.

There was no strong Pope, no Urban II, to spur this fervor onward, but someone else was on hand to do so. It was a mere abbot, but one who was greater than most Popes; it was Bernard of Clairvaux (klair-voh').

Bernard was born in 1090 of a well-to-do family near Dijon, (dee-zhone') in Burgundy, about 150 miles southeast of Paris. He was clearly not meant for soldiering, so he was given the only alternative for an upper-class youth in those times — an education in preparation for a clerical life. He lived gaily enough until, as a result of a long process of conversion, he suddenly decided, in 1112, to enter a relatively new monastery at Cîteaux (see-toh'), sixteen miles south of Dijon.

This monastery represented a new movement toward reform, for the older Cluniac movement had gone soft by now. This new movement is known as "Cistercian" from the Latin name of the town of Cîteaux. The Cistercians placed heavy emphasis on labor in the fields. They brought wasteland into use as pasture and eventually bred sheep and developed the production of a high grade of wool. However, the monastery had troubles at the start and was not doing very well until Bernard came along, with some thirty of his friends and relatives, whom he had persuaded to join him.

He spent three years in austerities and was then sent, in 1115, to found a daughter monastery of his own in a place about sixty miles north of Dijon. He named the place Clairvaux ("bright valley").

Thanks to the furious energy of his writings and teachings, the Cistercian reform took on an almost explosive expansion. Before his death, thirty-eight years after his coming to Clairvaux, there were 338 Cistercian monasteries spread all over western Europe.

His fame grew each year and so did the influence of his mystical religious views. He was devoted to the Virgin Mary, for instance, and he, more than anyone else, was responsible for the importance placed on her by the Church after his time. Without moving from his obscure post at Clairvaux, Bernard became the uncrowned Pope, with far more influence than those who occupied the Roman papal throne in his time. He lectured kings and admonished papal legates. It was his influence, for instance, that made it possible for Innocent II to become Pope against the claims of others. Bernard might have been Pope himself if he had wished, but he preferred his abbacy.

After the death of Innocent II, there were two brief papal

reigns and then, in 1145, a Cistercian monk, a disciple of Bernard, became Pope under the name of Eugenius III (and Bernard continued to dominate him as though Eugenius, Pope though he was, were still his pupil). The news of the fall of Edessa reached Europe just after the election of Eugenius III, and both he and Bernard were thunderstruck.

To Bernard it seemed that nothing less than a movement led by the great monarchs themselves could redress the balance, and the times were ripe for it. Louis VII of France seemed the obvious choice. Bernard had intervened in the king's feud with the Church and had negotiated a compromise. Louis's gratitude for this and his still-twinging conscience made him ready to listen to Bernard. (And Bernard was a contentious, quarrelsome, overbearing, harshly eloquent man to whom it was hard not to listen, anyway.)

On Easter Day, 1146, Bernard addressed the French court and, in a burst of enthusiasm, the young king (he was still only in his mid-twenties) took the cross from the abbot's own hand. Lords and knights crowded about, swearing their oaths to march to the Holy Land, and once again France was in turmoil.

The crusading movement had never quite stopped, but this new drive caught everyone's attention. What followed — an expedition eastward under the king himself — has been called the "Second Crusade."

One person remained unmoved, the Abbot Suger (who, like everyone else, had been lectured in his time by Bernard and who hadn't enjoyed the experience). Suger had guided Louis VI; he had advised the marriage of Louis VII to Eleanor of Aquitaine; and he was adviser to Louis VII now. He was unimpressed by the lure of the east and saw the crusade only as a source of trouble. Through it, the king's presence would be removed and the real problems, those at home, would grow more threatening. To be sure, the Anglo-Norman power had been neutralized by civil war, but how long would that last?

And surely, in the king's absence, the vassals would stir themselves and grow stronger.

Louis VII's queen, Eleanor, was delighted, however, at the prospect of a crusade. She visualized it as a long succession of knightly tourneys, with brave and gallant knights going out to perform prodigious feats of valor for love of the fair ladies whose gloves they would wear on their helmets. Not only did she strongly urge Louis eastward; she insisted on going herself, with all the court.

It was beyond the power of Louis to resist the thunders of Bernard, the pleas of Eleanor and the pangs of his own aching conscience. He placed Suger in charge of the kingdom during his absence and prepared to leave.

Bernard's preaching had, in fact, persuaded not only Louis, but another monarch, even more highly placed, to march eastward. This was Conrad III, who was then the German Emperor. Following separate routes (to avoid quarreling among themselves), the two armies, led by the mightiest monarchs in western Christendom, moved eastward in 1147 to inflict punishment upon the Moslems, while all Europe held its breath.

Both armies reached Constantinople and their leaders were feted by the Byzantine Emperor, Manuel, who considered himself Roman Emperor and his visitors merely barbarian kings. The humiliations which the western monarchs had to undergo in their negotiations with Manuel took some of the gloss off the romance of the crusading.

The German army was ferried across into Asia Minor by the Byzantines, who gladly led them into the interior to get rid of them, either by having them march to the Holy Land or having them wiped out. They didn't care which, and it turned out to be the latter. Few of the German Crusaders escaped the scimitars of the Turks, but Conrad III was among those few.

Louis VII was more cautious. He marched along the Asia Minor coast to stay in Byzantine territory as long as possible.

When he was finally compelled to face the Turks, he left his infantry to be destroyed and went by sea, with his knights, to the Holy Land. They reached Antioch, near the northern limit of the Latin kingdom. A hundred fifty miles to the northeast lay lost Edessa, now in the grip of the Moslems. Three hundred miles south was Jerusalem, which was in Christian hands still.

The leaders of Antioch, fearing for their own safety if the Moslem advance went unchecked, urged Louis VII to march on Edessa without delay. So did Eleanor, who still wanted her romantic knightly battles. Louis, however, had had enough. The march through Asia Minor had had precious little romance in it and a good deal of very unromantic misery. He had made up his mind that he would not fight and he did not. Instead, he led his army through safe, west-controlled territory to Jerusalem. Eleanor, in horror and revulsion, threatened Louis with divorce, but Louis went anyway, and she had to accompany him.

In Jerusalem, the French army got what spiritual comfort it could out of visiting holy sites and praying there. It even laid a brief, halfhearted siege to Damascus, 140 miles northeast of Jerusalem, but it did no real fighting, and eventually left for France again.

It had been a monumental and humiliating failure for Christianity, for France, for Bernard and, most of all, for Louis. In 1149, two years after they had started out, the survivors (including the two monarchs) returned with nothing accomplished and with lost battles and, worse, avoided battles, as all there was to show for their effort.

3

DUEL WITH THE ANGEVINS

DIVORCE AND REMARRIAGE

The Second Crusade had one result that was disastrous for France, for it brought Louis VII and Queen Eleanor to the final parting. Eleanor had always found her husband unheroic and the very opposite of the troubadouring ideal. She was utterly disgusted at his miserable showing in the east and she demanded a divorce.

Suger, who had ruled France well during Louis's absence, and who was given the title of "Father of His Country" on the king's return, was enormously relieved to have Louis back again, but was horrified at the possibility of divorce. If Eleanor were nothing more than a wife and a woman, she might leave and good riddance — but she carried Aquitaine with her, a realm that made up as large an area (and one that was more cultured) than that which Louis ruled in his own name.

To Suger's arguments, however, Louis turned a sullen and sulky ear. He was as humiliated by the fiasco in the east as Eleanor was, if not more so, and it was easy for him to persuade himself that it was all Eleanor's fault. She had insisted he go, filling his head with foolish romantic notions; and if she hadn't egged him on, he would have been spared the entire mess. At that, if she had only not insisted on coming along and weighing him down with a full court and with her constant din of advice, he might have been able to do better than he did, or at least not have done so badly in full view of the scornful women.

In addition, there was the more mundane fact that she had borne him only two daughters, and no sons, in twelve years of marriage. This was a serious matter for it placed the succession in jeopardy, and of what value was Aquitaine if there were no son to inherit it? In the case of Anglo-Normandy, Louis had only too clear an object lesson of what might happen to a strong kingdom if only daughters remained behind at the death of a king.

Suger had no chance to change Louis's mind, either. Turning seventy, and worn out with a lifetime of labor, he died in January, 1151. With Suger gone, and with both Eleanor and Louis anxious for a divorce, it was easy enough to trump up a sufficient reason to allow Pope Eugenius III to grant it. This he did in March, 1152.

The divorce, however, had results that far surpassed even the worst of Suger's fears, for immediately after Suger's death, the situation took a change for the worse, as follows.

While Louis had been away in the east, the Anglo-Norman situation had remained unchanged. Stephen still ruled an England that was descending into virtual anarchy. Geoffrey Plantagenet ruled over Anjou and an increasingly restive Normandy, whose lords resented having to owe allegiance to a hated Angevin.

As a result, Geoffrey, who wasn't feeling very well anyway,

decided in 1150 (shortly after Louis's return from the crusade) to transfer the dukedom of Normandy from himself to his and Matilda's son, Henry. Henry, who at that time was seventeen years old, had the advantage, as far as the Norman lords were concerned, of being the great-grandson (on his mother's side) of William the Conqueror.

Now the Anglo-Norman realm was split into three parts: England, Normandy and Anjou; and matters might seem to have improved further for France. Not so; in the space of the next four years there was a series of events, every one of which spelled further disaster for Louis.

First, Suger died and Louis was left without his shrewd guidance. Then, eight months later, in September, 1151, Geoffrey Plantagenet died and young Henry became Count of Anjou as well as Duke of Normandy.

It might have seemed that was an unimportant event. Now it was Stephen and Henry that divided Anglo-Normandy, rather than Stephen and Geoffrey. Geoffrey, however, had been rather third-rate in abilities and had possessed little drive. Henry, on the other hand, was young, vigorous, intelligent and enormously ambitious. Most of all, he was unmarried.

Perhaps Suger, if he had been alive, might have been able to estimate the depths of Eleanor's malice, but Louis VII could not. Anxious only to get rid of his unbearable queen, he went ahead with the divorce, convincing himself, now, that what was important above all else was to get sons. In March, 1152, there came the third event, for the divorce was made final.

Eleanor, herself, then took the next step, and it could have been dictated only by a desire to do Louis as much harm as she could. She was thirty years old and Henry of Normandy was only nineteen, but she was still a handsome woman and she was still young enough to bear children. What's more, most important of all, Aquitaine was still hers to bestow upon a husband, and she chose Henry. Henry might have resisted a woman almost old enough to be his mother, but he couldn't resist Aquitaine, so in May, 1152, less than two months after Eleanor's divorce, they were married.

Eleanor couldn't have liked her new boy-husband very much, and she certainly grew to hate him in time (a hate that was vigorously returned), but if she meant to do harm to Louis she had succeeded. The realm that belonged to her immediately came under the control of Normandy. It meant that all of western France was under the united rule of Henry; even Brittany, which remained independent in theory, was a Norman puppet in actual fact. Louis VII found himself facing a vassal who actually controlled lands in France far more extensive, far more cultured and far richer than the royal domain, and there was nothing he could do about it.

Things rapidly grew even worse. A year later, Stephen's son Eustace died. Stephen himself was in poor health and his remaining son was clearly unfit for rule. He therefore made the best of it by offering to make Henry his heir if Henry would agree to allow Stephen to live out his life as king. Henry, quite certain he would not have long to wait, agreed.

Stephen obligingly died in October, 1154, and before the year was over, Henry of Normandy was crowned King Henry II of England.

What existed now was an "Angevin Empire," so called because Henry II was, on his father's side (which was what counted, dynastically), of the House of Anjou.

Louis VII could now plainly see what had happened. Because of his quarrel with the Church, which had led to his foolish willingness to go adventuring eastward on the Second Crusade, and because of the failure of that crusade, which had led to his divorce from Eleanor, all the painstaking work of his father and of Suger was undone. The Anglo-Norman kingdom had been reunited and to it was added Anjou and Aquitaine.

To anyone watching these events it would now seem that it would be only a matter of time before all of France would be swallowed by the descendants of that dread Norman, William

ENGLAND

London ●
Canterbury ●

ENGLISH CHANNEL

Bouvines ●

EMPIRE

Rouen ●
Château Gaillard

NORMANDY

Mantes ●
Paris ●

CHAMPAGNE

Troyes ●

BRITTANY

MAINE

ANJOU

BURGUNDY

AQUITAINE

Albi ●
Toulouse ●
Muret ●
Béziers ●

NAVARRE

CASTILE

ARAGON

BARCELONA

SPAIN

MAP III

Angevin Empire ▬▬▬▬

The Angevin Empire — 1180

the Conqueror. But, somehow, the appalling nature of the crisis seemed to pull Louis VII together. He had made his last mistake; from now on, he was the shrewd and patient Capetian, waiting catlike for any mistake on the part of his enemy.

Grimly, he held on to what he had and strengthened himself where he could. He married again, but his second wife died after bearing him a single child — a third daughter. He then married a third time, and his new wife, Alice of Champagne, bore him first a daughter and then, in 1165, presented him with a son at last, whom Louis named Philip.

(By that time, however, Eleanor of Aquitaine had borne her new husband, Henry II, four sons and three daughters. A fifth son was destined to arrive in 1167, so that she gave birth to ten children altogether in an age when each childbirth was as dangerous as a pitched battle — and remained robust through it all. She was a remarkable woman in many ways.)

Louis VII could not fight Henry II directly; he was not strong enough; but he was not without weapons, either. For one thing, feudal theory was on his side. Henry, however powerful he might be, was Louis's vassal and owed him obedience. This Henry could not lightly flout, for he had vassals of his own and he could scarcely teach them that it was safe to defy an overlord. Thus, in 1159, when Louis occupied a section of the Mediterranean coast which Eleanor claimed as part of her heritage, Henry voluntarily gave it up rather than fight his overlord.

Then, too, there were conflicts within Henry's dominions, and Louis VII, who could not fight battles well, was a past master at handling disorders in the enemy camp. Thus, between 1164 and 1170, Henry was preoccupied with a Homeric struggle against Thomas Becket, the Archbishop of Canterbury, and throughout that period Louis VII consistently supported Becket. The longer the quarrel lasted, and the more it kept Henry's passions and energies turned inward, the better for France.

After Becket was assassinated in 1170, Henry's sons (too

many for the good of the Angevin realm) were old enough to quarrel among themselves and with their father. Louis VII at every point did what he could to encourage such quarrels and did so with great skill.

So it came about that Henry II, though he seemed to have all the cards on his side, could make no headway against his shrewd and patient adversary, who had seemed so feckless when it was a matter of battle rather than political infighting.

PROGRESS AND PARIS

Meanwhile, as the dynastic quarrels simmered endlessly, France, both on Louis's side of the boundary line and on Henry's side, was steadily progressing in material wealth and prosperity.

Windmills, for instance, were being built in France during the reign of Louis VII, the idea having reached the west from the Arab world, which was further advanced technologically than Europe was in those days, and from which the Crusaders were bringing back all sorts of ideas. (The intellectual ferment caused by the Crusades was far more important in the long run than battles, either lost or won.)

The windmill does the work of a water mill, but more erratically, since the wind does not blow as steadily as water flows; nor does the wind always blow from the same direction. The windmill therefore required more sophisticated engineering than the water mill did. On the other hand, the wind blows everywhere, and windmills made it possible to produce useful power for the grinding of grain, and for other purposes, in regions that were distant from streams.

Thanks to the growing group of men skilled in mechanics through their work on mill machinery, the mechanical clock was introduced some time in the twelfth century. Earlier, the passing of time had been recorded by the periodic ringing of a bell ("cloche" in French, from which the word "clock" is derived) by a watchman who kept his eyes on an hourglass. This was replaced by clock hands which moved automatically, through the impulse of a gradually dropping weight.

By modern standards, the weight-driven clock was a poor device which did not serve to tell time closer than a large fraction of an hour, but it was a great advance on anything that had preceded it. It made men generally far more conscious of time, as they watched the slowly moving hands in the church steeple or town house, and made a beginning for the time-bound portion of western culture. Through making men aware of the *constancy* of time, it helped lay the groundwork for the eventual development of experimental science.

Other advances gained from the east improved western shipping. Increased use of the triangular lateen sail made it easier to take advantage of light winds; the sternpost rudder made it easier to steer. Most of all, the coming of the magnetic compass made it easier to keep a fixed direction when out of sight of land. Gradually, it became possible to sail with confidence in the open sea, and the change began which was eventually to send west European mariners over all the watery globe.

Advance in shipping meant more trade, and a wealthier economy. As a result of two centuries of Capetian rule (plus efficient Norman rule in its part of France), the nation, which had been almost entirely agricultural up to about 1150, was beginning to develop industry and commerce.

This meant an accelerated growth of towns, which were centers of manufacture and trade. These towns were outside feudal theory, which was based entirely on land and agriculture.

The townsmen gathered together to protect themselves against both military and economic disaster. Their union was called a "guild" (from a word related to "gold" and referring to the union dues the members had to pay). The guild gradually divided on craft lines; each different line of work having its own "craft guild." The guild regulated the standards and rules of work, made it possible for members to be protected against cutthroat competition, unemployment and so on.

The richer townsmen, the "bourgeois" or "burghers" (from the word for "castle," the central citadel of a town), gained a social position higher than that of the peasantry and lower than that of the landowning aristocracy. They were a "middle class." Military leadership was reserved for the aristocracy, so the middle class capitalized on its education (necessary for business and commerce) to begin replacing the clergy in service to the State as lawyers and administrators.

Paris was a special case. As the home of the king and the court, it had a prestige that did not depend on its trade or industry, although it had that in gathering plenty. It was a center of the aristocracy and the clergy. In the twelfth century it began to be a center of learning.

Teachers and students flocked to Paris, and there the learning of the day (chiefly those aspects which dealt with the philosophy of religion) were expounded and listened to. Since books were few and expensive, teaching consisted of a professor reading from a book to the assembled crowd of students and then commenting on it. Sometimes two professors would engage in a "disputation," in which each would advance his own theories before audiences of delighted students (a kind of intellectual tennis match).

The most famous of the early teachers was Peter Abelard, who was born in 1079 of a family of minor aristocrats. During the reign of Louis VI, Abelard was an enormously popular lecturer. Students flocked to him avidly, for he was not only an effective orator but he was "modern" as well. He argued, as far as possible through reason, rather than by merely citing authorities.

Indeed, in his book *Sic et Non* (*Yes and No*) he took up 158 theological questions concerning which he cited authorities. In each case, he cited ancients of impeccably pious credentials on each side, and left the matter unsolved and even undiscussed by himself. Without uttering a single word, so to speak, he amply demonstrated the absolute intellectual bankruptcy that comes of merely citing authority.

For all his brilliance, or because of it, he was an unpleasant fellow, intellectually arrogant, and unsparing of others' feelings. In disputations, Abelard would delight in defeating others, including his own teachers, with contemptuous ease, through dialectical brilliance that would have the students cheering him and laughing at his opponents. He was nicknamed the "Indomitable Rhinoceros," which shows what his effect must have been on those pitted against him.

Naturally, he made many bitter enemies among those he mocked, among those who were less popular and among those whose beliefs he unsettled. What's more, Abelard gave his enemies the chance they were waiting for, when, at the age of forty, he fell in love with Héloise, a girl half his age, whom he was tutoring. She was beautiful and intellectually brilliant and both she and Abelard behaved with the kind of foolish romanticism that the troubadours sang of. (The view, usually, is that Peter seduced Héloise, but how can that be when she was willing to be loved and when, from their behavior and correspondence afterward, one might reasonably suspect that she seduced him?)

In any case, Héloise's uncle, furious at this love affair (which eventually resulted in a child), took his revenge by hiring ruffians to seize Abelard and castrate him. Thereafter, Abelard was a broken man, wandering from monastery to monastery, and hounded by his enemies, of whom the chief was Bernard of Clairvaux.

Bernard's mystical views were diametrically opposed to Abelard's reliance on reason, and Bernard was as disputatious and as arrogant as Abelard himself, and far more powerful and dangerous. In the end, Bernard won out and had Abelard's works declared heretical. He would have gone on to have Abelard formally tried for heresy and perhaps executed, but Abelard died in 1142 before the trial could come to pass. Before dying, Abelard wrote an autobiography, *The History of My Calamities*, the first important work of the sort since St. Augustine's autobiography seven centuries before. After Abelard's death, Héloise, who never ceased to love him, saw to his burial, and when she died in 1164 she was buried beside him.

Abelard's views remained influential, however, and the rule of reason which he attempted to establish *was* established despite the opposition of Bernard of Clairvaux. The rational view has reigned in western intellectual life ever since — though never without opposition from mystics.

One of Abelard's students, an Italian known as Peter Lombard, wrote *Book of Sentences* about 1150, in which he, too, quoted authorities. He did not use Abelard's mocking spirit in doing so, however, but carefully selected those authorities which would support a moderate view and would take due account of the role of reason. There was some opposition but it remained a standard text for generations. Peter Lombard's fate was other than Abelard's, for he became Bishop of Paris in the last years of his life.

Another of Abelard's students was a young Englishman, John of Salisbury, whose influence was political as well as theological. He was on the side of the Church against the State and supported Thomas Becket against Henry II. Indeed, he may have been the deciding influence on Becket's views and actions and he was present when Becket was assassinated at the altar of the Canterbury Cathedral. Thereafter, he felt it prudent to retire to Louis's dominions out of the reach of Henry II. He became Bishop of Chartres (shahr'tr), fifty miles southwest of Paris, in his last years.

Abelard, Peter Lombard and John of Salisbury were all theologians, little concerned with the world of nature. There was, however, also the beginnings of "natural philosophy" (the study of nature — something eventually to be called "science") stemming, by way of the translation of Arabic commentaries, from the works of the ancient Greek philosopher Aristotle.

There was Thierry (tyeh-ree') of Chartres, for instance, who may also have been among the teachers of John of Salisbury. Thierry was among the first, in the early twelfth century, to promote Aristotelianism. He endeavored to reconcile the Scriptural descriptions of the universe with those of Aristotle.

About Abelard and his disciples there gathered a permanent clot of students, who formed the nucleus of what was to be the University of Paris, which was definitely in existence by 1160. This was not the first of the universities of the Middle Ages, but it was destined to be the most famous. Its intellectual vigor was to help make Paris famous throughout Europe as a center of culture — a position it was to keep down to our own time.

In secular literature, there was, of course, the troubadour ballads, which reached northern France through the influence of Eleanor of Aquitaine. Such material reached its peak with the work of Chrétien de Troyes (kray-tyahn'duh-trwah').

Chrétien de Troyes seems to have been a native of Champagne, of which Troyes (ninety miles southeast of Paris) was the capital. He was patronized by Marie, the older daughter of Louis VII and Eleanor, who married Henry, Count of Champagne, in 1164.*

At the time, the tale of King Arthur, a legendary British king who fought off invading Saxons in the sixth century, was extremely popular. It had first been told by Geoffrey of Mon-

---

* It was the sister of Henry of Champagne who was Louis's third wife and who the next year became the mother of Philip, heir to the throne, so that Marie's stepmother was also her sister-in-law, and Philip was both her stepbrother and her nephew. Royal marriages produced complicated relationships, some of which could always be found, at need, to make a marriage invalid.

mouth a generation before, as part of his thoroughly fictional history of Britain. Geoffrey wrote in Latin, but a younger writer, Wace, adapted it about 1155 and retold it in Norman-French, in which form it grew exceedingly popular in France.

Chrétien, using the Arthurian legend as background, proceeded to weave tales of courtly love that cast a spell over his contemporaries and have never lost their effect down to this day. It is in Chrétien's version, for instance, that we first find the mystic search for the Holy Grail. It was also there that Sir Lancelot was introduced, a knight who became the epitome of ideal chivalry and who, in popular consciousness, outweighs King Arthur himself.*

The troubadour-inspired Arthurian romances (plus other strictly fictional tales of such historical events as the Trojan War and the conquests of Alexander) replaced the chansons de geste in popularity. They introduced knights who were gentler and more courteous. They played up the beauty and worth of women, and helped raise their status in the real world.

Their universal popularity also popularized the various French dialects outside France and began the process whereby French was to succeed Latin as the language of culture — a position it was to keep into the nineteenth century.

By the twelfth century, there were three French dialects which outweighed all the rest. There was the Norman-French of the Angevin Empire, which was to have an important influence on the development of the English language. There was the Provençal of the south and of the troubadours. And there was the Francien of the court and of the University of Paris. It was the role of the university that made Francien of prime importance to the intellectual world.

---

* Lancelot's love for Guinevere, the wife of King Arthur, is the typical situation to be found in troubadour tales, so that the modern musical *Camelot* is the direct descendant of the romances that Eleanor of Aquitaine brought northward with herself.

THE THIRD CRUSADE

Louis VII's last years were busy ones, as he continued to stir up trouble within the hate-filled family of Henry II.* He kept the pot boiling and even managed to get advantage out of the existence of a powerful enemy. Louis's lords, fearful of Henry II, drew closer about the French throne. Louis's reputation, in his old age, for mildness and justice, encouraged his lords to bring their disputes before him for judgment, thus enhancing the royal prestige.

When Louis VII died in 1180, he managed to leave a strong realm to his son, whom he had had crowned a year before.

The new young king, Philip II, only fifteen years old at the time of his succession, inherited the dangerous situation of having a vassal far stronger than himself. He was a true Capetian, however, and he addressed himself to the situation with a vigor that belied his age.

He was called "Philip the God-given" at first, because his father had waited through three wives and a quarter of a century for his birth (said to have come in response to Louis's ardent prayers). Eventually, however, he was to be called Philip Augustus, because he augmented (that is, enlarged) the realm.

Not many, perhaps, would have been willing to predict such a nickname when Philip first succeeded to the throne. Physically, he was of unimpressive appearance, and had had little time for an education, coming to the throne with no knowledge of Latin. Furthermore, Philip's youth and inexperience raised hopes for power in the hearts of some of the French lords.

In particular, Henry, Count of Champagne, uncle to the new

* Interestingly shown in the motion picture *The Lion in Winter*.

king, thought he had the chance to control the realm and took up arms. At once, Philip showed himself to be young in years only. He made a politically inspired marriage which won him friends against Henry of Champagne and then managed to persuade Henry II, the Angevin, to support him as well.

It might have been to Henry II's advantage to support Henry of Champagne, but he had no reason to suppose the boy-king would be dangerous, or that the Count of Champagne might not be the more dangerous of the two. Besides, Henry had the feeling that vassals must not be allowed to rebel against their king. With both kings against him, Henry of Champagne was forced to give in.

Philip II, secure on his throne, was not minded to return the favor, however. He continued to support Henry's sons. When the oldest of those sons died, Richard, the second, became heir to the throne and took the field against his father. Philip promptly joined Richard and the two became boon companions.

But while this united war against old Henry II continued, there came grisly news from the east once more.

Since the disgraceful Second Crusade of Louis VII, forty years before, conditions in the Holy Land had continued to deteriorate for the Christians. The greatest Moslem hero of the era had arisen in the person of Saladin (sal'uh-din), who united all of Egypt and Syria under his rule and who pressed heavily on the Latin kingdom. In 1187, Saladin actually took Jerusalem itself.

A thrill of horror swept the west at the news, but Richard found something joyful in it. He was his mother's son, a romantic brought up in the troubadour tradition. He even wrote verses himself and sang them sweetly. Indeed, he was the perfect exponent of the courtly love in which the fair maiden is sighed over but never approached, since he was a homosexual.

Like his mother, Richard longed to go on a crusade and win fame in knightly battles in the Holy Land. The capture of Jerusalem by Saladin was the perfect excuse, and he vowed to take an army eastward as soon as he was firmly established on his throne.

Philip II, however, was no romantic at all, but a highly practical and unemotional politician. He knew all too well the results of his father's crusading and the last thing he wanted was to go wandering off to the world's end, while his realm needed him so badly. Not only was he deeply engaged in removing the great danger of the Angevin Empire (including Richard himself when the time came for it) but he was also striving to continue the consolidation of the royal realm, in the careful style of his father and grandfather (and their faithful adviser, Suger).

Philip II established a new class of royal administrator, strictly responsible to himself, to rule the various corners of the realm, administer the king's justice and help keep the lords firmly under the royal sway. He continued to encourage the growth of towns and chose administrators from among the burghers. He also strengthened the army and made it semi-permanent in order to reduce the need to scrabble for men at the moment of crisis, or to depend too heavily on the private equipage of the lords.

Most of all, he paid attention to his capital city of Paris. He built walls about it, paved its streets, began the structure that was eventually to become the Louvre and continued the construction of the great cathedral of Notre Dame, the cornerstone of which had been laid in his father's time. It was under Philip II that the process began which was to end by making Paris the city which the western world united in considering the most charming in the world.

And while all these plans were humming through his mind, some already in process, some in preparation — here was this great fool, Richard, spoiling for a fight, and thinking of nothing more than engaging in storybook tournaments in the east.

Richard demanded that Philip join him in the promise to go on the crusade and Philip had to. For one thing, Richard and he were allies and Philip did not wish to do anything to offend the other at this time. For another, public opinion was strongly pro-crusade at this point, and it would have looked bad for Philip to have refused to agree to fight the infidel for the sake of Christ.

Being Philip, he turned the situation to good use. He took advantage of public fear of Saladin, the reconqueror of Jerusalem, to lay a new tax on his people, the so-called "Saladin tithe." It was intended to raise the money for the crusading venture and surely no good Christian would refuse to pay it. The Saladin tithe was the beginning of a new financial policy that was the very early forerunner of modern taxing procedures.

By and large, Philip did not feel too worried. He was reasonably sure that when Richard became king, royal responsibilities would drive all thought of crusading from his mind. In this, at least, he was wrong. In 1189, Henry II was finally hounded to death by his sons, Richard became king and, to Philip's horror, promptly began preparing to go crusading.

He called on Philip to do likewise. Philip desperately wanted to refuse and began to make the usual polite explanations of difficulties, but public opinion was overwhelming. Philip *had* to go, and, bending to necessity, he agreed to participate in what came to be called the "Third Crusade"; in 1190, they set off. (Philip had no Suger to leave in charge of the kingdom. He appointed a Council of Regency instead, one that included no less than six burghers.)

Once again, as forty years before, the German Emperor agreed to come, and the three greatest kings of Christendom went marching off to war.

This time, things looked well. The German Emperor was Frederick I (usually called Frederick Barbarossa, or "Redbeard"). He was far greater than Conrad III had been. He was in his late sixties by now but had proven himself a fierce warrior and there were no signs that old age had as yet softened him. Philip II, though warfare was not his specialty, was at least going on a crusade without a frivolous queen accompanying him. And then, finally, there was the large, blond knight, Richard I, going along. Surely it could not fail.

And, indeed, the Third Crusade was the only one to vie with the first in legendry and success.

Even so, its success was limited. Frederick Barbarossa, leading his troops overland, reached Asia Minor and there was accidentally drowned while bathing in a small stream. With him gone, his army broke up and played no further part.

That left the two kings, who went by sea, separately. They met in Sicily and quarreled endlessly. It was plain that each distrusted the other far more than either hated Saladin. As far as each king was concerned, the Moslems could remain forever undefeated if such a defeat would mean an advantage for the other.

Nevertheless, each had to keep moving eastward. Philip II, who was anxious to get the whole thing over with, delayed far less than Richard did, and reached the Holy Land on April 20, 1191. There he found the Crusaders desperately trying to salvage some scraps of the coast. They were laying siege to the coastal town of Acre, eighty miles north of Jerusalem. Soon, Richard arrived as well.

Acre had been besieged for nearly two years before the kings came, with little real effect. In that time, the defensive had far the advantage, and strongly walled positions, manned by resolute defenders, could be defeated, generally, only by treachery, starvation or disease. Of these, disease at least was apt to strike the besiegers as the besieged in those days of nonhygiene. Both sides had lost heavily in the course of the siege and both sides were ready to give up. The arrival of the kings, however, gave a lift to the besiegers and reduced the besieged to despair. In July, 1191, the city was taken. As many as 100,000 men had died on both sides.

To Philip II, the capture of Acre brought little to cheer about. He was a far more capable man than Richard was — in everything but actual fighting. At Acre, however, Richard was in his element. He led, shouted, exhorted, fought and left Philip entirely in the shadow; it was as though the French king weren't there.

Both kings shared in the general sickness afflicting the army and both recovered. Philip, however, was by no means well even after his recovery and had had enough. Acre was taken; he could point to that as an accomplishment and it was sufficient for the purpose. He left his army behind, but he himself returned to France before the end of 1191.

Richard loudly proclaimed this to be a desertion and thereafter took over sole leadership of the crusade — something which suited him better anyway.

Back in France, Philip II turned against the real enemy, which, as far as he himself was concerned, was the Angevin Empire. Strictly speaking, the domains of a crusading ruler were considered inviolate while the ruler was fighting the enemies of Christ, but Philip didn't have to attack the Angevin realm directly.

Richard had left behind his younger brother John as regent, and John was every bit as faithless as Richard. Philip began a shrewd campaign to make it clear to John that French support was available if the regent were in the mood for a little usurpation.

Richard, still in the Holy Land, heard the news and grew uneasy. He had fought gallantly and won victories but, though coming within eyeshot of Jerusalem, had not yet succeeded in taking it. Was he to continue in the east while losing his realm at home, or was he to abandon Jerusalem? It was a hard choice, but he finally decided on home, and left the Holy Land in 1192.

On the way back, however, he was taken prisoner in Germany and was held for ransom. Philip II, when the news reached him, must scarcely have been able to believe his good luck. He exerted every effort to have Richard turned over to himself or, at the very least, to have him kept in prison. Prince John was rather in sympathy with this view, but public opinion in favor of the great crusading hero was too strong to withstand. The ransom was raised in the Angevin dominions and, in 1194, Richard returned to his realm.

He did not return in any good humor, however. He was in a fury against Philip II, naturally enough, and began an unrelenting war against him.

The art of war had improved, as had other aspects of western society, thanks to the new knowledge brought back by Crusaders. The metal stirrup, suspended from the saddle, had come into wide use in the west for the first time and had served to lengthen the advantage of the armored knight. It gave him a secure seat and made it possible for him to put the full weight of himself and his horse behind the thrust of the spear.

Castle design became more subtle and efficient, too. Vulnerable corners were avoided, for instance. Richard had learned castle design well and in 1198 was building Château Gaillard ("Gallant Castle") on a precipitous cliff, three hundred feet above the Seine River, fifty miles downstream from Paris. Built with walls within walls, and strongholds within strongholds, it was intended to serve as an impregnable barrier that would prevent Philip from penetrating the Angevin heartland while serving as a basis for raids into the royal dominion.

It worked admirably, and while Philip fended off his bitter enemy as best he could, he lost all the battles. There is no telling how badly things might have gone for France then, were it not for Richard's incurable knight-errantry. He fought for small causes as ardently as for large, and in 1199, in a battle for an unimportant castle, fought over a trivial matter, he received an arrow wound which became infected and killed him.

PHILIP AUGUSTUS!

Succeeding Richard was the far less warlike John, and Philip was saved.

The succession was not an entirely peaceful one. Indeed, on the occasion of every transfer of kingship in the Anglo-Norman history after the death of William the Conqueror, there had been some question as to who was to rule. This time was no exception.

Richard had had a brother, Geoffrey, who was older than John. Had Geoffrey lived, he would have been heir, but he died before Richard. His wife, however, was pregnant at the time of her husband's death and some months later she bore a son whom she named Arthur. Arthur was twelve years old at the time of Richard's death.

The question now was whether a younger brother could take precedence over the son of an older brother in inheriting the crown. According to later notions of "legitimacy" there is a strict order of inheritance and Arthur would have been the "true king," not John. In 1199, however, the matter of legitimacy was by no means well established and there were other matters to consider instead.

The Anglo-Norman realm was in a death struggle with France; was this a time for a boy to become ruler? Furthermore, Arthur had been educated at King Philip's court and was more a Frenchman than a Norman. Could he be trusted to be more than Philip's puppet?

Richard, who knew he would have no sons, had first intended to make Arthur his heir. However, he hated Philip more than anything else in the world and, distrusting the boy's

French education, he decided on John as his heir in 1197. Eleanor of Aquitaine (still alive!) also supported John over a grandson she scarcely knew and so did the anti-French lords of England and Normandy.

So John succeeded, but by no means with the unanimous consent of his vassals. There were lords in the Angevin domain, outside England and Normandy itself, who supported Arthur, and Philip knew that.

The Capetians had consistently supported pretenders to the Anglo-Norman throne at every opportunity. France had supported Robert Curthose against William II, William Clito against Henry I, Matilda against Stephen, and Henry's sons against Henry II. It was the best way of keeping the Anglo-Normans off balance. Philip himself had supported Richard against Henry II, and John against Richard. He was quite ready now to support Arthur against John.

To prevent this from happening, John had to come to quick terms with Philip, at considerable disadvantage to himself. Philip accepted the terms but held on to Arthur for future use and waited for an opportunity to renew hostilities under an occasion favorable to himself. He had not long to wait.

In 1200, less than a year after Richard's death, John had married, with considerable haste, a young lady (only thirteen years old, in fact) named Isabella, who owned considerable land in southern France. The land, of course, was what he chiefly wanted. John divorced his first wife and it was with Isabella that he was crowned.

Unfortunately for John, Isabella, at the time of her hasty marriage, had been engaged to a member of a powerful French feudal family who also wanted that land. The family felt aggrieved and appealed to Philip II.

Philip listened gravely. John, as far as his lands in France were concerned, was Philip's vassal and Philip had a duty to judge disputes between vassals. In 1202, he therefore summoned John to appear before him to answer the charges.

John would not, of course. His dignity as King of England made that impossible and Philip knew he would not. When John failed to come, he was in contempt, and Philip could, again quite according to the letter of feudal law, declare John deprived of the lands he held as vassal.

Naturally, that meant nothing unless Philip was prepared to take them by force, but that was exactly what he planned to do, and with loud proclamations to the effect that he had right on his side, he took the field.

John had to fight.

In the shifting fortunes of war, John, in 1203, came to the relief of a castle where Eleanor of Aquitaine was being besieged. The besieging army included Arthur among its leaders. Not only did John rescue his mother, but he also captured Arthur.

Arthur was promptly imprisoned and was never again seen. Exactly what happened to him no one knows, but the general opinion is that John had him quietly executed. This gave John undisputed control of the throne, but it meant an enormous propaganda defeat for him. Philip had skillfully placed him in the wrong from the standpoint of feudal theory, and now the French king worked hard to spread the view that John had murdered his nephew, the rightful king.

Many of the French vassals turned away from the royal murderer and switched to Philip's side, as he stood there, shining in conscious rectitude. At once, the Anglo-Norman dominions began to fade away.

Nor was it a matter of mere propaganda. Even while the poison of Arthur's imprisonment and presumable execution was doing its work, Philip was preparing to carry through an astonishing feat of arms. It was an age of castles and Philip made ready to lay siege to the greatest castle of them all, Richard's own Château Gaillard, thoroughly modern and widely thought to be impregnable.

In the summer of 1203, Philip encircled it and settled down

to the siege. To keep his army busy, he kept it working away at the castle in a variety of ways. He used catapults to throw large rocks over the walls, and battering rams to bang away at them. He tried to mine the walls also — that is, he dug the ground away from under them in spots, while shoring them up with timbers; then he burned the timbers. He even sent soldiers through a drainpipe in hope that they would penetrate the interior.

What he was waiting for all the time, however, was for starvation to do its work. By the coming of cold weather, the pinch of hunger was making itself felt inside the castle. At all costs, the defenders had to hang on, for who knew when disease might not strike down the besiegers, or when dissension might not break out among them, or when a relieving army might come? To stave off utter famine, therefore, the defenders sent out of the castle some four hundred women, children and old men.

The French army did not let them pass, nor did they kill them. They kept them in no man's land, hoping that the defenders, out of pity, would take them back and starve the faster. Neither side would give in, and, in a competition of heartlessness, both sides watched the poor outcasts, reduced even to cannibalism, die of starvation and exposure in the course of the winter.

In the end, starvation did its work and in March, 1204, Château Gaillard surrendered and Philip had a stunning victory that utterly broke Angevin morale.

In June, Philip's forces marched into Rouen, the Norman capital, and by 1205 he was in control of virtually all of northern France. He was Philip Augustus indeed.

Eleanor of Aquitaine died in 1204, just a few weeks after the surrender of Château Gaillard. She was well over eighty years old. She had been the wife of two kings and the mother of two kings. She had been imprisoned and she had triumphed. She had been humiliated at the failure of her first husband in a crusade. She had been overjoyed at the great feats of her son in another crusade. She had been the occasion for the establishment of the Angevin Empire and she lived just long enough to see it melt away.

Yet parts of her own heritage remained. The southwestern coast of France, with its great seaport of Bordeaux, remained loyal to John. England continued to hold coastal Aquitaine, usually called Guienne (gee-en'), for two and a half more centuries.

4

THE CLIMB UPWARD

THE ORTHODOXY OF PHILIP

After the end of the Angevin Empire, France was free to expand without the constricting effect of the rival power that had held it by the throat for half a century. And it did expand. For a century afterward, it climbed upward in wealth and influence.

Philip II himself saw France through the first stages of the climb. He did so not merely by his successful war against the Angevins but by warring against religious division within the wide areas nominally subject to him.

One group, relatively easy to take care of, was the Jews.

The Jews had lived in western Europe since Roman times, surviving occasional periods of hostility but, on the whole, not too badly treated. They could not hold land in the feudal system for they could not take the Christian-oriented vows required, but, in an agricultural society, their penchant for trade and commerce was useful and they played the role of a middle class.

The western Jews even managed to develop an intellectual life of their own, based on the Old Testament and on the voluminous commentaries (the "Talmud") developed over the centuries in Judea and Babylonia. About 1000, Gershom ben Judah headed a rabbinic academy in the Rhineland and was the first to bring to western Europe the Talmudic lore of the east.

Toward the end of the eleventh century, the leading Jewish scholar was Rabbi Solomon ben Isaac, who had been born in the French town of Troyes in 1040. Usually known as Rashi (rash'ee), from the Hebrew initials of his name, he wrote highly regarded commentaries on every aspect of the traditional Jewish law.

But then came the crusading fever. The ignorant crowds, fanned into wild anti-Moslem zeal by the winds of propaganda, sought out whatever enemies of Christ they could find. The Moslems were far away and dangerous, but the Jews were close at hand and helpless. Mobs destroyed the Jewish communities in many towns, and western Europe experienced the first wave of what in later centuries were to be called "pogroms."

Worse than wild periodic bursts of anti-Semitism, which passed, was a permanent economic change. The rise of a native middle class in France, for instance, made the Jews less necessary from an economic standpoint. The French burghers themselves would do. Philip II could therefore parade his Christian orthodoxy without economic danger. Almost at the beginning of his reign, he began to harry the Jews out of France.

The deterioration of the Jewish position in the twelfth century began their drift eastward to less advanced lands, which still welcomed a ready-made class. Thus it came about that in later centuries it was in eastern Europe that Jews were found in greatest concentration (and where they were eventually to find new persecutions).

The orthodox Christian could, however, find offense closer to home. Not all Christians believed according to the official doctrine as handed out from the Church hierarchy. There were "heretics" who had views of their own, for all that they accepted Jesus.

In Bulgaria, sometime before 1000, there came the beginnings of a puritanical sect that believed the world and its material content to be a creation of the Devil. They therefore rejected the Old Testament which made it appear that God formed the world and found it good. In order to be assured of salvation, it was necessary, they believed, to refrain as far as possible from any connection with the world. The new sect disbelieved in marriage, in sex, or in eating and drinking beyond the bare essentials. Death was a positive good, and, if all men died and thus freed themselves of their material bodies, so much the better.

The tenets drifted westward and caught root in southern France. The puritanical attitude grew popular as a reaction, in part, against the worldly corruption of much of the Catholic priesthood, and the heresy flourished.

The men of the new sect called themselves "Cathari" from a Greek word for "pure." Outstanding among these puritans was Peter Waldo, a rich merchant of Lyon (lee-one'), which is now in southeast France but which was then, despite its French culture, part of the German Empire. In 1170, Waldo, following the advice of Jesus literally, sold his goods, gave them to the poor and began to gather men about him ("the poor men of Lyon" or "Waldensians"), who preached voluntary poverty.

The city of Albi, nearly 200 miles southwest of Lyon, was another center of Cathari strength. In Roman times, it had been the capital of a Gallic tribe known as the Albigenses. As a result, the sect came to be known as Albigensians and the name was sometimes used for all the heretics in southern France and northern Italy.

The Church approved the feelings about poverty and puritanism within limits, but wanted them guided by the hierarchy. They could not sympathize with the desire of the Cathari to get rid of the churchly administrative structure. Waldo, for instance, had the New Testament translated into Provençal so that each person could read and interpret it for himself. The Cathari did not feel it necessary to obey priests and bishops against the dictates of their own conscience.

Indeed, the Cathari in their various forms were almost like certain Protestant sects that came to exist three centuries later.

The Church might easily have crushed these heretics but the Cathari found sympathizers among a number of the southern lords. These lords may well have been attracted by the doctrine, though it may also be that they saw a chance to expropriate Church lands and wealth if the heretics won out.

The strongest supporter of the Cathari was Raymond VI, Count of Toulouse (which was forty-five miles southwest of Albi). He succeeded to the title in 1194 and resisted papal blandishments to change his attitude.

In 1198, however, Innocent III ascended the papal throne, and, under him, the medieval papacy reached the peak of its political power. Its prestige had been greatly enhanced by the crusading movement and it could now, under the lead of a firm and resolute man, bring even strong kings to heel. Innocent was such a man.

He sent a legate to Raymond to urge him to take measures to stamp out the heresy, but Raymond refused. Innocent grew firmer in his insistence, and Raymond in his refusal, and then, in 1208, the legate was killed. The tale was quickly put out that the murder had been carried through at Raymond's order and an angry Pope Innocent declared a crusade against the heretics. It became as legal and praiseworthy (in the eyes of the Church) to kill heretics as to kill Moslems.

Innocent had hoped that Philip II would take over the leadership of the crusade, but Philip saw no reason to do so.

It was sufficient to allow his lords to do the job, stay at home and reap the reward of his orthodoxy and their efforts. As for the lords, eager for all the religious benefits that would come from going on a crusade, and for loot as well, they flocked to the task.

Prominent among them was Simon de Montfort (mone-fawr'), who had fought in the Holy Land against Moslems and who knew exactly how a Crusader should fight. In 1209, the northern Crusaders took the town of Béziers (bay-zyay'), near the Mediterranean coast, a hundred miles east of Toulouse. The town was put to the sack, but the question arose as to how to tell which of the town's inhabitants were damned heretics and which were good Catholics. Simon de Montfort (or perhaps a legate of the Pope) had an easy solution.

"Kill them all," he said, "for the Lord will know his own." And so several tens of thousands of men, women and children were killed.

Raymond VI, fearing he could not withstand the ravaging barons of the north without help, turned to Pedro II of Aragon, a Spanish kingdom lying just south of the Pyrenees. The Aragonese culture and language was close to the Provençal, and besides, Pedro was Raymond's brother-in-law, so he answered the call.

The crucial battle took place on September 12, 1213, at Muret (myoo-ray'), a town about twelve miles south of Toulouse. The forces of Raymond and Pedro, which were laying siege to the town, were superior in number to those of Montfort, but the allies cooperated imperfectly. Montfort, in a daring maneuver, led his knights out of the city as though he were trying to escape and then wheeled back to fall upon Pedro's troops in a surprise charge, while Raymond's remained inactive. Pedro II was killed in action, and when his forces broke, those of Raymond were demoralized and were quickly swept along as well. It was a complete victory for the northerners.

The heretics held out stubbornly, but one by one their strongholds were wiped out. Montfort himself died in action in 1218 outside the walls of Toulouse and it was not till 1226 that the heresy was thoroughly stamped out in blood and cruelty. (Indeed, remnants of the Waldensians continued to survive all difficulties and to remain in isolated Alpine valleys right down into the twentieth century.)

With the Cathari, the flourishing Provençal culture was destroyed and the way was opened to the spread of the Capetian power to the Mediterranean. As an example, Provençal lost its status as a separate language and slowly gave way to Francien.

In dying, however, the independent Provençal culture had its effect on the ruder world of the north. For instance, Roman law (as systematized under the Byzantine Emperor, Justinian, in the sixth century) had been rediscovered in Italy shortly after 1100. Roman law was taught first in the University of Bologna and from there it spread to the Provençal University of Toulouse. With the assimilation of the south accomplished, Roman law, with its tenets more humane and orderly than those based on old Teutonic doctrine, reached Paris.

The "Albigensian Crusade" left, however, an evil legacy in the form of an almost paranoid fear of heresy on the part of many.

As long as the enemies of the Church were Jews and Moslems, they could easily be recognized. Heretics, on the other hand, who believed in Jesus and revered his teachings, were usually harder to identify. Very often, they simply sounded like unusually virtuous Christians (almost to the point, in fact, where virtue was itself grounds for suspicion of heresy).

If heretics remained a minor danger, they could be dealt with locally. The Cathari, however, had required a major war before they could be destroyed, so more drastic methods for dealing with heresy were put into action.

A judicial body called the "Inquisition" came into being in 1233. It dealt with suspicions of heresy, inquired into the matter (using torture, if necessary, something which was common judicial procedure at the time) and then, if the suspicion were confirmed, handed the heretic over to the secular authorities to be put to death.

The Inquisition served to suppress dissent of all kinds and in those districts where it was most active, it had a deadening effect on intellectual activity and cultural ferment. Where it best succeeded in creating unity of opinion, it did so by establishing an intellectual desert.

THE LAST ANGEVIN FLICKER

Despite Philip's official orthodoxy and his harsh actions against those who did not fit into the rigid Catholic structure, he did not hesitate to oppose the Church in personal matters.

In 1193, for instance, Philip was twenty-eight, and a widower. He already had a six-year-old son and heir, but an unmarried condition offered a king a chance for a stroke of politics. Philip therefore agreed to marry Ingeborg, the sister of Canute VI of Denmark, so that he might possibly make use of the Danish fleet against the Angevins (the formidable Richard was at war with him, then).

Ingeborg arrived. What went on during the wedding night no one knows, but whatever it was, it didn't suit Philip. The next morning, he repudiated her, fleet or not, and arranged to have an assembly of bishops annul the marriage. When the humiliated Ingeborg refused to return to Denmark, Philip had her placed in a convent and three years later took another wife. The Danish king, furious at the insult to his sister, appealed the matter to the Pope who was then Celestine III.

Celestine ordered Philip to leave his new wife and reinstate Ingeborg, but Philip paid no attention. And then Innocent III succeeded to the papacy.

In 1200, Innocent III lost patience with Philip and placed France under an interdict. Philip might have held out even so, but he was facing his duel with John and he wanted no complications in the form of lords who would plead they could not fight for him because of papal thunders. Most reluctantly, he gave in and agreed to take back Ingeborg. He didn't really; he still kept her in the convent; but he had to grant her the title of queen.

Then, after Philip took Château Gaillard and overran Normandy, he had the grim pleasure of watching John of England run foul of the masterful Pope Innocent in his turn. John fought the matter out more stubbornly than Philip had, for the English king was involved in a difficult dispute over principles of control over bishops and Church money, not over a personal marital difficulty. The dispute endured for years.

The French king waited patiently for Pope Innocent to come through with a threatened deposition of John. In that case, Philip could, if he wished, invade Guienne, or even England itself, maintaining that he was only fulfilling the orders of Mother Church, and some English lords, accepting the view, might defect to the French side.

John knew perfectly well that Philip was ready for just such an invasion in just such a case. He also knew that his own vassals, some annoyed at John's ill success in battle, others at the discomforts of the battle with the Church, and all at John's harsh policy of taxation necessitated by the loss of French revenues, were restive.

John was forced at last, therefore, to make a humble submission to the Pope in 1213. That, to Philip's keen disappointment, ended England's difficulties in that direction. John then made ready to reverse the situation and to invade France. He had not yet given up hope of re-establishing the Angevin Empire.

For this purpose, he had made an alliance with the German Emperor, Otto IV, whose mother had been an older sister of

John's. Together, uncle and nephew planned a pincer attack against Philip. John was to take an army to Guienne and attack Philip from the southwest. Otto, in alliance with the Count of Flanders, would simultaneously invade France from the northeast.

Unfortunately for the allies, they did not achieve synchronization. Had Otto and John acted together, Philip would have had to divide his forces and might then possibly have been defeated. As it was, Otto delayed, and John found himself attacking from Guienne alone. There, he was defeated.

When Otto finally moved, along with those Flemish and English contingents that had joined his army, it had become a one-front war and Philip could move his entire force to the northeast.

The armored cavalry, which bore the main brunt of the fight, was about equal on the two sides, but Philip managed to maneuver Otto onto ground where the French forces would have the advantage. The two armies met on July 27, 1214, at Bouvines (boo-veen'), a village ten miles southeast of Lille, for one of the very few decisive pitched battles in that age of war-by-siege.

It was, however, another one of those battles in which knight met knight with much noise and little damage. (It was only the unarmed footmen who had to fear massacre.) At one point indeed, Philip himself was seized and pulled off his horse. The enemy soldiers then tried to find some chink in his armor through which they could stick a lance — but failed. Before they could do anything about the metal shell, Philip was rescued.

In the end, the result of the mutual battering was that Otto fled and his forces were driven from the field. The victory of Philip II was complete and England's hope for a restoration of its French dominions was smashed for over a century.

John's failure made his condition still more precarious in England, where his lords moved into clear rebellion. They

forced concessions from John in 1215, these being summarized
in what came to be called the "Magna Carta," thus beginning
a process which fixed limitations on the royal power in England
and kept it from ever becoming as absolute as it did on the
Continent.

Nor were all the lords satisfied even then. Some agreed to
offer the crown to Louis, the older son of Philip II, as a way of
blackmailing John into still further concessions. Louis accepted
the offer and led an army into England in May, 1216.

This is the only invasion of England, after the Norman conquest, by a foreign army, and it had some successes. Prince
Louis even occupied London for a time. John, however, died
in October, and the English lords then began to flock about
John's nine-year-old son, who succeeded as Henry III. Louis
was defeated in 1217 and left England (though not before
accepting a ten-thousand-mark bribe to do so).

On July 14, 1223, then, when Philip II died at Mantes
(mahnt), thirty miles west of Paris, he could look back on a
forty-three-year reign filled with accomplishment and solid
deeds that meant far more than the flashiness of his great oppo-
nent, Richard. Philip left a royal realm which had doubled in
size over that which he had inherited. He had destroyed the
Angevin Empire, which, at his accession, had been stronger in
France than he was. He had further extended the power of the
central government over the feudal lords, had steadily increased
the prosperity of the land * and had left a substantial surplus in
the treasury.

It was in his reign, too, that an important literary advance
took place. A French nobleman, Geoffroi de Villehardouin
(vee-lahr-dwan'), took part in the "Fourth Crusade." This was

---

* Of course, we must not judge prosperity by modern standards.
The economy was still primitive, and during Philip's reign eleven
famines were recorded. Then, too, with cities largely built of wood
and with fire-fighting techniques virtually nonexistent, life was precarious in that respect. The city of Rouen burned down six times in
twenty-five years.

diverted from its intended goal and, in 1204, captured and sacked the great Byzantine capital of Constantinople, which never entirely recovered.

When de Villehardouin returned, he published a chronicle, *Conquest of Constantinople*. This was not only a well-written book and a most valuable history, but it was the first piece of historical prose of the Middle Ages that was not written in Latin. It was written in Francien. Combining this with the destruction of the Provençal culture, we can, from this point on, speak of the Parisian dialect as French, and consider it a virtually national language. This meant that, for the first time, a French nationalism transcending provincial boundaries might exist and be ready for exploitation by those kings clever enough to take advantage of it.

Perhaps the most impressive sign of the increased strength of the Capetian dynasty, however, is an apparently small one. Since 987, seven Capetian kings had ruled in Paris. Each of the first six, in order to assure the succession, had had his son crowned in his own presence, thus binding the lords to the new king in advance. Philip II, the seventh in the line, had felt no need for that. He had so established the Capetian monarchy in the hearts of Frenchmen that he was quite sure that no one could possibly dream of disputing the succession. Besides, his son Louis was a mature man of thirty-six at the time of Philip's death and had won laurels for himself in the invasion of England.

And so it came about. Philip's son succeeded to the throne without trouble and reigned as Louis VIII. He is sometimes called Louis the Lion-Heart, an obvious reference to his father's great adversary, Richard, and therefore a slap at the English, whose territory he had invaded.

He was not, however, as successful as the nickname might indicate. He carried on Philip's policies but struck no sparks. He attempted to drive the English out of Guienne but failed.

With greater success, he continued the task of extirpating the Albigensian heresy in the south.

He established one pernicious precedent which, in years to come, was to prove almost fatal to France; that was the policy of being too good to younger sons.

The first Capetian kings had to work too hard to wrest control of the royal lands from the lords to give much of it away. Then, when land and power grew, there was the fortunate fact that Philip II was an only son and therefore got it all. Philip, in turn, had two sons, but wisely let the younger be satisfied with a minor title and again all went to his successor.

Louis VIII, however, had four sons, and while the oldest was to inherit the kingdom, parental love saw to it that the three younger sons each became lord of a sizable province. This was called an "appanage" from a Latin phrase meaning "to furnish support," since the revenues could support the younger sons in a style becoming a scion of the royal family.

To be sure, the provinces chosen were from among those recently conquered from the Angevins or from the south, and did not touch the original royal domain. Also, in theory, the appanages were still in complete subjection to the royal authority and could be taken away. However, there was always the chance that if the king were weak or careless, an appanage could descend from father to son till long usage and distant relation would make it seem un-French and its ruler an independent sovereign.

What Louis VIII did, then, was to start a custom that succeeded in establishing a new kind of lord, more powerful and more dangerous than the old, if only because the new lords were themselves Capetians and could aspire to the throne. The time was to come when the existence of appanages would nearly destroy the kingdom.

Then, something else unprecedented in Capetian history took place. The first six successors of Hugh Capet had each reigned a long time, never less than twenty-nine years and for an average length of thirty-eight. This was one of the many strokes of good fortune for the dynasty, for a long reign usually fixes a particular king in the mind of the subjects and makes the succession of a grown son seem almost a matter of course.

But in 1226, having ruled only three years, Louis VIII died while campaigning in the south. His oldest son succeeded as Louis IX, but he was only twelve years old, and the son of a mere three-year king.

THE SAINT-KING

There was trouble, of course. The accession of a boy-king would always be the signal for attempts on the part of the aristocracy to gain power. In fact, this was a chance for the lords to reverse the steady process of centralization carried through by the Capetian kings; as it turned out, the last really good chance.

The new king was, however, fortunate in his mother, a woman who was more than a match for all the men who now gathered together wolfishly to pluck selfish advantage at the cost of France, generally. She was Blanche of Castile, a younger daughter of Alfonso VIII, king of Castile, and, through her mother, a niece of the English kings, Richard and John. She was married to the prince who later became Louis VIII when she was only twelve years old, as part of the temporary peace agreement between John and Philip in 1200.

Despite her Angevin inheritance she was completely French. When her husband invaded England, she was heart and soul with the project. When, after John's death, Louis was driven back, she personally took charge of attempts to send supplies across the Channel.

When her husband died, she at once took over the regency, running the kingdom on behalf of her son with a strong hand. She maintained the royal prerogatives, turned back the threat from a league of lords and defeated a halfhearted English invasion of Brittany.

During her regency, Raymond VII of Toulouse, the son of the ill-starred Raymond VI, was finally defeated and the Albigensian heresy wiped out. Blanche saw to it that Raymond's heir, a daughter, was married to one of her younger sons. Louis IX himself was married by Blanche to Margaret, who was heiress of Provence, that section of the Mediterranean coast east of the Rhone River. Through these marriages, the royal power was brought south to the Mediterranean. The vision of Suger of a century before, in connection with the ill-starred marriage of Louis VII and Eleanor of Aquitaine, was now brought to fruition by Blanche, and permanently.

What's more, Blanche was in charge of the education of her son, and she brought him up in the strict tradition of Christian piety and virtue. He always remained a mama's boy to an extent, but he was a strong king, nevertheless. Her teachings made him sufficiently mild and gentle in his private life, however, to win over the hearts of his people and the admiration of most historians.

His Christian virtues are exemplified by the fact that he was faithful to his wife (who bore him eleven children), which was not royal custom in those days — or later days, either. He wore a hair shirt next to his skin, which, of course, itched and irritated him, and induced skin disorders. This was in line with the theory of those times that it helped keep one's mind on higher things if the body was mistreated. As a gesture of humility, Louis would kiss lepers and have poor people brought in to dine with him. He insisted on the dregs of society, so that beggars were brought in sometimes who smelled so badly that the soldiers of the guard (no flowers themselves, no doubt) objected.

Louis IX also improved justice by abolishing trial by combat (in which the more skillful fighter, or the man who could hire the more skillful fighter, was sure to win the suit) and insisted on using actual evidence to judge between the right and wrong of an affair.

In only a few respects did his piety lead him to cruelty. He promulgated stiff laws against blasphemy, gambling and prostitution, and insisted on the most barbarous treatment of Jews and heretics.

It is no wonder that a quarter century after his death, he was canonized by the Church (not many kings are and still fewer deserve it as clearly as Louis did). Louis IX is usually known as St. Louis for that reason.

Louis was twenty years old in 1234, when he began to rule in his own name, taking over the kingdom which his mother had handed him intact and stronger than ever. He showed at once that his direct control would not change matters for the worse. When Henry III of England tried to encourage feudal rebellions in the south and to support these by English invasion, Louis reacted strongly and promptly and re-established order.

This was a period of time in which England was weakened by constant squabbling between king and lords, and the German Empire was in virtual anarchy. France was the one strong power in western Europe, and Louis IX kept it strong by staunchly maintaining the royal prerogatives on every side as his mother had, even (despite his piety) against the Church.

He further increased the efficiency of administration, pushing hard against bribery and corruption. He issued laws covering the entire kingdom so as to increase its feeling of unity. He established a uniform coinage for the realm, outlawed local warfare, the private carrying of arms, and other aspects of the more anarchic side of feudalism. He also began increasing royal control over the towns in order to weaken the great mercantile families who, at their worst, had become almost middle-class lords in their independence and in their callous treatment of the lower classes.

In all this, Louis was aided by the growing prestige of Roman law as the basis of government. In place of Teutonic tribal decentralization, Roman law supported a strong central executive. Louis used its tenets to justify the increase of his own power at the expense of lords, burghers and priests.

Under him, France continued to advance culturally. The University of Paris was now a definite and already renowned institution. Robert de Sorbon (sawr-bone′), who was Louis IX's chaplain and confessor, endowed a foundation for impoverished students of theology, and out of this grew the great school that still bears his name, the Sorbonne.

Scholars flocked to Paris to study and teach from all over Europe. Among the great names which are to be found in the University's annals in this period are Roger Bacon from England, Albertus Magnus from Germany and Thomas Aquinas from Italy.

The influence of Aristotle's philosophy grew as his books became available through translation from Arabic, and Thomas Aquinas, who came to Paris in 1256, completed what Abelard had begun. With Aquinas, the victory of rationalism in theology was final, for he succeeded in creating a complete synthesis of Aristotelian philosophy and Catholic doctrine. His teachings remain the fundamental basis of the Catholic system of theology to this day.

Albertus Magnus was an accomplished alchemist who is credited with the discovery of the chemical element, arsenic. He was the first individual in history to whom the discovery of a particular chemical element can be attributed. Roger Bacon emphasized the importance of experiment and observation over authority and deduction and is therefore one of the forerunners of modern science. He described spectacles and gunpowder in his writings and both came into use over the next century.

An actual experimenter in science, one whose work is valuable even by modern standards, was Peter Peregrinus (pehr-uh-grigh'nus), who was an engineer in Louis IX's army. In 1269, while taking part in the slow and dull siege of an Italian city, Peregrinus wrote a letter to a friend in which he described his researches on magnets. His work helped make the magnetic compass a sure and delicate device for use on shipboard, since he showed how a magnetized needle could be made to pivot and how it might be surrounded by a circular, graduated scale.

The spinning wheel was introduced in the thirteenth century. In place of the twisting by hand which slowly converted a fuzzy yarn into a tight, strong thread, there was a large wheel, easily driven by a foot treadle. It made spinning both easier and faster. It is also the first example of the transmission of power by means of an endless belt, something very common, on a much huger scale, in modern industry.

Romantic fiction continued to grow in popularity after Chrétien de Troyes had shown the way. Thibaut IV (tee-boh'), Count of Champagne, was a most successful writer of lyric verses in the troubadour tradition. He was born in Troyes in 1201 and was brought up in the court of Philip II. Some of his early verses were thought to have been addressed to Blanche of Castile, and indeed he took her side against the other lords during her regency. This won him enemies and he was accused of having poisoned Blanche's husband, Louis VIII, though this is extremely unlikely.

A longer piece of romantic literature is the thirteenth-century fictional work *Aucassin and Nicolette*. It gives an account of two young lovers who are first separated and then reunited; and the story is full of lovers' laments, suspense, narrow escapes, with all crowned by a happy ending. It is the "boy meets girl; boy loses girl; boy gets girl" plot that is still popular today and is likely to be popular forever.

An even more elaborate and ambitious production is the

Roman de la Rose. This deals with the allegorical wooing of a rosebud (symbolizing a young maiden) growing in a garden that symbolizes aristocratic society. All sorts of abstract qualities are personified in a fashion that allowed trenchant comments on the life of the times. The first part was written about 1240 by a French poet, Guillaume de Lorris, and it was completed about 1280 by another French poet, Jean de Meung.

Louis IX himself collected manuscripts and encouraged literature. What's more, he was the occasion for the first great biography in the vernacular. Jean de Joinville (zhwahn-veel'), who served and admired Louis, wrote his biography after the death of the saintly king. (Joinville himself is remarkable as one who, among the short-lived people of medieval times, managed to attain the great age of ninety-three.)

Louis's encouragement of literature did not extend to the more popular forms, however. These displeased him with their licentiousness.

Rollicking students of the growing universities relieved the hours of serious study, for instance, by writing gay, satirical and often libidinous verse praising wine and women and poking fun at the clergy. They called themselves "goliards," apparently a distortion of "Goliath," after a mythical bishop who was the subject of some of the songs. The Church did not find the goliardic verse at all amusing, but many other people did and such things were hard to control, even by the severest cleric, or even by the king.

There were also "fabliaux" (rather like what we would today call anything from "comic anecdotes" to "short stories"), usually intended to raise a laugh. The best known of the fabliaux writers wrote under the pseudonym Rutebeuf (ryoot-bawf'), and he did not hesistate, in his writings, to make fun of the Pope or even of Louis IX himself.

The most famous of the fabliaux is a connected series of popular verse, elaborated in the course of the thirteenth century, and called *Le Roman de Renart* (*The History of Reynard the Fox*). This is an allegorical tale of animals who clearly represent human counterparts. The tale tells of the manner in which Reynard, through unprincipled shrewdness, defeats and humiliates the other animals, even the more powerful, such as the wolf, bear and lion.

The fabliaux were clearly middle-class literature. The clergy and the aristocracy were the villains, and Reynard, in particular, personified the clever man of the people, who, with power arrayed against him, had to get by on his wits.

The growing vigor of the French language was such that it spilled over beyond France's boundaries even this early. An Italian scholar, Brunetto Latini (lah-tee′nee), wrote an encyclopedia of knowledge between 1262 and 1266, while in exile in France. The natural thing to have done at that time would have been to write it in Latin. He chose, instead, to write in French.

THE LAST CRUSADES

Perhaps the most remarkable, and most useless, aspect of the reign of Louis IX, but one that was well-suited to his piety, was his single-handed revival of crusading zeal.

Since the time of the Third Crusade, a half-century before, the whole concept of crusading had lost its idealism and had become a matter of crude power politics, heretic hunting or worse. The Fourth Crusade had all but destroyed the great Christian city of Constantinople, and the dreadful bloody war in southern France had been dignified with the name of a crusade.

Worse yet, in 1212, a kind of mania seized the teen-age children of France and Germany. The idea spread that children would succeed where the soldiers had failed. Because of their innocence, the children would be guided to the Holy Land and to victory by God. Southward they wandered to the Mediterranean which, they were convinced, would part for them. Many perished on their way. Those who reached the sea and who waited vainly for the parting were approached by mariners who offered to take them over. The mariners did so, too, and sold them into slavery.

More crusades of the usual kind also took place. Some of them are given numbers. The "Fifth Crusade," which took place between 1218 and 1221, was a complete failure. The "Sixth Crusade," 1228–1229, was a success in a way. It was conducted by the German Emperor Frederick II, very much against his will. He actually recovered Jerusalem in 1229, but by negotiation, not by battle. Jerusalem remained Christian for fifteen years before being retaken a second time by the Moslems in 1244.

About this time, too, a still greater danger than the Turks menaced Europe. The Mongol tribes of central Asia were united under the remarkable leadership of Temujin (tem′oo-jin), who later called himself Genghis Khan (jen′gis-kahn′) or "Very Mighty King." And so he was, for before he died in 1227, just after the accession of Louis IX, Genghis Khan had conquered all of China and much of the rest of Asia, with only India and Indo-China behind the barrier of the Himalayas remaining free.

Under Genkhis Khan's son and successor, Ogadai Khan (og′-a-digh), the Mongols swept into Europe and took all of Russia. In 1240, they moved farther west still. They handily defeated the Poles, Hungarians and Germans, and the only force that seemed to stand in the way of their reaching the Atlantic after the total subjugation of Europe was the army of Louis IX.

It seems doubtful that this army, or any European army of the time could have withstood the mobile Mongol horsemen under the leadership of their remarkable general, Subotai (sub′-oh-tigh′), — but the test never came. In 1241, Ogadai Khan died and the Mongol armies in Europe returned to Asia to take part in an election for his successor. They never came back to western Europe, although Russia remained under their domination for centuries.

Louis IX was unaware of his close call, however; his eyes remained fixed on the Holy Land and on the much older menace of the Turks.

At the time, Constantinople was still in the hands of Frenchmen, thanks to the manner in which the men of the Fourth Crusade took and nearly destroyed the city. The hold was tenuous, however, and the "Latin Emperor," Baldwin II, himself of Capetian lineage, made begging visits to France in 1236, pleading for help. This affected Louis strongly. Then in late 1244, there came an illness during which he thought he might die and, as he lay recovering, there came the news that Jerusalem had once more fallen to the Moslems. Louis felt he had been saved from death for a purpose and he promptly made a formal vow to go on a crusade.

It took some time to disentangle himself of affairs at home, and Louis's mother, Blanche of Castile, pleaded with him not to go. Louis might conceivably have listened to his revered mother, but then, in 1245, Baldwin II was back in Paris, and he carried with him something he said was the very crown of thorns which Jesus had worn on the Cross. Louis would not have dreamed of doubting that he held in his hands the veritable object that had played its part in the Crucifixion twelve centuries before. He had a lovely church, the "Sainte-Chapelle," built to house it and then intensified his preparation.

In 1248, he sailed away with his army on what is known as the "Seventh Crusade," leaving his mother to be regent in his absence. He was the third French king to go crusading.

It was Louis's plan not to strike at the Holy Land directly. This was in line with the greater sophistication of the crusading movement. It had become quite clear that holding the

Holy Land was very much like holding the tail of a lion, leaving its head and claws free to strike back. One had to strike at the head, the main center of Moslem power, and the tail would then fall by itself. The main center at this time lay in Egypt, and it was toward Egypt that Louis IX led his army.

In particular, Louis was considering the events of the Fifth Crusade, a generation earlier. In 1218, Crusaders had attacked Egypt and had laid siege to Damietta (dam-yet'uh), a city at the eastern mouth of the Nile. The siege lasted eighteen months and the city was taken. The Egyptian sultan then offered to restore all Moslem holdings in the Holy Land, including Jerusalem, if the Crusaders would give up their holdings in Egypt. Unfortunately, success had fired up the enthusiasm of the papal emissary and he refused, ordering the Crusaders to conquer all of Egypt, even though the Nile was in flood and it was almost impossible to advance. Naturally, the Crusaders met complete defeat.

Louis reasoned that Damietta was as important to the Egyptian sultan now as then. If he took it, he could exchange it for Jerusalem. So he landed his army at the mouth of the Nile and by June, 1249, with far greater ease than was the case with the Fifth Crusade, he took Damietta.

Exactly as had happened thirty years earlier, the Egyptian sultan offered the same exchange: Jerusalem to the Crusaders if they would give back Damietta. Unbelievably, Louis IX, despite the lesson of the Fifth Crusade, made precisely the same mistake. Uplifted by an initial victory, he refused Jerusalem and decided, instead, to capture the Egyptian capital of Cairo, over a hundred miles upstream.

Louis IX had learned enough from the Fifth Crusade to wait until the Nile flood was over. He made his way safely to Mansura (man-soo'ruh), about forty miles upstream, and there he finally met Moslem opposition. Louis did well. On February 8, 1250, he launched a surprise attack that succeeded admirably, but Robert of Artois, the king's brother, overcome by success, launched a pursuit with his own columns instead of waiting to cooperate with the rest of the army. His eagerness for personal glory ended with the destruction of his men.

The Moslems could then counterattack effectively against Louis's weakened and dispirited forces. Louis had to retreat, while disease inflicted further ravages. The Moslems pursued and on April 6 closed in, virtually annihilated the army and took its leaders, including Louis himself, prisoner.

Louis was able to ransom himself by turning over 800,000 gold livres and agreeing to give up Damietta. He then went, with that remnant of his army which survived, to the Holy Land. He remained there four years, hoping to enlist the aid of non-Christian enemies of the Moslems — including the Mongols and a violent Moslem sect called "Assassins," who used hashish freely (hence their name) and who practiced political murder to achieve their ends.

Meanwhile, back in France, Blanche, capable to the end, had kept the peace in his absence and had raised men and money for him, including the money needed to ransom him. She died in 1252, and was, on the whole, probably the most remarkable woman (save one) in French history.

When the news of his mother's death finally reached Louis, the king realized he must return. In 1254, he was back in France, the whole venture a failure. The fact that Louis's crusade had ended so ignominiously, although he himself was a byword for piety, went far toward discrediting the entire crusading movement.

Louis IX himself felt the ignominy. Having failed against the Moslems, he wanted no further war with Christians and bent every effort to reach a final settlement with England and end the chronic warfare that had continued since the time of William the Conqueror.

In 1258, he signed a treaty in Paris with the representatives of Henry III of England. This treaty was not written in Latin, as was the custom, but in French; and not in Norman-French, either, which even then was still the official language of the English court, but in Francien. This treaty was the first step toward making French the general language of diplomacy among the European powers, a position it was to retain for six centuries.

By the terms of the treaty, England finally accepted the loss of Normandy and Anjou, together with other provinces which Philip II had taken nearly half a century before. In exchange, Louis recognized Henry's possession of Guienne and his right to the title of Duke of Aquitaine (inherited from his grandmother, Eleanor). Out of anxiety to keep the peace and out of a feeling of feudal justice, he even turned over to the English some sections in the southwest which had been under French control.

This last was done against the expressed wishes of the inhabitants of the regions which were being turned over (a sign of the increasing nationalism among the French). It was also against the gloomy distress of Louis's advisers, who pointed out that Henry gave up what he did not possess while Louis gave up what he did.

Louis went ahead anyway, gambling on a permanent settlement and final peace. (When the gamble failed a century later, under conditions Louis could not have foreseen, Louis's concessions helped place France at an unnecessary disadvantage.)

Louis made a similar treaty with James I of Aragon, allowing him to keep the province of Roussillon (roo-see-one'), just north of the Pyrenees on the Mediterranean coast, provided he give up all claims to wider dominions.

Having disengaged himself from the enemy, both English and Aragonese, in the southwest, Louis inadvertently began an unnecessary entanglement in Italy that was to keep France involved, generally to its harm, for centuries. It came about in this fashion —

During the first part of Louis's reign, the German Emperor was Frederick II, who spent most of his reign in a violent struggle with the papacy. He died in 1250, while Louis was a prisoner in Egypt, and the contest for the succession began at once. This contest was centered in Sicily and southern Italy, where Frederick II had preferred to live and from which he had ruled his Empire.

The papacy feared that any son of Frederick would continue the fight against papal power, and it moved heaven and earth to wipe out the hated line. Frederick's son, Conrad IV, succeeded in seizing control of Naples, but died in 1254.

Frederick had, however, an illegitimate son, Manfred, who now took up the fight with considerable success. Throughout Italy, he led the antipapal forces, and successive Popes were forced to look abroad for some foreign prince who would fight against Manfred, defeat him and then rule in southern Italy and in Sicily as a royal friend and ally of the Pope.

The strongest kingdoms outside the German Empire were England and France. In 1255, Pope Alexander IV tried to have Edmund, the son of Henry III of England, take over the fight against Manfred. This fell through.

Ten years later, another Pope, Urban IV, offered the same deal to Charles of Anjou, the youngest brother of Louis IX, and this time things were different.

They shouldn't have been. It had been Capetian policy to avoid foreign adventures. Except for the Crusades and for the short-lived invasion of England in 1216, all Capetian wars had been fought on French soil, with the sole purpose of internal unification, never of foreign conquest. This was an intelligent policy that had conserved France's strength and put it where it counted and was in sharp contrast to the opposite policy of the German Empire, which ruined that realm with painful results that have made themselves felt to the present time.

But Charles of Anjou was tempted. The east lured him. He had fought in Egypt with his royal brother and had been imprisoned there with him. Nor was it Egypt and the Holy Land that hung dancing before his eyes; it was something more wonderful; nothing less than the city of Constantinople which, for a thousand years, had ruled the East and which still wore the halo of Roman glory, even though, in actual fact, it was far gone in destruction and decay.

The Latin Emperor, Baldwin II, who had been so instrumental in maneuvering Louis into the Seventh Crusade, was himself a Capetian, for his father's father had been a brother of Louis VII. To be sure Baldwin II had, in 1261, been ejected from his feeble throne, and the native Byzantines took over the shadow of their Empire once more under the Emperor, Michael VIII; but that might be reversed. After all, Charles of Anjou had married his daughter to the son of Baldwin II, so he could claim a connection. Why should not another Capetian, himself, reign as Roman Emperor in Constantinople? And would not Sicily and southern Italy — and the support of the Pope — be a perfect base for such an eastward thrust?

Charles could do none of this without Louis's permission, of course, and he set about obtaining it. Charles, born a few months after Louis VIII's death, was the baby of the family, and Louis IX included among his virtues a love of family. He could not resist and, probably against his better judgment, sent Charles off adventuring and thus entangled France in Italy.

In June, 1265, Charles managed to make his way to Rome, eluding Manfred's fleet. There he was crowned King of Naples and Sicily, collected an army and moved southward into Naples. On February 26, 1266, battle was joined near Benevento, thirty miles northeast of Naples. There Manfred, who handled his army unskillfully, was defeated and killed.

The son of Conrad IV, Conradin (kon'ruh-deen), who was the grandson of Frederick II, took up the antipapal fight. On August 25, 1268, his forces met those of Charles at Tagliacozzo (tahl'yah-kawt'soh). Charles kept part of his forces hidden and in reserve. When Conradin's army defeated the rest and dispersed in pursuit, Charles' reserve emerged and could defeat Conradin's tired contingents piecemeal.

Conradin fled, but was captured and taken to Naples, where Charles had him hanged. In this way, the line of Frederick II was utterly wiped out and Charles of Anjou found himself secured on the throne as Charles I of Naples and Sicily.

While all this was going on, a new sultan had come to power in Egypt. This was Baybars (bigh-bahrs'), a slave who managed to seize the throne after having been made commander of the bodyguard of the previous sultan. In 1260, he was the very first ever to inflict a defeat on the all-conquering Mongols, who in half a century had not lost a battle. Under him Egypt became more powerful than ever, and almost all the holdings still in western possession in the Holy Land fell to him.

Louis IX, uneasy at these new disasters for the Crusaders and ever mindful of the humiliating failure of his own effort, longed to try again, and began to dream of attacking Egypt once more.

Charles of Anjou, from his new eminence, had other ideas, however. Charles still had his eye on Constantinople and to him it was the Byzantines who were the enemy. Indeed, he viewed Baybars of Egypt as a potential friend and ally. Charles did not want Louis to attack Egypt but argued instead that he ought to attack Tunis which was, after all, also Moslem.

Tunis, however, was much closer to France and lay just ninety miles west of the westernmost tip of Sicily. A united French-Sicilian force could surely establish a strong base there, which would place the control of the central Mediterranean firmly in Capetian hands. Then, one could move eastward in strength and at leisure. (Charles visualized this eastward thrust as against Constantinople, but presumably he didn't bother explaining that detail to his idealistic brother.)

In 1267, Louis IX, now fifty-three years old and feeling the full weight of his years, announced his plan to go to Tunis and began his preparations. His advisers were horrified. His old friend Joinville, who had accompanied him on his earlier crusade, told him flatly that he was a fool and refused to accompany him a second time. Nevertheless, Louis left France

on July 1, 1270, on the "Eighth Crusade," and landed at the·
site of ancient Carthage.

Almost at once the army was struck by plague, and Louis
himself, the only monarch ever to lead two crusades, caught
the disease and died on August 25.

So, ingloriously, ended Louis's venture almost as soon as it
started. It put an end forever to the notion of crusading glory.
The crusading movement continued sporadically, but there
was never to be anything called a "Ninth Crusade."

5

AT THE PEAK

SICILIAN KNIVES AND FLEMISH PIKES

With Louis at Carthage was his oldest son, Philip. Immediately upon Louis's death, he patched up a truce with the Moslems and returned to France where he was crowned as Philip III (sometimes known as "Philip the Bold"). This is another sign of the firmness with which the Capetian dynasty had established itself. Even though the heir to the crown was outside the realm on the occasion of the king's death, none moved against him. Philip succeeded as a matter of course and without trouble.

Philip continued to strengthen the royal grip on southern France, but his reign was a rather colorless one. In his time, the real Capetian glamour was to be found in Charles of Anjou, the king's uncle, who still ruled in Naples and Sicily and whose ambitions were not deflated by the fiasco before Tunis.

Charles decided to attack the Byzantine Empire directly, and crossed the southern Adriatic to land an army in the Balkans. By 1277, he had entrenched himself over a considerable portion of the Byzantine dominions and had even managed to have himself proclaimed King of Jerusalem. This was not through conquest, of course, for he was never near Jerusalem. It was merely a worthless title inherited by a number of men after Jerusalem's fall and carried only social prestige with it. Charles paid money to the current holder for the right to call himself by the title.

Charles' weak point, however, was in the Italian dominions he had ruled. He had handed out lordships to the French nobles who had accompanied him to Sicily, and he placed crushing taxation upon the Sicilian population to help finance his vaulting plans. The Sicilians, who remembered the great days of Frederick II, remained strongly attached to his house. Though Frederick's last male descendant, Conradin, was dead, Manfred had had a daughter who had married Pedro III of Aragon.

The Sicilians therefore turned to Pedro, who was willing to take on the burden. He made an alliance with Michael VIII of Constantinople, who was himself in a life-and-death struggle with Charles.

But it was neither Pedro nor Michael nor both together who carried through the key stroke against Charles. It was the Sicilians themselves, rendered desperate in their hatred of their arrogant French masters.

On March 31, 1282, at the time of vespers (the evening prayer) the Sicilians arose. How far it was spontaneous and how far encouraged by the emissaries of the wily Michael VIII, we cannot know, but the results were bloody and final. Every Frenchman the Sicilians could reach was killed; every man whose French accent (if nothing else) betrayed him. Thousands died in this so-called "Sicilian Vespers" and within a month the rebels held the entire island.

Charles came roaring back from the Balkans, all thought of

Byzantine conquests postponed. He might have retaken the island, but by now Pedro of Aragon was in Sicily and his forces controlled it.

Pedro invaded southern Italy, defeated Charles' fleet near Naples and captured Charles' son. Philip III of France came to the aid of his uncle Charles by launching an invasion of Pedro's home kingdom of Aragon (how one foolish foreign adventure leads to another), and was roundly trounced.

Charles of Anjou died in 1285, all his ambitions having come to nothing, and Philip III died a month later.

And while the warfare between Christians continued, the Moslems were methodically sweeping up the few remaining cities and castles which the Crusaders were still holding in the Holy Land. Their last fortress, Acre, taken a century before by Richard the Lion-Heart, fell in 1291, and it was to be more than five centuries before a Christian army was to be again in the Holy Land.

Philip III of France was promptly succeeded by his oldest son, Philip IV, often called "Philip the Fair," where "fair" carries the connotation of "handsome" rather than "just."

Philip IV was a strong king, who continued the policy of Louis VI and Philip II, that of extending the direct royal control in every direction by every means. By his time, the steady enlargement of the royal domain meant that fully half of France was under the direct rule of the king or of other members of the Capetian family. Nor was the king any longer merely the most important of the lords. He was another class of being altogether. He was the supreme power of the land, the chosen of God, and all were his subjects equally, the lord as well as the peasant.

The only part of France ruled by an equal was, of course, Guienne, which was controlled by the English king. Philip invaded the English dominions and did pretty well because the English king, Edward I (the son of Henry III, and a much more forceful and capable ruler), was strongly engaged in

Scotland, which occupied the northern portion of the island of Great Britain. To make sure that Edward I would continue to be so occupied, Philip made an alliance with the Scots in 1295, initiating a policy to which the French would cling for three centuries.

But if the French had a natural ally on the borders of England, the English could return the compliment. On the northeastern rim of the French dominion were the towns of Flanders. They had flourished under Capetian protection when it had been Capetian policy to encourage the towns as a makeweight against the lords. By the time of Philip IV, however, the lords were quiet and presented no problem. It was the towns which cried avidly for enlarged privileges. Capetian policy turned antiburgher and the wealthy towns of Flanders now (and, indeed, for some time past) found in France their chief enemy.

That meant that the English were their natural ally. This was not only a matter of a common enemy, but of common economic advantage. Flanders found that English sheep (in response to England's generally miserable climate) produced longer and thicker wool than Flemish sheep did. The Flemish weavers therefore bought English wool and exported Flemish cloth and both nations profited. Nor did the Flemish need to fear English aggression since a stretch of sea separated the two lands. This was not an unpassable barrier, of course, but it was better than the nothing-but-flat-land that separated Flanders from the rest of France.

In 1297, then, Edward I was able to mount an invasion of northern France, thanks to the help of the Count of Flanders. Nor was this the first time the two regions had combined in an actual military alliance. There had been Flemish contingents in alliance with John in the campaign that had ended with the Battle of Bouvines.

In the face of this invasion, Philip IV was constrained to call off his own warfare in the southwest. But then Edward I had to return to England to face the Scots again, and that left a vengeful Philip IV ready to deal with the Flemings. He marched into Flanders, beat down its count and forced him in 1300 to accept French control of the area.

Defeat by Philip was bad enough for the Flemings, but the situation was made worse by the fact that Flanders was suffering a recession. Textile factories were being set up in Italy and the competition was cutting into Flemish profits. In addition there had been a series of bad harvests and food supplies were low. The Flemish, exasperated by economic woes, found the French control insupportable and reacted as the Sicilians had done twenty years before.

On May 18, 1302, at the time of matins (the morning prayer), there was a popular uprising in the town of Bruges (broozh) near the seacoast, 170 miles north of Paris, and some three thousand French were massacred.

There was no Pedro of Aragon to call in for protection, however, and the Flemish townsmen made ready to face an angry Philip IV by themselves. That they could even dream of doing so was the result of certain slow changes in the art of warfare that had been gradually building up.

For centuries the armored knight had been supreme in the battlefield, and there had been a race between opposing factions to make their own knights ever stronger and more formidable. By the end of the thirteenth century, the knight had become a kind of one-man tank, riding a huge, armored horse. The whole thing was heavy, formidable and slow.

The armor itself, solid sheets of metal now, instead of the earlier chain mail, was much less vulnerable, but it was also heavier and had become so expensive that it was almost ruinous to attempt to support many knights. That was one factor, indeed, in the decline of the feudal aristocracy. It was getting so that only the king could support a large army of properly equipped knights.

Through the thirteenth century, then, there was a search for new weapons that would break the stalemate of knight against knight, and that would be inexpensive.

One such weapon was the crossbow. At its most advanced this was a steel bow firing steel arrows or "bolts." It was so stiff that it had to be drawn back slowly by means of a hand crank. The bolts were, in consequence, fired with much greater force than ordinary arrows could be and, at short range, could penetrate armor!

The great disadvantage of the crossbow was that it was so time-consuming to load. A group of crossbowmen could advance with their weapons cocked. They would launch their bolts at the opposing armies and these might do considerable damage. The bowmen themselves, however, would then have to retreat hastily. They had "shot their bolt" and by the time they could load again, the opposition horsemen (or, sometimes, the proud knights on their own side) would have ridden them down.

Crossbows made their appearance as early as 1066, when William the Conqueror used them in his conquest of England, but didn't receive their full development till after 1200. They seemed to be a horrible weapon of war because they enabled a low-born archer to kill a knight occasionally and even the Church tried to have them outlawed (except against infidels, of course), but there was really no need to. So important was the disadvantage of slow reloading that the crossbow never proved really decisive in any of the great battles of the Middle Ages.

Quite otherwise was a much simpler weapon, the pike. This was a long, wooden spear, fitted out with metal points and, sometimes, with a hook to the side of the point so that the pike could pull as well as push. Spears in themselves were among the oldest of weapons, but the pike was a particularly long and sturdy variety designed to reach the horse-and-rider before the horseman's sword or spear (necessarily short if it were to be handled on horseback) could reach the footman.

A single man with a pike was, of course, no match for a horseman, but a closely standing group of pikemen could present a forest of metal points that, if firmly maintained in the face of a cavalry charge, could turn back the horses.

Flemish pikemen had been in evidence at the Battle of Bouvines, but they were not used against the French horsemen. They defeated the French infantry, but as the battle was decided by the clash of knight against knight, the value of the pike was overlooked.

What counted most was that the crossbow and the pike were cheap enough to be in the reach of almost everyone. The lowborn were making a beginning in the use of weapons that could counter the horse and armor of the well-born aristocrats.

None of this, however, was in the mind of the French who were readying to chastise the Flemish. Robert of Artois (grandson of Louis VIII and son of that brother of Louis IX who had ruined the possibility of success in Egypt) took command of the French army and made ready to associate the name with disaster for a second generation. Around him gathered fifty thousand, including a large contingent of well-armored knights.

Facing them were a mere twenty thousand Flemish pikemen.

The two armies met on July 11, 1302, at Courtrai (koor-tray'), twenty-five miles south of Bruges. The Flemings had chosen the ground well. They were on land that was crisscrossed by canals and one canal ran immediately before their line, with the land sloping upward toward them on its other side. To one side was marshy ground.

There, rank on rank, with their pikes presenting a porcupine front to the enemy, the Flemings waited.

Robert of Artois sent forward his footmen and ordered a volley of crossbow bolts. But the footmen were mired in the soft ground and the bolts did insufficient damage, so the knights made ready to end the battle with a charge.

The tales of chivalry and of courtly love had emphasized the glories of knighthood, and the tales of the Crusades supported this, for even Christian defeats in that distant land were glamorized and distorted into tales of immense knightly valor. There was no occasion for the French knights, then, to think that they needed to do anything but charge. Against them was nothing but a low-born mob and it would have been beneath knightly dignity to attempt anything in the way of fancy tactics. All that had to be done was to spur straight ahead and ride the rabble down.

This they attempted to do without artifice of any kind and in several waves. They rode over their own crossbowmen, splashed through the canal, mired themselves in the marsh, and heaved their way up the slope, while the Flemish townsmen, pikes ready, waited calmly.

The French line was in utter disorder in no time. Some knights were hurled off their horses by the press of those who followed. Some fell into either the canal or the marsh and their heavy armor would not allow them to rise again. And then the Flemings were upon them.

Now the way knights fought among themselves was to deal a few thwacks back and forth till one or the other sounded the cry of surrender. The beaten knight was then treated with a great deal of ceremonious courtesy and was held for ransom. This sort of thing is admired by shortsighted people who forget that such gentle consideration was only for knights. The low-born footmen who were compelled to accompany an army and who had neither horses on which to escape nor armor for protection were usually slaughtered ruthlessly without a chance to surrender. After all, they had no way of raising a ransom.

Consequently, when the low-born townsmen had the knights at their mercy, they did not in the least follow the rules of chivalry. Those rules were only for knights. Methodically, the long pikes rose and fell and quite remorselessly, the mired knights were slaughtered. Robert of Artois himself was killed and seven hundred other knightly nobles of high degree met their death.

The number is known because seven hundred pairs of golden spurs were collected by the Flemings so that the Battle of Courtrai is far better known as the "Battle of the Spurs."

Philip IV did not accept the defeat at Courtrai as final, of course, and led new armies into Flanders. He won victories enough to salve his pride but the Flemish towns preserved their essential independence, and Philip did not think it wise to push matters too far.

The Battle of Courtrai pointed a valuable lesson. Warfare was more than a set of single combats between knights fighting as though they were at a tournament or living in a kind of Arthurian fairytale born in the mind of a troubadour. Foot soldiers, well disciplined and adequately armed, could stop a disorganized rabble of horsemen and wreak havoc upon them.

The lesson was there to be learned but the French nobility did not choose to learn it. Reluctant to leave their troubadour world and their crusading mythology, they blamed their defeat at Courtrai on the poor choice of ground. (A few years later, Swiss pikemen defeated German knights just as remorselessly, and there the result was blamed on the mountains and not on the existence of firm and resolute low-born warriors.) The French aristocracy spent more than a century suffering periodic disasters as bad as that at Courtrai, or worse, before they finally learned that knighthood had come to be a thing for storybooks only.

THE POPES BOW

Though the military defeats in Sicily and in Flanders were spectacular, they were only pinpricks after all. Under Philip IV's steady and somewhat ruthless hand, the process of centralization went on and France grew ever stronger. Three centuries of Capetian rule had unified the country to the point where, by the fourteenth century, there were only four regions under the nominal overlordship of the French king that remained strong enough to take independent action if they wished. All were on the outskirts of the realm.

There was Guienne on the southwest, which was, of course, ruled by the English king, and Flanders on the northeast, which was, as often as it dared be, in alliance with England. In the east was Burgundy, under a duke of distant Capetian descent, which was usually working hand in hand with the royal government. And in the northwest was Brittany, which was a special case. In the sixth and seventh centuries it had received a steady influx of British refugees fleeing the Saxon armies that invaded Britain. The land received a distinct Celtic tinge, therefore, including a Celtic language, Breton. Its people felt less French than did those of any other province, but it did not pursue an actively anti-Capetian policy. Rather it did what it could to remain neutral and reserved. When it was forced to take sides, it did so as mildly as it could.

But territorial centralization was not enough. France needed economic centralization, too, if the government was to be strong. The feudal system might be virtually dead from the military and political standpoint, but it still existed financially. Philip IV found himself tied down by a medieval system for raising money that was extremely inefficient and that was based on the intricate legal interrelationships of various vassals and of vassals. The royal income never kept up with rising costs, and Philip IV, who found himself presiding over a realm larger and inevitably more expensive than those of preceding kings, had to dig for money in every possible way.

What's more, the court, mired in the glue of feudal tradition, had to experience the frustration of watching subjects grow wealthy while the nation remained poor. The burghers were flourishing. About 1200, the Italian mathematician Leonardo Fibonacci (fee-boh-nah'chee) had introduced a new number

system to Europe, which he had borrowed from the Arabs —
hence called "Arabic numerals." These, much more easily handled than the time-honored Roman numerals, were gradually
adopted by merchants. About 1300, moreover, double-entry
bookkeeping was devised in Italy. Both advances served to increase efficiency and make decisions both faster and more certain (having rather the effect on fourteenth-century business
that computers had on twentieth-century business), and the
burghers prospered.

It is no wonder that a monarch like Philip IV would not stop
at questionable methods to keep the government abreast of the
prosperity. He debased the coinage, for instance, putting in
less gold and silver and keeping the excess for himself. He ruthlessly squeezed those sections of the population with which the
people, generally, were out of sympathy. He forced vast sums
out of the Jews and out of the Italian moneylenders. When he
had squeezed the Jews dry, he expelled them from the kingdom.
He sold knighthoods to the rich burghers for large sums. (This
gave them social prestige and freedom from taxation, so that it
was really a long-term loss in exchange for a short-term gain.)
Philip IV also offered freedom to serfs (peasants who were not
exactly slaves but who could not leave the land they cultivated
for their lords), not out of humanity, but in return for money,
if they could find it.

One source of money that always dangled temptingly before
monarchs in the Middle Ages was the swollen coffers of the
Church. Many a medieval king had not been able to resist help-
ing himself to some of that money, but the Church always
fought back and, almost always, won out. King John of England
had tried and Pope Innocent III had forced him to knuckle
under.

But times were changing, and the medieval Church was passing its peak of power. The last to recognize this were the Popes
themselves.

On December 24, 1294, a Pope was elected who took the

name of Boniface VIII. He was a choleric, arrogant man who viewed the papal power as though it were still what it was in the time of Innocent III and was impulsively rash enough to say so.

He considered himself the arbiter of royal quarrels. He gave official approval to the rule of Aragon over Sicily, which had been a fact, even without his approval, ever since the Sicilian Vespers. He also strove to bring about peace between Philip IV and Edward I in the war that was going on at the time of Boniface's accession.

He naturally wanted peace because, under the pressure of war, both kings were taxing the clergy without papal permission. The war continued and so did the taxation, and the short-fused papal temper went off. In 1296, Boniface VIII issued an official announcement, or bull,* called *Clericis laicos,* which threatened automatic excommunication of anyone who taxed the clergy without papal permission.

The English government was rather daunted by this, but Philip IV wasn't. His need for money rose superior to all else and he prepared to break a cardinal point of Capetian policy. Until then, the Capetians might have quarreled with the Pope over personal problems, but hardly ever on basic principles. England and the German Empire wasted energy and effort on battles with the Church over attempts to control the clergy and squeeze money out of clerical coffers, but France made very few attempts of the sort. In fact, when the Pope had to flee from German armies, he could always count on safety in French dominions.

Yet now Philip IV moved into open enmity with the Pope. He began by forbidding the export of any gold or silver from the realm. This at once cut off a substantial portion of the

---

* Papal bulls were so called because they were sealed with a small ball of lead or "bulla" — the same source from which "bullet" (a little bulla) comes. Papal bulls, always in Latin, are named after their first two words.

papal revenues and this came at a bad time for Boniface, for he was having trouble with the local Roman nobles. Very much against his will he was forced to backtrack, and even to make a conciliatory gesture in 1297 by raising Louis IX, Philip's grandfather, to sainthood. What was more important was that he allowed the French clergy to be taxed to support Philip's wars in Flanders.

But then in 1300, Boniface VIII proclaimed a Jubilee or Holy Year to celebrate the thirteenth centenary of Jesus' birth. Hordes of pilgrims came to Rome; incredible quantities of money flooded into the treasury through their pious offerings. Boniface was filled with joy at this evidence of the power of the papacy and its capacity to elicit veneration from the people. Between that, and the financial cushion the Jubilee had brought, he was ready to try battling Philip again.

The occasion came in November, 1301, when a French bishop was tried for various crimes by a royal court. This was dead against papal theory, which held that churchmen could only be tried in clerical courts. At once there began a violent battle of words between king and Pope. Boniface used the usual papal thunders, but Philip IV tried a new weapon, not at the disposal of earlier kings — the growing feeling of national pride among the French.

To the Pope, there was still a single "Christendom," which might be distinguished within by different kings and different languages but was united by the single heritage of the Roman Empire, by the single Latin language, by the single Emperor, and most of all by the single Church, led by the single Pope.

Philip knew better. The strengthening and extension of the royal domain; the heroic tales of the Crusades, so largely French; the popular literature in the vernacular — all helped make Frenchmen feel themselves to be Frenchmen first and members of Christendom only second.

Philip boldly began to issue propaganda against Boniface, therefore, accusing him of a variety of crimes in language that

made him appear an Italian priest, a foreigner, a non-French-
man, rather than a Pope.

Philip also called together an assembly of representative
members of the three "estates" — the nobility, the clergy and
the burghers — so that he might consult them, get their agreement to his line of action and give the nation a feeling of par-
ticipating in his decisions. This had been done on a local or
provincial scale in earlier times, but this was the first time all
France, generally, was drawn together. This national meeting
came to be called the "Estates-General" therefore. (It suited
Philip to have such a meeting in another way. When the
Estates-General authorized a new tax, it was the will of the
nation making the decision, and not arbitrary royal tyranny —
and the tax would raise that much less antagonism.)

It was difficult even for the clergy to forget that they were
French when they thus participated in what was visibly the
French people deliberating as one.

Boniface might have backed away in the face of Philip's clear
intention of taking extreme measures, if necessary, but the
Battle of Courtrai took place at just this time and Boniface felt
that Philip would have to retreat. In November, 1302, four
months after the battle, he triumphantly issued the bull *Unam
sanctam*. In this bull, Boniface clearly and explicitly stated that
the Pope was ruler not only in the spiritual sense but also in the
temporal sense; that all the kings of the world owed allegiance
to the Pope; and that all who denied this were heretics. No
Pope prior to Boniface had ever dared make such a sweeping
and all-embracing claim.

Philip did not allow himself to be downcast either by the defeat at Courtrai or by the papal claim. Instead in May, 1303,
he called a conference at Paris which even French churchmen
attended, and had his lawyers draw up a bill of particulars
against Boniface. Boniface was accused of religious offenses:
of heresy, of sorcery, of setting up images of himself in churches
that he might be worshiped, of having forced his papal prede-

cessor to resign and then of having him killed. More effectively, perhaps, he was accused of crimes against French national feeling: of calling the French heretics and threatening to destroy them, of saying he would rather be a dog than a Frenchman, and so on.

The only retort Boniface could make was to excommunicate Philip, to declare him unfit to rule and to declare all his vassals freed of any allegiance to him.

It was just possible that some of Philip's vassals might feel tempted to take advantage of this and plead piety, so Philip moved quickly. The bull of excommunication was to take effect on September 8, 1303, and on that day Philip had a force of men in Rome ready to take action. They were under the lawyer, Guillaume de Nogaret (noh-guh-ray'), who had been a leader among those who had drawn up the bill of particulars against the Pope. Taking advantage of the feuds among the Romans and allying himself with the Colonna family, which hated the Pope to the death, Nogaret surprised the Pope at his summer home in Anagni (ah-nah'nyee), thirty miles east of Rome.

The Pope was taken into custody and manhandled. The Colonnas would have killed him on the spot, but Nogaret prevented that, knowing well that if the business were carried too far it might boomerang.

Boniface was soon released and returned to Rome, but the bull of excommunication was never issued and the Pope, nearly seventy years old, and broken by the humiliation of what had happened so soon after he had claimed to be lord of the earth, died within weeks.

He was succeeded on the papal throne by Benedict XI. The new Pope was a partisan of Boniface, but he did what had to be done. He gave in to Philip IV, and made no attempt to carry on the fight. He contented himself with excommunicating Nogaret.

What had happened was quite clear. Previous Popes had fought successfully against monarchs by taking advantage of feudal principles. They had always had the ability to turn the great lords loose against the king and to deprive the nation of churchly functions. Now Popes could do so no longer. In the new spirit of nationalism it was harder to drive lords to rebel and easier to make the clergy serve the people even against the will of the Pope. Where the choice had once been Pope before king, it had now become king before Pope.

The papacy remained influential and, in some places, powerful even down to this day. After the "Terrible Day of Anagni," however, the papacy could never again lord it over monarchs. As a political "great power" it had been broken in a single day, and at what had seemed the peak of its power.

But Philip IV was not satisfied. He wanted more. It was not enough that the Pope give in to him. He wanted a Pope who would be an outright puppet.

He therefore put his full weight to bear on the election of another Pope, when Benedict XI died in 1304 after reigning for only a year. Philip's candidate was the French Archbishop of Bordeaux. The Archbishop was elected on June 5, 1305, and took the name of Clement V.

An ailing man and a weak personality, Clement V was, from the start, under the harsh influence of the French king. Philip forced him to agree (probably in advance of the election, as the price of his support) to move his seat from Rome to the papal possession of Avignon (a-vee-nyone') on the Rhone River, 400 miles northwest of Rome. Avignon was French, and it was now a French mob which might threaten the Pope and not an Italian one.

Clement was forced to create enough French cardinals to make sure that French Popes would continue to be elected. (In point of fact, seven successive Popes, beginning with Clement V, did reside in Avignon, over a period of sixty-eight years. This, because of its similarity to the seventy years in which the Jews were in exile in Babylon is sometimes referred to as "the Babylonian captivity of the papacy." Even afterward, when the Popes returned to Rome there was a further forty-year period during which there were claimants to the papacy still in Avignon.)

Clement was also forced to annul the bulls *Clericis laicos* and *Unam sanctum,* thus abandoning, in theory, what the papacy had lost in fact. He even had to lift the sentence of excommunication from Nogaret.

Finally, he bowed his head and agreed not to interfere with what Philip IV planned to do in connection with the Templars.

THE TEMPLARS DIE

The organization of the Templars originated in the Holy Land after the First Crusade. In 1119, a certain knight devoted himself to protecting the pilgrims flocking to Jerusalem. Others joined him and soon a band of fighting men, professing poverty and utter devotion to Jesus, formed. These warrior monks received, as their first headquarters, a section of the palace in Jerusalem lying next to what was considered to be the site of the Temple of Solomon. They therefore called themselves "Poor Knights of Christ and of the Temple of Solomon." This was shortened to "Knights Templars," or even just "Templars."

The warrior monks fought heroically during the Crusades, but they also received rich endowments from those who felt guilty, perhaps, that they were not themselves fighting in the Holy Land. The "Poor Knights" were soon poor no longer, but became a large, disciplined order, with branches all over Europe, and with rapidly accumulating wealth. It was strongest in France, naturally, for it was the French nobility which bore the burden of the Crusades.

Even after the Crusades dwindled and the Crusader position in the Holy Land grew hopeless, the Templars continued increasing in strength. Their power, wealth and their unassailable position as pious and chaste warriors for Christ made them a state within a state and a church within a church. They could not be controlled by either bishops or kings and they behaved and were treated as though they were a sovereign power.

With the wealth they had, they became the moneylenders of Europe, charging interest just as the Jews did, but in a devious way that enabled them to pretend they were following Christian principles and that it wasn't interest. Furthermore, they could collect more efficiently than Jews could, for they had far more power and were far less liable to be murdered by mobs acting as defenders of the faith.

Toward the end of the reign of Louis VII, the Templars had been awarded a tract of land just outside Paris. There they built a headquarters called "the Temple," which was the prime center of the order. By the time of Philip IV, the Temple, under the Grand Master of the Templars, Jacques de Molay, was the financial nucleus of western Europe, a kind of medieval "Wall Street."

There is, however, nothing as unrelenting and as dangerous as a powerful debtor. As the Templars grew ever more arrogant and secure there was bound to come a time when they lent money (and demanded repayment — *that* was the point) to someone who was powerful enough and sufficiently unscrupulous to strike back.

That someone was Philip IV. He was in debt to the Temple, and despite his exactions from Jewish and Italian moneylenders (whom he could plunder at will without thought of repayment), despite his higher taxes, he knew he would never be able to repay the Temple or to satisfy the hard-eyed knights who made it up. The only alternative was to disband the Temple, destroy the Templars and appropriate their wealth.

For that, he needed the cooperation of the Pope. Clement V, it is supposed, promised such cooperation as part of the price for becoming Pope. Nor could he back down, for Philip IV blackmailed him continually with the threat of placing the dead Boniface VIII on trial and irretrievably blackening the reputation of the papacy. And then, too, it may be that Clement was not entirely averse to smashing the Templars; they were, after all, rich, powerful and not submissive to clerical authority.

What about the people? Many had been alienated by the arrogance of the Templars, but there was such a thing as superstitious awe. Ah, but the Templars had a weakness: their organization was secret and people are always ready to believe the worst about secret rites. It would be simple to maintain that the Templars, in secret, committed all kinds of religious and sexual abominations, denying Christ, worshiping idols, practicing homosexuality. The Templars could even be made to admit all this under torture, and in that century (as in others, including our own), people are willing to believe confessions extorted in this manner.

To have this work, though, there must be no one powerful enough on the other side to start a counterpropaganda. Jacques de Molay happened to be safe in Cyprus, so Philip had the Pope recall him to France in order to discuss, supposedly, a new crusade. Unsuspectingly, de Molay came back.

To the last minute, Philip maintained the friendliest and most flattering attitude toward the Templars and then — acted. On October 13, 1307, the king's officers arrested every Templar in reach, up to and including de Molay. There was no resistance, no flight. Surprise had been successfully carried through.

Nor was there any delay. The Templars in custody were put to the question at once, with torture, of course. The torture was continued till they confessed; and they were told, while still under torture, that others had already confessed. The only alternative to confession was death by torture and, in Paris alone, thirty-six Templars died rather than confess. De Molay was not among them, however. He broke, and that made it the harder for the others. Templars confessed to all the abominations it was demanded they confess to. Philip IV then saw to it that news of the confessions was broadcast throughout the nation, making use of public opinion against the Templars, as earlier he had done against Pope Boniface.

Those Templars who confessed did not save themselves. They were placed under humiliating punishments and were finally burned at the stake by the orders of the pitiless Philip. Jacques de Molay himself was the great demonstration piece. He was forced to confess over and over, was put through years of humiliation and misery, though he was an old man approaching seventy years of age. Finally, he was burned alive on March 19, 1314, before Notre Dame — and at the last moment, he seized the occasion to deny everything to which he had been forced to confess.

The Templars thus went down in blood; Philip's debts were abolished; the possessions of the Temple were divided between Church and State.

The whole procedure had terrible consequences. It encouraged belief in witchcraft and placed the highest sanctions on the use of torture, and on the cruelest treatment of anyone accused of heresy. What Philip did out of cold-blooded need for money helped fasten five centuries of horror on Europe in the name of religion.

There is a story that de Molay, at the stake, called upon king and Pope to meet him at the bar of heaven within the year. If he did, the call was answered. Pope Clement died on April 20, 1314, one month after the flames had consumed de Molay, and King Philip died on October 29 of that year.

At the time of Philip's death, France stood at the peak of its medieval power, and was clearly the leading power of Christian Europe. This, traditionally, had been the role of the two Empires, the German and the Byzantine. In Philip's time, however, the Byzantine Empire was reduced to the city of Constantinople plus a few small scraps of territory here and there, while the German Empire had been in virtual anarchy since the death of the Emperor Frederick II.

About 1306, in fact, a French lawyer, Pierre Dubois (dyoo-bwah′), who had been a representative at two of Philip's Estates-General, published a pamphlet which was ostensibly about a crusade to recover the Holy Land. Chiefly, though, it urged Philip to form a European league of nations under the leadership of France — one in which all disputes would be settled by arbitration instead of war, in which there would be universal education and in which Church property would be secularized. There have been few men as far ahead of their own times as Dubois.

It was another measure of Capetian success that members of the family sat on thrones outside France. Though Charles of Anjou had lost Sicily as the result of the Sicilian Vespers, his son, Charles II, surviving imprisonment by the Aragonese, managed, with papal help, to hold southern Italy. He reigned as King of Naples till 1309, when he was succeeded by a younger son, Robert I, who ruled till his death in 1343.

The older son of Charles II was elected King of Hungary as Charles I, and under his son Louis I (called "Louis the Great") the land reached a peak of prosperity. Louis ruled Hungary from 1342 to 1382 and over Poland as well from 1370 on.

The reign of Philip IV, however, was not entirely successful. It had, in fact, three notable failures.

First, despite his best efforts, both fair and foul, Philip did not solve the financial problems of the government. His income was ten times that of Louis IX, but it did not match expenditures even so. What's more, because of inequitable taxation and primitive methods of collection, the French people were weighed down with financial exactions even though the government ran at a loss.

Second, the Estates-General did not accomplish its purpose. In England, a similar organization developed into Parliament, which gave the land a government of unexampled efficiency and enlightenment. That came about, though, because in England the lower nobility and the middle class stood together against the absolutism of the monarch and the anarchy of the great nobles. In France, unfortunately, the division between the nobility and the burghers proved unbridgeable and the Estates-General never became an effective arm of the government.

Third, and on the short-term basis most important, Philip IV, so shrewd otherwise, failed to learn the lesson of the Battle of Courtrai. So did the French military, generally. They were to pay for this heavily.

THE THREE SONS

Philip IV's oldest son succeeded as Louis X. He is called in the histories "Louis le Hutin," where the final word may be translated as "Stubborn" or "Quarrelsome." That may describe his characteristics as a man, but as a king, the young man (he was twenty-five at the time of his accession) showed no strength. His uncle Charles, son of Philip III and a younger brother of Philip IV, easily dominated the new king and was the real ruler.

Philip III had given his younger son, Charles, the county of Valois (val-wah'), a section of territory some thirty-five miles northeast of Paris, as an appanage. For that reason, Louis X's uncle is known as Charles of Valois.

Under Louis X and Charles of Valois, there was a reaction against the policies of Philip IV. Both the nobles and the clergy won back some of the power taken from them by the harsh Philip. An attempt to carry on Philip's external policies by invading Flanders bogged down in torrential and unseasonable rains in the summer of 1315.

And then, on June 5, 1316, the king died of pleurisy caught, it is said, by overdrinking cold wine, after having overheated himself at ballplaying. He was twenty-seven years old at the time of his death.

He was not much of a king but his death left France in a peculiarly delicate condition.

Over a period of three and a quarter centuries, France had been ruled by twelve Capetian kings. Some were better or stronger than others, but the first eleven had one thing in common — each had passed on the crown to a son. Never once was there a disputed succession and this went a long way toward accounting for France's steady rise in power and prosperity over this period. (England had much more trouble in this respect and had suffered anarchy when Henry I had died without a son.)

And now the twelfth Capetian king had died and had left no son. He had a four-year-old daughter, Jeanne (or Joan), however, and might it not be that she could ascend the throne? Granted that it was the universal practice among royalty to give a son precedence over a daughter, even over an older daughter; surely, if there were *no* sons, a daughter might succeed. Daughters succeeded to land and titles in many cases. Eleanor had succeeded to the huge duchy of Aquitaine, and Matilda had come within a hair of making herself accepted as Queen of England.

Nevertheless, female rulers usually had no recourse but to marry and then it was the husband who actually ruled, as Eleanor's husband, Henry II, had ruled in Aquitaine. This made any queen a rather uncertain quantity. Who could tell whom she might marry — someone, perhaps, who would be utterly repugnant to the nation generally. And a child queen was worse still, of course.

Then, too, in this particular case, there was still another problem. Jeanne was the daughter of Margaret of Burgundy, Louis X's first wife. In the later years of Philip IV, she had been tried for adultery and had been convicted. She was imprisoned for life but died soon after her husband's accession to the throne. (Rumor had it that Louis X had had her killed so that he could marry again.) Under these conditions, who could be certain that Jeanne was a true daughter of the king?

Finally, Louis X's second wife, Constance of Hungary, against whose fidelity there was not the slightest whisper, announced that at the time of her husband's death she was pregnant — and, of course, the child that was on its way might be a boy.

Charles of Valois would have been willing to see Jeanne become Queen of France, since, with any child monarch, his own ascendancy might continue. Public opinion was in favor of awaiting the result of the pregnancy, however, and he possessed himself of patience.

There was another person, all hot-eyed and eager, and that was Philip, Louis X's younger brother. If Jeanne was excluded from the succession and if the expected child were also a girl, surely he himself would be the logical successor. He was in the provinces when Louis X died, but now he hastened back and loudly proclaimed himself regent on behalf of his unborn possible-nephew.

On November 12, five months after the king's death, the queen's baby was born and it was a boy. It was named Jean (John) and goes down in history as King John I of France. The joy at his birth, however, was turned to gloom when the baby died within a week. The thirteenth Capetian king in the direct line was gone.

That put the problem back where it was except that there was no hope of further children.

The regent, Philip, solved the problem by acting quickly, announcing himself to be King Philip V, and setting the coronation date for January 9, 1317. The only one who might have thought of disputing the point was Charles of Valois, but if the thought did occur to him, he decided against it.

Immediately upon his accession, Philip V called together a gathering of nobles and clergy, for the purpose of making his position tight and secure. He had the gathering proclaim that the rule in France was that no woman could inherit the throne. This established a precedent that was to persist throughout French history. No reason was given for the rule; it was simply proclaimed; for otherwise Philip V could not be king.

In later times, the theory arose that there was a so-called "Salic law," dating back to the Salian Franks who had begun the conquest of Roman Gaul in the fifth century, to the effect that the throne could not be held by women, but this was a very doubtful precedent. It looked good only because in all the history of France and of the Frankish kingdom that had preceded it, the supply of logical male candidates had never failed and no woman had ever had the occasion to test the rule.

Philip V (also called "Philip the Tall") tried to regain the ground lost to the lords and clergy under Louis X. For the purpose he strengthened the burghers, granting them the right to bear arms under certain conditions. He tried further to unify coinage and measures in the nation, but was opposed by those who profited by the old ways, or were simply used to them. He called numerous meetings of the Estates-General to discuss monetary problems, not always successfully.

It is always useful for a king to have some unpopular segment of the population he can hound, and use as a lightning rod to attract the dissatisfactions of his subjects. However, the Templars were gone, the heretics of the south were gone, and there weren't even many Jews left. Philip therefore found a novel and particularly helpless minority to destroy — the lepers. They were accused of conspiring against the government and many were put to death — surely a peculiar state of affairs, when a skin disease became a capital crime.

Philip V died on January 2, 1322, having reigned five years and having attained the age of twenty-eight. Philip had had a son but he had died in 1317, while still a child. That meant Philip V was survived only by a daughter and, again, a pregnant wife. Again the nation waited, but this time, the baby was a girl.

By the precedent Philip himself had established, neither could succeed, and the crown passed quietly to the third and youngest son of Philip IV. He reigned as Charles IV and is also known as "Charles the Fair."

Under him, petty warfare began in the southwest against the possessions of England. The English, still there, were now under the rule of Edward II, a weak king and, as it happened, a brother-in-law of Charles IV. Charles' older sister Isabella (a daughter of Philip IV) had been married to Edward II in 1308, when she was sixteen and he, twenty-four. It was an unhappy marriage, as might be expected since Edward II was a homosexual who devoted himself to male favorites and who treated his wife with scorn. Naturally, Isabella took lovers.

In 1326, she and her lover, Roger de Mortimer, rebelled against the king, forced him to abdicate and in 1327 had him brutally killed. Charles IV naturally supported her, partly because she was his sister, but chiefly because any English civil war was useful to France. As a result of Edward II's misfortunes, the warfare in the southwest ended with some French gains, since Isabella needed peace at any reasonable price to consolidate her English rule.

The quick shifting of kings in France since the death of Philip IV might have been disastrous for the kingdom, had it not fortunately coincided with Edward II's reign in England. Nor, perhaps, did it seem that France had much to fear from England in any case. France was no longer a badly divided nation facing a centralized Anglo-Norman kingdom.

Instead, France had a homogeneous population of 15 million under a centralized rule. If some Frenchmen were under English rule in Guienne, they were far from England itself, which had a population of less than 4 million. Nor could any English city compare with the French metropolis of Paris with its population of 200,000.

But then, in January, 1328, Charles IV fell ill and died, the third (and last) son of Philip IV to die after a comparatively brief reign. If the deaths of his older brothers had posed a problem for the succession, that was as nothing to what happened now.

6

CATASTROPHE!

COUSIN VERSUS NEPHEW

For the third time in a dozen years, a French king died, leaving behind only one daughter and a pregnant widow. In those dozen years, three sons of Philip IV had died and two infant grandsons as well. The male line of Philip IV was extinct, unless, of course, Charles IV's queen, who was expecting in two months, was delivered of a boy.

Well, then, what now? Wait for the queen's delivery, certainly, but what if it were to prove a girl? There was no fourth brother of the last three kings. To be sure, Philip IV still had one surviving daughter, Isabella, who was now ruling England, along with Mortimer. By the precedent set in 1317, however, she could not be queen, any more than any of the granddaughters of Philip IV.

Queen Isabella of England, however, introduced a compli-

cation. Though she could not become queen herself, she had a
strapping son of sixteen, a large and promising youth, who was
Edward III of England (still ruling in his mother's shadow).
The precedent of 1317 simply said that women could not inherit the French throne; it did not say they could not transmit
the inheritance.

To the English, the inheritance could certainly be transmitted. Even though the English had not accepted Matilda
as queen two centuries before and had preferred a more distantly related male, they had accepted Matilda's son eventually and he had reigned gloriously as Henry II. What's more,
Henry II assumed the kingship even though his mother was
still alive at the time of coronation. By this precedent, the
English could argue that Edward III, the nephew of the last
three kings of France and grandson of Philip IV, was not only
King of England, but also rightful King of France.

To the French, however, this, whether right or wrong, logical or not, was absolutely insupportable. The new nationalism
which Philip IV had so assiduously cultivated made it un-
thinkable that the French monarchy should be placed under
an Englishman. Some alternative had to be found and some
rule had to be established to make the alternative possible.

Philip III had had two sons. The older had reigned as Philip
IV, and the younger was Charles of Valois, who had been the
real power behind Louis X. The male line of Philip IV had died
out, so the natural thing was to turn next to the male line of
Charles of Valois. Charles himself had died in 1325, but he
had left behind a son, Philip of Valois, who was thus first cousin to the last three kings of France and nephew of Philip IV.
His relationship was somewhat more distant than Edward's
but it was through his father, whereas Edward's was through
his mother.

The Estates-General met and decided that if a woman had
no right to be queen, she had no right she was capable of
transmitting. It followed that only those could rule France

who could trace their ancestry back, *through males only,* to some preceding king of France.

This was added to what later came to be called the Salic Law, though there was no mention of that precise term at the time. The Salic Law (to give it that name) not only ruled out Edward III, it also ruled out any sons that the granddaughters of Philip IV might have. In fact, provided that the widow of Charles IV did not have a son, Philip of Valois was the only male who could qualify for the throne and, provided the rule was accepted, there was no disputed succession after all.

When Charles IV's widow was finally delivered on April 1, 1328, and the baby turned out to be another daughter, Philip of Valois at once claimed the throne and became Philip VI of France.

Philip VI was, of course, as much a Capetian as any of the earlier kings, since he descended, through an unbroken succession of males (of whom only one, his father, was not a king) from Hugh Capet. For the first time since Hugh Capet, however, there reigned a king whose father had not been a king, but merely a count of Valois. Therefore, it is customary to consider Philip VI and his descendants to be of the House of Valois.

For a time all looked well. Young Edward III blustered a bit, but accepted the French decision and made no immediate attempt to claim the crown. He formally went through the rites admitting Philip to be his overlord in 1329. In 1330, he took over the government from his mother, and then, in 1331 as complete ruler of the land, he went through the rites again.

But then trouble came; trouble that arose in Flanders.

Ever since the Battle of Courtrai, the towns of Flanders had been maintaining considerable independence not only with respect to the French monarchy, but even against their own counts. They continued to shore up that independence by orienting their sympathies toward England. The English in their turn were always eager to encourage the Flemish towns

to retain as much independence as possible, since that left
them a thorn in the French side and helped keep the pressure
off English possessions in the southwest. The sympathies of
Edward III toward Flanders had a personal basis, too, since
in 1328 he married Philippa of Hainaut (ay-noh'), a district
in eastern Flanders.

It was to French interest to keep Flanders under firm control, and the French aristocracy, moreover, continued to be
anxious to gain revenge for the Battle of Courtrai and to wipe
out the disgrace of that defeat.

When the towns rebelled against their count, Louis of Nevers (neh-vair'), Philip VI eagerly led an army against the im-
pudent Flemish burghers.

Once again, the Flemish pikemen waited stolidly for the
onset of the French knights. This time, the pikemen, who
were fighting at Cassel, thirty miles west of Courtrai, did not
have as good a choice of ground as their predecessors, a quarter-century earlier, had had. The French knights, when they
charged on August 23, 1328, did not do so as recklessly, either.
The French army was large enough to surround the unsup-
ported Flemish footmen. The pikes were hard to breach and
the Flemish fought fiercely, but little by little the knights bore
in and when the wall of pikes broke, they charged and killed
the Flemish virtually to a man.

This battle confirmed the French knights in their faith in
their cavalry tactics, and in their dismissal of the Battle of
Courtrai as a military freak. In consequence, the very fact
that the Battle of Cassel was a victory made more certain the
coming catastrophe for France.

Philip's victory in Flanders, having made the sullen Flemish
more subservient for the nonce, raised the value of ruling the
territory. The westernmost section of Flanders (in which the
Battle of Cassel had taken place) was called Artois (ahr-twah')
and for many years a certain Robert claimed to be its count and
called himself Robert of Artois — though he is not to be con-

fused with Robert of Artois who died at the Battle of Courtrai.

The county was now in the hands of Eudes IV (yood), Duke of Burgundy, by virtue of the claims of his wife, Joan, who was the older daughter of Philip V. Robert's case was that he himself, though a more distant relative than Joan, was a male and inherited through males and should therefore take precedence over a female. Years before the Battle of Cassel, Philip V had decided in favor of his son-in-law, and Robert had, in fury, gone so far as to take up arms against the king. He was forced to capitulate, however, in 1319.

He then decided to gamble on the deaths of the sons of Philip IV without male heirs and allied himself with Charles of Valois, marrying a daughter of his. He ardently supported the claims of Philip of Valois to the throne and he was an important factor in pushing through the acceptance of Philip as king.

Robert reasoned that it was he, now, not the Duke of Burgundy, who was closely related to the king by marriage. What's more, Philip VI had gained his title by placing male inheritance above that of female and was bound to stick to the precedent. Surely Robert would now be confirmed in his title. After Philip VI's victory at Cassel, when Artois was completely pacified, Robert raised the point.

Philip considered the matter, but, regardless of what his personal feelings might have been, Eudes of Burgundy was still far stronger than Robert of Artois, and it was more politic to confirm the former in his possession. Robert, taken aback and embittered, determined that if he could not have his county, he would certainly have his revenge and, in 1334, he went to England with that in mind.

Edward III of England was rather a throwback to Richard I the Lion-Heart. Edward was a knight who fancied himself doing great deeds. It was he who made Saint George the patron saint of England, because in legend Saint George was portrayed as a knight dressed in full armor, killing a dragon.

Furthermore, he took to calling himself Edward Plantagenet, since he was great-great-great-grandson of Henry II, the son of Geoffrey Plantagenet. This was a transparent attempt to call back the great days of the Angevin Empire a century and a half before.

Naturally, such a monarch was bound to lend an ear to the insidious temptations of the hate-filled Robert of Artois. Robert pointed out that Philip VI, in denying Robert his county of Artois, was proclaiming the right of female inheritance over a more distant male. In that case, was not Philip himself admitting that Edward III's claim through the female (his mother) was superior to that of the more distant male claim of Philip?

The argument was actually a bad one since the assembly that had decided on Philip VI as King of France applied the rule of noninheritance and nontransmission by the female to the kingship only. There wasn't the slightest hint of making it a general rule for all landownership.

And yet, bad or not, the argument was an attractive one to a king who hungered for glory, and it could be (and was) used with great effect in rousing public opinion in England and in convincing Englishmen that there was justice on their side in any war with France.

DISASTER BY SEA

England and France began inching toward war, each redoubling its efforts to keep the enemy occupied elsewhere. France subsidized the Scots and encouraged them to raid and invade the northern English border, while the English labored to keep resistance alive in the Flemish towns.

There began what would today be called a "cold war" in Flanders. The French arrested English merchants there, while Edward III placed an embargo on wool exports.

Yet actual hostilities did not erupt. One of the reasons was that there was not much Edward could do, and France could afford to wait and let Edward stew. In case of need, French forces could strike at Guienne at will and keep England occupied there. As for the island itself, Philip had no real interest in it; the Scots could do his work for him there.

For Edward to wait in his turn would be the equivalent of backing down, but he didn't know what else to do. Edward was to prove himself a master at the art of fighting battles (that is, he was a great "tactician"). But at the art of warfare generally, which is much more than battles alone, he was not skilled; he was a poor "strategist." So he dithered.

The Flemish towns, however, grew restive. The cold war was affecting their livelihood and they wanted matters brought to a head. A rich merchant of Ghent, Jacob Van Artevelde (ahr'tuh-vel'duh), took the lead and began to urge a league of Flemish cities that would present a united front against Philip VI and against Louis of Nevers, the Count of Flanders. To make such a union successful, they had to have the support of England, and so Flemish emissaries began to join their voices to that of Robert of Artois, and to urge Edward to declare himself King of France.

Philip, relying on Edward's inability to move, escalated the conflict by declaring Guienne forfeited to the French crown in May, 1337, and beginning its occupation. Edward's hand was forced. It was either do something or capitulate. In October, 1337, Edward III formally declared himself rightful King of France.

This is considered as beginning what is usually called "The Hundred Years' War," because the English tried to maintain this claim by force of arms for about that period of time —

actually closer to a hundred and twenty years. It is a poor name, though, for the next century was not continually filled with fighting, but included long periods of virtual peace.

Declaring himself King of France did not, however, make it any easier for Edward to decide how to fight the war. Somehow, he would probably have to invade France and for the purpose, he needed Continental allies. There were, to begin with, the Flemish cities, now more or less united under the strong no-nonsense rule of Van Artevelde, who was enthusiastically pro-English. Edward also obtained the alliance of the German Emperor, who was then Louis IV.

With all this settled, Edward took what small forces he could afford to raise and sailed to Antwerp, safely in Flemish territory. There he tried to persuade the Flemish to undertake strong offensive action, and tried also to talk the Empire (divided and feeble, as usual) into supplying manpower.

While all were willing to encourage Edward to fight, none, however, was overpoweringly eager to join him. Everyone preferred to remain on the defensive. Twice, Edward III led an army to within sight of French forces and twice nothing came of it. Philip VI didn't need to fight; he had only to let Edward thrash about uselessly and all would be well for France.

So for two and a half years, the war consisted of tiny actions in Guienne where the French slowly bit into English territory, and other tiny actions in the north, where Edward III tried to enlarge a patch of English-held territory on the Channel coast in northeastern France. All that England gained by this slow warfare was virtual bankruptcy.

Philip finally could not resist the impulse of hastening the sure defeat of England. It seemed to him that there was only one push needed; some morale-destroying move like merely landing some French soldiers in England. Edward III would then surely agree to peace on French terms.

In order to carry out this move, Philip began to collect ships

and men at Sluys (sloys) on the Flemish coast.* Edward III
could tell quite easily what Philip was planning and it seemed
to him that the only safe response was to attack those ships
and try to abort the invasion before it began.

He therefore sailed toward Sluys with a fleet of 150 ships
under his personal command in order to attack the 190 ships
gathered by the French. Battle was joined on June 24, 1340.

The French fleet had awaited the attack in the medieval
style of fighting on the defensive. They kept their ships in
harbor, tied them together, and did their best to convert them
into an extension of the land. Fighting on the French side
were some mercenaries under a Genoese corsair, Barbavera,
who urged the French to hoist anchor and move out to sea
so that they could maneuver and break contact if necessary.
The French admirals, filled with knightly ignorance, considered the suggestion typical low-born cowardice and stayed
where they were, waiting for the English to come to them.

The English didn't bother. They stayed at a distance, maneuvering leisurely so as to get the wind and the sun at their
backs. Then, still at a distance, they let loose galling flights
of arrows at the massed and waiting French soldiers on board
their immobilized ships, including special arrows designed to
damage sails and rigging. The English ships, maneuvering
freely, could concentrate against those ships that seemed to be
in trouble and could board at will just where boarding would
be most effective. It was as though men with their fists free
were fighting men who were tied hand and foot. The French
fleet was almost totally destroyed (only Barbavera and some
of his ships escaping when the Genoese desperately cut the
ropes that tied them to the rest of the fleet). The sailors were
slaughtered without mercy.

The Battle of Sluys initiated a period of English supremacy

---

* Sluys is located well inland now, but in 1340 it was on an inlet
of the sea (an inlet now silted up) and was well able to hold large
quantities of shipping.

at sea over the French that was to last, with minor exceptions, for six centuries. What it did immediately was to place the Channel firmly under English control. From this time on, it was almost always possible for the English to ship men and arms freely into France; it was almost never possible for the French to do the reverse.

Yet though Sluys was a great English naval victory and though the Channel was a clear highway for England, Edward III still could do nothing. Neither then nor later did he know how to exploit the battle victories he was capable of winning. Since he was still virtually bankrupt, he was forced to agree to a six-month truce on September 25, 1340, one that left the questions at issue unsettled.

The truce did not lead to peace, however. Neither did other truces established later. There was a constant scattering of warfare here and there always, whether there was a truce on or not. In Brittany, for instance, there was a dispute over the succession to the ducal throne, with Philip VI supporting one candidate and Edward III the other. On the whole, victory leaned toward Philip's candidate.

There was also continued fighting in Guienne, where Philip pressed French attempts to turn the confiscation of the area from theory into fact. On the whole, the French had the better of it here, too.

Even Flemish friendship with England was shaken in July, 1345. Van Artevelde, who was now the virtual dictator of Flanders, proposed that the Count of Flanders be formally deposed and that the title be granted to the oldest son of Edward III. This oldest son, Edward, Prince of Wales, was fifteen years old at the time.*

---

* In later centuries, he was to be known as "the Black Prince" because he was supposed to wear black armor. Actually, he was not known by that name in his own lifetime and there is no evidence that he wore black armor. The first recorded use of the nickname came two centuries after his death. Still, it is as the Black Prince that he is universally known now.

Van Artevelde's suggestion had some merit. The Black Prince of Wales was half-Flemish. Nevertheless, the Flemings would not have a foreign ruler. Their friendship with England was a purely political one and no more. There were riots and on July 24, 1345, Van Artevelde was caught by a mob and killed.

So despite the naval victory at Sluys, Edward III after nearly a decade of war was losing on three fronts: Brittany, Guienne and Flanders.

All that kept his cause alive was that France was having troubles, too. It was on French soil that all the fighting was taking place and it was costing Philip money. He had to raise taxes. In 1341, for instance, he placed a tax on salt for the first time; a tax that was particularly inescapable, and therefore onerous, since salt was a basic necessity to life.

Dissatisfaction bubbled up everywhere and some of the nobles took advantage of this to lead revolts in Normandy and Brittany. Philip had to deal with them firmly and chop off a few heads. He then called meetings of the Estates-General to allow petitions for redress to be made, and to attempt to conciliate the grumbling burghers by making economies in administration.

Edward now decided, in desperation, to try the kind of blow Philip had planned before the Battle of Sluys. The Channel was English; why not land an army in France? This would be a serious gamble, for if the army were defeated, it was certain that England would have to give up. On the other hand, it might not even have to fight. French war-weariness might lead to French concessions if the English army made any progress at all.

DISASTER BY LAND

On July 12, 1346, Edward landed his army at St. Hogue in

Normandy, where the French coast juts northward into the Channel about 200 miles west of Paris. It was the first time English forces were in Normandy since John's time a century and a half before. For some reason, Edward's ships then sailed away, leaving the English army isolated in France.

Quickly, Edward marched southeastward, taking the city of Caen (kahn) on July 27. He continued marching in the general direction of Paris. His intention was to pull French troops away from Guienne and Brittany, defy the French king by passing near Paris, and thus win an enormous propaganda victory. If he could fight a battle on his own terms, so much the better.

When he reached the Seine River, however, he found the bridges down. This was disconcerting, as he didn't want to be trapped against a river. He raced upstream and found a repairable bridge only fifteen miles from Paris, repaired it and crossed on August 16. He then headed northward to Ponthieu (pone-tyoo'), a coastal district, some ninety miles north of Paris. Ponthieu, with its capital of Abbeville (ab-veel') belonged to England and had been a possession of the English royal family through marriage since the time of Edward I, Edward III's grandfather. Immediately to the north of Ponthieu were Artois and Flanders, where the army could be reinforced by the Flemish, if necessary, and where Philip would probably not care to follow.

The English march from Normandy, past Paris, and toward Flanders, had achieved its purpose of winning a propaganda victory, but it had not been carried out without losses. Edward's army was shrinking. Philip's best bet would have been that of a steady harassment while avoiding an actual battle. He could have inflicted losses at minimal risk and sent Edward back to England with scarcely a man following him. What price propaganda victory then? And Edward's financial troubles would probably keep him from repeating the stunt for years and possibly force him to peace altogether.

Unfortunately for France, this cold-blooded strategy was impossible. To have an English army march at will through the countryside and then allow it to leave without being openly crushed in a great battle went against all the knightly virtues. Philip VI had to catch the English army and destroy it.

Caught off-guard by the invasion, Philip was slow in gathering his army and didn't even start till after Edward had crossed the Seine. That lost the French their best battleground, but there remained one important river left between Edward and a secure line of retreat. That was the Somme River which ran through Abbeville.

Edward was hastening for the Somme. He reached it near Abbeville and again found all bridges either down or heavily guarded. The French army was thirty miles upstream and would be on him the next day. He was willing to fight, but he preferred to do so north of the river, on the side toward Flanders. He had to find a ford and he offered a large reward to anyone who could tell him of one. A local Frenchman came forward to collect the money and to point out a place where the river could be crossed, though only at low tide. Edward waited for low tide, then sent his army splashing across on August 24, 1346. He completed the task just as the French came within sight.

Edward then proceeded to the town of Crécy (kray-see'), ten miles north of the river, and there he found what he considered suitable ground for a battle. On the morning of August 26, the day on which he knew the French would be upon him, he carefully disposed his forces.

Edward's army was unusual in several respects. In the first place, it was a disciplined array of professionals who were well and regularly paid (in comparison with the French feudal army, undisciplined, and with its knightly contingents despising the rest).

Second, Edward had with him a novelty in the form of weapons making use of gunpowder. It was nearly a century, now, since Roger Bacon had talked of gunpowder; and it had been known to the Chinese centuries before that. Gunpowder itself was no secret; not even a novelty.

But how could gunpowder be bent to the task of warfare? Its explosive force could be used to hurl heavier projectiles more forcefully than anything ever used by earlier armies, but how to contain that force? One could imagine a tube open at one end. At the closed end, gunpowder could be tamped, with a round ball of stone or metal pushing against it hard. If the gunpowder were made to explode, the ball would be hurled along the tube and out the open end.

What one would need would be a metal tube strong enough not to burst when the gunpowder exploded; it would have to be straight and of even bore so that the ball could emerge smoothly with a minimum loss of energy; and the ball itself would have to fit tightly at all points so that the explosive force would not leak around it with loss of energy.

In short, the bottleneck was not in the discovery of gunpowder, or in the concept of its use. It lay in the purely technological problem of devising a practical cannon. The first mention of such a cannon came in 1324 in connection with the use made of them by citizens of the city of Ghent in Flanders.

They had been improved in the half-century since and now Edward had picked up the device from his Flemish allies. Even now, the cannon weren't much, being too small and uncertain of aim to do much direct damage, but the noise might be expected to help frighten the enemy horses. The Battle of Crécy was the first major engagement at which cannon were used and it is notable in the history of warfare for that reason. Nevertheless, it was nearly a century before such "artillery" became decisive.

Third, the English army was almost entirely on foot. It had been hard enough ferrying men across the Channel; horses would have been impossible. Nor was Edward concerned about that. He hadn't attempted to pick up horsemen in France, for instance, and what horses he did have he hid in a nearby wood. He did not plan to use them.

Edward had seen that the armored knight was outmoded. For a thousand years, the horseman had been king of the battle-field and the decision had come as a result of the simple shock of horse against horse, while footmen were considered of no account. And yet, if footmen could somehow gain the weapons to counter the horsemen, it was obvious cavalry would be finished. There are far more footmen than horsemen, and foot-men can be more easily trained. The individual footman is more dispensable and more easily replaced. In fact, if the foot-man has the necessary weapons, the horseman becomes a sitting duck, if only because the horse itself is so large and vulnerable a target.

The pike, properly handled by masses of stolid footmen, was such a weapon, as the Battle of Courtrai showed, but Edward had something even better and that was the fourth amazing thing about his army. It was the longbow.

The longbow was apparently invented by the Welsh. It was more than six feet long and it fired arrows that were three feet long. A skilled longbowman could shoot an arrow accurately for 250 yards and reach an extreme range of 350 yards. It had twice the range of the average crossbow and what was much more important was its speed of firing. While the crossbow-man was cranking up his device, the longbowman, snapping forward the arrows from the quiver on his back, could fire five or six times. If equal numbers of longbowmen and crossbow-men were to encounter each other, the latter would be bound to be riddled if they came within range. The longbow was the nearest approach to a pregunpowder machine gun ever known.

The longbow was, of course, a long-range weapon and if the enemy could somehow come to close quarters it would not prove as useful as the pike. Coming to close quarters against thousands of trained longbowmen was a great deal easier said than done, however.

The English had picked up the use of the longbow during the campaign in Wales by Edward I, and they had perfected its use against the Scots, when it had enabled them to win several battles on a hugely one-sided scale. They had also used it at the Battle of Sluys and in one or two minor skirmishes. It was at Crécy, however, that the French (and western Europe generally) were to be introduced to its virtues.

And yet it was never accepted on the Continent. That was because it had faults as well. The best bows were made of yew wood and and yew trees were specially grown in England for the purpose. They were not common elsewhere. Worse yet, the proper use required tall men with great strength and stamina, for it was necessary to exert a pull of a hundred pounds in order to draw the string back to the ear. (Longbowmen had to cut their hair short to make sure the bowstring did not entangle itself in the hair when drawn back. This started an English military tradition of short hair.) Furthermore, to exert this pull smoothly, while holding the bow firmly, taking quick and accurate aim, and seizing another arrow immediately after firing, took years of training.

The difficulties of making good longbows, and the greater difficulties of finding men large enough and strong enough, and training them long enough, kept Continental military forces wedded to the crossbow. That at least could be fired by anyone after minimal training. So the longbow remained an English monopoly and for decades kept English armies the greatest, man for man, in Europe, perhaps in the world.

But let us get back to Edward at Crécy. He lined up his unmounted men-at-arms along a ridge, with the right flank anchored at a stream. They were only 4000 in number and were thinly spread along the line, but Edward counted on their playing no role but to serve as cleanup fighters, or to counterattack if necessary. At either flank, and in the center, he distributed his 8000 longbowmen. Pitfalls were dug before the lines just in case some horsemen got that far.

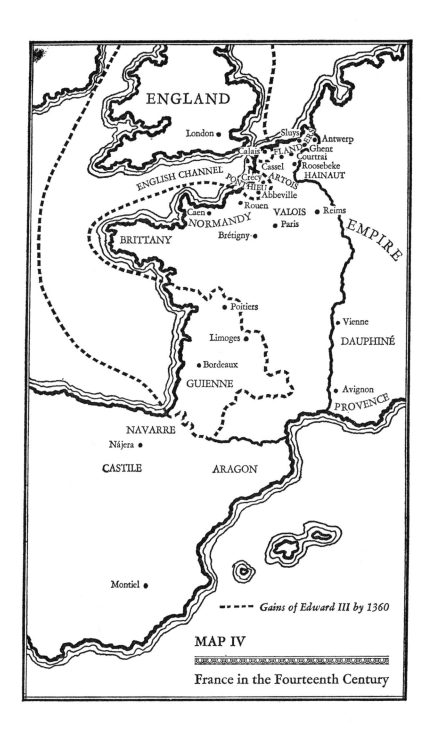

ENGLAND

London •

Sluys •
Calais • Antwerp
FLANDERS • Ghent
Cassel • Courtrai
Crécy • Roosebeke
ENGLISH CHANNEL PONTHIEU ARTOIS HAINAUT
Abbeville •
Caen • Rouen •
NORMANDY VALOIS Reims •
Paris •
BRITTANY Brétigny •

EMPIRE

Poitiers •

Vienne •
Limoges • DAUPHINÉ

Bordeaux •
GUIENNE Avignon •
PROVENCE

NAVARRE
Nájera •

CASTILE ARAGON

Montiel •

- - - - - *Gains of Edward III by 1360*

MAP IV

France in the Fourteenth Century

Edward then took up his own stand in a windmill from which he could oversee the entire battle, and waited. His entire fighting strength was about 20,000 men.

When Philip VI arrived at Crécy at the head of his men, it was late in the day. He headed about 60,000 men altogether, three times the size of the English army. These included 12,000 armored knights and 6000 skilled Genoese crossbowmen.

Conditions were far from good for the French to begin with. Edward had deliberately disposed his line so that the French, on arriving, would have to make a sharp left turn, which was certain to throw their undisciplined hosts out of order. Then, too, a brief rainstorm had muddied the ground and left the footing somewhat precarious. Finally, the French would have to charge against the English by moving westward, with the late afternoon sun in their eyes.

The best thing for the French to have done would have been to stop, reconnoiter the ground carefully and wait for morning. The men would then have recuperated from the fatigue of the chase, the ground would be hard, and the morning sun would be in the eyes of the English. Philip attempted to arrange that this be done, but the unruly knights would have none of it. To wait would not be knightly. The French army was facing foot soldiers who were only one-third their own numbers and they wanted immediate battle.

Philip therefore ordered his corps of mercenary crossbowmen to move forward and attack. The crossbowmen were tired, for they had marched on foot with all their equipment, and their leader suggested waiting. The knights, however (who were on horses), considered this cowardice and ordered them forward.

The crossbowmen therefore advanced with shouts, raised their weapons and fired. The English remained in a firm, disciplined line and waited for the Genoese to laboriously crank their weapons, reload and come closer. When the Genoese were close enough, there was the signal to fire and, from three points in the English line, thousands of arrows converged upon the luckless crossbowmen. The effect was that of a hailstorm with hard points and those crossbowmen who were not transfixed retreated hastily.

By now, though, the French knights could wait no longer. Instead of watching for a signal and charging in unison, everyone was restlessly pushing forward on his own, trying to be the first to gain knightly glory. The result was endless confusion, and when the retreating Genoese didn't get out of the way fast enough, the cry went up to "Run those rascals down. They but impede progress."

The knights lunged forward, and many of the crossbowmen were indeed ridden down, but this served only to increase the disorder in the French ranks. The English found themselves facing not an army but a mob; a mob, what's more, that never came close.

Over and over, groups of knights charged in some sixteen separate waves. Over and over, the longbowmen tirelessly mowed them down. By the time the French disengaged, after night had fallen, some 1550 knights were lying dead on the field, together with enough dead of other groups to equal the entire strength of the English army. The English casualties were virtually nonexistent. It was the Battle of Courtrai all over again, magnified into tenfold disaster for the French.

Legends concerning the battle grew up later among the English. The most famous one involved the young Prince of Wales, the Black Prince Edward, who was at the battle and in the fight though he was only sixteen years old. The legend states that the contingent that was nominally under the lead of the Black Prince was having heavy weather and a courier was sent to King Edward to ask for supporting troops.

But when Edward found that his son was still unwounded and still fighting, he sent the courier back with the stern message that there would be no help. "Let the boy win his spurs" (that is, his knighthood), he said. The victory was won and Prince Edward was indeed knighted on the battlefield by his father.

It is not at all likely there is any truth in this story, however, since in actual fact there was little knightly melee in the battle and the English men-at-arms lacked work.

Fighting on the French side was John, King of Bohemia, whose pleasure was war, and who fought not only on his own account but as a free-lance knight in the service of others. The French King Charles IV had married John's sister, and Philip VI's son and heir had married John's daughter. There was thus a marriage tie with both the current and the preceding king of France and it was not surprising that John of Bohemia was fighting on the French side.

What was surprising, however, was that he was actively fighting, despite the fact that he was fifty years old, and had been blind for ten years. He insisted on having his followers lead him into the thick of the fighting so that he might participate. He struck about with his sword at random until he was killed. The tradition arose that the Black Prince himself slew the blind old man and adopted John's crest (three ostrich feathers) and his knightly motto, "Ich dien" ("I serve").

The whole story is fishy. In the thick of *what* fighting? Blind John was probably struck down by an arrow and young Prince Edward probably never got close to him. (What credit in killing a blind old man, anyway?) The Prince of Wales' mother had among her titles that of Countess of Ostre-vant ("ostrich feather") and there is a Welsh phrase "Eich dyn" meaning "Behold the man." These rather than the blind king are the possible sources of crest and motto.

The Battle of Crécy was one of the decisive battles of world history. It made of England itself (not of England as merely part of the Angevin Empire) a great military power, a position it maintained long after, though sometimes just barely. It marked the beginning of the end of the medieval feudal army and showed that the armored knight was useless in battle, thanks to the development of new weapons for footmen.

This did not mean that horsemen were of no use at all. They still had the advantage of mobility. They could not fight appropriately armed footmen alone, but if two groups of footmen were closely engaged, a squadron of horsemen, charging down upon the flank or rear of the enemy foot could do decisive damage. It meant then that battles would be fought by combinations of different kinds of fighting men and that the good general would have to know how and when to make use of each. Edward III could do this; it was his great, inborn talent. The French were not to learn how for nearly a century.

Precisely because the French did not understand what had happened from the standpoint of military theory, the immediate effect of the Battle of Crécy was to destroy the morale of the French fighting men. The victory of the English seemed so incomprehensible to them. How could a few low-born footmen win so one-sided a victory over the flower of the French knighthood. There seemed something superhuman about the English, and the French cowered at their approach. Scarcely a major battle was fought for nearly a century in which the French weren't half-beaten before ever an arrow flew.

The exultant English, on the other hand, did not always understand the military facts of the matter, either. They preferred to accept the flattering suspicion that one Englishman was as good as ten Frenchmen and fought the war forever after on that assumption. As long as the French half believed that also, things went well for the English, but the French recovered sooner than did the English from this misapprehension. It was the French, eventually, who learned how to harness the next new advance in military technique to their purposes, and that was fatal to the English imperial hopes.

Despite the one-sided victory at Crécy, Edward III was in no position to imagine conquering France and making himself its king by sheer force. France was still too large and his army far too small. Indeed, his chief concern was to bring his army safely back to England and to leave behind him some improved base in the nearby coastal regions of France, for use in future invasions.

He therefore marched to that part of France which was nearest England, where stood the French port of Calais (ka-lay'). In September, 1346, within a month of the great victory, Calais was placed under siege.

Now came one benefit of the Battle of Crécy. The King of France, paralyzed by what had happened to him, and with his knighthood dead, could not bring himself to attempt any action to aid the hemmed-in citizens of Calais. The English controlled the sea and all the land approaches to the town. With nothing to fear from the French, they sat unhurriedly down in enemy country and waited for the surrender.

It was only after the siege had lasted ten months that Philip made a gesture. He scraped together another army and marched toward Calais. By then, though, the English were entrenched, the shores were commanded by English ships, and the French soldiers were not overjoyed at tangling with the dread Edward. The French army had to march away again and leave Calais to its fate.

Calais surrendered in August, 1347. Edward, angry at the town's long resistance, had it in mind to visit undiscriminating slaughter on its inhabitants. His own officers, however, objected. They told him that if he did so, the English would themselves hesitate to put up stern resistance against possible

French besiegers in future, for fear of being treated according to such a precedent. Queen Philippa added her pleas on behalf of the citizens of Calais, and they were spared.

Nevertheless, Edward evicted most of the population and replaced them with English, converting Calais into a town that, for two centuries, was to serve as England's base in France.

Yet Edward's army had continued to suffer by attrition and could do no more. The invasion of France had cost Edward 400,000 pounds, an enormous sum for those days and, glory or not, the English had to have peace. Edward therefore agreed to a truce with Philip and took his army out of France. He returned to an England that was almost drunk with jubilation, while Philip, in unbearable humiliation, kept trying to deal with the dissatisfactions of his own subjects.

But once disasters begin to come, they come in battalions. France had suffered a disaster at sea at the Battle of Sluys, and a far worse disaster on land at the Battle of Crécy. Now there came a disaster worse than either, worse than both together, worse than anything mere medieval armies could do; something that placed not only France, but England, too, and all Europe under a terror beyond that which mere armies could create.

It was the plague.

The plague is essentially a disease of rodents and is spread from rodent to rodent by fleas. Every once in a while, however, when the fleas spread the disease to rodents such as house rats which live in close conjunction with human beings, the disease spreads also to men. Sometimes it affects the lymph nodes, particularly in the groin and the armpits, causing them to swell into painful "buboes" — hence "bubonic plague." Sometimes the lungs are affected ("pneumonic plague") and that is even worse, for then contagion proceeds from man to man via the air and there is no need for the intervention of rats and fleas.

Sometime in the 1330s, a new strain of plague bacillus made its appearance somewhere in central Asia; a strain to which human beings were particularly susceptible. Men began to die, and even while Edward and Philip fought out their trivial battle over who was to rule over France the grinning specter of death was striding closer to Europe. By the time Calais fell, the plague had reached the Black Sea.

In the Crimea, the peninsula jutting into the north-central Black Sea, there was a seaport called Kaffa (kah'fah) where the Genoese had established a trading post. In October, 1347, a fleet of twelve Genoese ships just managed to make it back to Genoa from Kaffa. The few men on board who were not already dead were dying — and thus the plague entered western Europe. In early 1348 it was in France and in mid-1348 it had reached England.

Sometimes one caught a mild version of the disease, but very often it struck virulently. In the latter case the patient was almost always dead within one to three days after the first symptoms. Because the extreme stages were marked by hemorrhagic spots that turned dusky, the disease was called the "Black Death."

In a world innocent of hygiene, the Black Death spread unchecked. It is thought to have killed some 25 million people in Europe before it died down (more because all the most susceptible people were dead than because anyone did anything) and many more than that in Africa and Asia. About a third of the population of Europe died, perhaps more, and it took a century and a half before natural multiplication restored European population to what it had been at the time of the Battle of Crécy. It was the greatest natural disaster to strike mankind in recorded history.

Its short-term effects were marked by the abject terror it inspired among the populace. It seemed as though the world were coming to an end, and everyone walked in fear. A sudden attack of shivering or giddiness, a mere headache, might mean that death had marked you for its own and had given you a couple of dozen hours to live.

Whole towns were depopulated with the first to die lying

unburied while the initial survivors fled to spread the disease to wherever it was they fled to. Farms lay untended; domestic animals (who also died by the million) wandered about uncared for. Whole nations (Aragon, for instance) were afflicted so badly that they never truly recovered.

Distilled liquors (alcoholic drinks produced by distilling wine, thus producing a stronger solution of alcohol than could be formed by natural fermentation) had first been developed in Italy about 1100. Now, two centuries later, they grew popular. The theory was that strong drink acted as a preventive against contagion. It didn't, but it made the drinker less concerned, which was something. The plague of drunkenness settled down over Europe to match the plague of disease and remained behind after the disease was gone.

Everyone suffered, those who lived in crowded quarters the worst, of course. Towns suffered more than the countryside and indeed the gradual urbanization of the west received a setback from which it did not recover for a century. Monastic communities were also particularly hard hit, and the quality of monastic life in some ways never recovered.

Even the highest were vulnerable. In 1348 and 1349, three archbishops of Canterbury died of the plague. In the papal capital of Avignon, five cardinals and a hundred bishops died. A daughter of Edward III, Joan, was on her way to Castile to marry the son of its King Alfonso XI. She died of plague in Bordeaux on her way there. And in Castile, so did King Alfonso. In France, Philip's queen, Joan of Burgundy, died.

The terrified populace had to take action. Knowing nothing of the germ theory or of the danger of fleas, unable to keep clean in a culture which was rather suspicious of cleanliness and considered it unholy, they could do nothing useful. They could, however, find a scapegoat and for that there were always Jews available.

The theory arose that the Jews had deliberately poisoned wells in order to destroy Christians. The fact that Jews were dying of the plague on equal terms with Christians was not allowed to interfere with the theory, and the Jews were slaughtered without mercy. Of course this did nothing at all to diminish the scourge.

Viewed from a longer range, the Black Death (which kept recurring at intervals — though never again as bad — after the first attack had died out in 1351) destroyed the medieval optimism of the thirteenth century. It placed a kind of gloom on the world and bred a growth of fatalistic mysticism that took a long time to dispel.

It also helped destroy the economic structure of feudalism. There had never been a surplus of labor on the fields and in the towns but with the devastation of the plague (which fell more violently upon the low-born than upon the aristocracy) there was a sudden extreme shortage. Savage laws were promulgated by governments in order to keep serfs and artisans from taking advantage of the suddenly increased value of their muscles and skills, but no laws could counter the economic facts of life.

Serfs who recognized the great need for their services dickered for better treatment and greater privileges and often got them. Artisans charged higher prices. Prices and wages rose and to the difficulties produced by war and plague were added those of economic dislocation and inflation.

Under the double blow of the Battle of Crécy and of the Black Death, the very basis of feudalism, both military and economic, was destroyed. In western Europe, it had to die. It took its time about it, but there was never a question of its surviving after the mid-fourteenth century; only of how long it would take before human beings realized that it was dead.

7

THE SLIDE DOWNWARD

THE KING IS TAKEN

Philip VI died on August 22, 1350, but not of the plague. He is sometimes referred to in history books as "Philip the Fortunate," a name applied to him because he would not have become king but for the fortunate (for him) fact that three brothers died in succession without leaving sons. It is a remarkably unfitting nickname, however, for his reign had been marked by unparalleled misfortunes.

And yet, in one respect, he enlarged France.

A section of territory on the east bank of the Rhone River, with its capital at Vienne (vyen), was ruled by Humbert II. He was known as the Dauphin ("dolphin") because, it is suggested, a dolphin had been on the coat of arms of a twelfth-century ancestor. The region he ruled was called Dauphiné (doh-fee-nay').

Humbert II spent so much money on wars and other extravagances that he was reduced to bankruptcy and, in 1349, sold his title and his land to France. King Philip handed both title and land to his oldest son, John, and, when John became king, he transferred title and land to his oldest son in turn. This became a long-standing custom and, for the next four and a half centuries, the oldest son (or grandson, if the sons were dead) of a reigning king of France was called "the Dauphin."

When John II became king, he found France in turmoil. The plague had about run its course and had left France in ruins, but now that men had stopped dying, the problem of the war with England (virtually suspended during the Black Death) intruded again.

Never since the time of Hugh Capet himself had the prestige of the Capetian line been so low. The mere fact that Edward III had for years been claiming to be King of France and that this claim had not been smashed made it conceivable that others might argue their right to the throne, too.

For instance, if women had been allowed to transmit the royal inheritance, then the claim would never have reached Isabella, the mother of Edward III. Instead, when Louis X and his short-lived baby, John I, had died, the throne would have passed through his daughter, Jeanne, to her son, Charles.

As it happened, Jeanne ruled as Queen of Navarre (nuh-vahr'), which was a small kingdom in northern Spain, straddling the western end of the Pyrenees, with its northern tip in what would now be extreme southwestern France. Its early history belongs with the other small kingdoms of medieval Spain, but, in 1235, a French nobleman succeeded to its throne and since then it had become a French appanage.

Jeanne's son, Charles II of Navarre, was eighteen years old at the time John II became King of France. Charles was an unscrupulous young man who could and did twist and turn, side with anyone, do anything to advance his own ambitions. He is known to history as "Charles the Bad," a nickname first given him when he suppressed a revolt in his territories with needless cruelty.

Charles, as grandson of Louis X and great-grandson of Philip IV, was quite aware of the fact that if Edward III could really enforce his contention that women could transmit the French kingship, then it would be himself, Charles the Bad, who was rightful King of France.

John II, as aware of this as Charles himself, tried to keep the young man quiet by granting him the hand of his daughter in marriage. This didn't work. With the king as his father-in-law, Charles merely demanded his rights more loudly and began by claiming certain lands which had belonged to his mother. These, John had granted to a new Constable (as the commander in chief of the French army was called) whom he had appointed. Charles the Bad therefore had the Constable assassinated and began to negotiate with the English.

John tried to counter this first by bribing Charles with a grant of lands in Normandy. When this didn't work and Charles continued to plot with the English (intent as he was on higher stakes), John had to risk counteraction by the growing number of French nobles who were drifting to Charles' side, and arrested the troublemaker in April, 1356. Charles' young brother, Philip, maintained the Navarrese interest and continued to side with England against France.

This was the first time in the course of the dispute over the succession that the English had a chance to make massive use of disaffection among the Capetians themselves, turning one against the other. The Anglo-Navarrese combination, though bad enough for France, was only a dim portent of things to come.

Meanwhile, John II was trying to mollify the people. The Estates-General met in 1355 in a furious heat over steadily increasing taxes.

For once, there was a forceful nonaristocrat to lead in the fight for fiscal reform. This was Etienne Marcel, a cloth mer-

chant who was the wealthiest man in Paris and the acknowledged representative of the middle class. Not only did he
demand that taxation be imposed by the Estates-General, rather
than by the king, but that the Estates-General be allowed to
supervise the collection. He invented a cap of red and blue to
be worn by his supporters and spoke of the "will of the people."
He was a French Revolutionary born four centuries ahead of
his time.

What made this middle-class revolt the more serious was that
Charles the Bad had been gaining support by being ostenta-
tiously antitax, so that when he was arrested many were convinced it was for his sympathies with the people.

If Marcel had been able to make his demands stick, if the
Estates-General had really been able to take over control of
the power of taxation (as the English Parliament was able to
do), then France might have followed the same road toward
representative government that England did.

Unfortunately, the middle class was really powerful only in
Paris. In the provinces, conservatism remained strong and
there was hostility to Paris as a hotbed of radicalism. Marcel
could never count on any broad national support, therefore.
Furthermore, the chaos in the land and the constant threat of
the English played into the hands of authoritarianism. The
necessities of war could not be denied and the pressure for
reform had to be abated.

The focus of the English danger was now in the southwest.
There the Black Prince, no longer a boy but a fierce warrior of
twenty-five, had landed in September, 1355, and had been con-
ducting bold raids far inland with relatively small forces. He
was not interested in battles really, just in loot.

Eventually, John II (who had been spending his time trying
to reassert control over those Norman castles which were under
the control of Charles the Bad and his party) decided to tackle
the Black Prince directly.

He may have looked forward to battle, in fact, for John II

was a quixotically chivalrous man. Though he was very nearly as dishonest and conniving as Charles the Bad when it came to politics and to dealing with his subjects, he had an exalted opinion of how he ought to behave to fellow knights. Despite the lessons of Courtrai and Crécy, he still believed in the tournament theory of warfare. He was therefore called "John the Good," where "good" does not mean "virtuous" particularly, but merely one who lives up to the rules of chivalry.

John the Good was far worse for France at this time than Charles the Bad.

Southwestward, John marched his large feudal army, which numbered as high as 40,000 men, to cut off the considerably smaller raiding parties (perhaps 12,000 all told) led by the Black Prince. The Black Prince's army, consisting mostly of Frenchmen from Guienne, but including three to four thousand English longbowmen, was laden down with loot and would have preferred to march back to security without a fight.

That, however, could not be. John's army, spurring wildly on, caught up with what seemed to be its prey on September 17, 1356, just ten years after the Battle of Crécy.

The meeting place was in south-central France about seven miles southeast of the city of Poitiers (pwah-tyay') and about 180 miles southwest of Paris. The English had disposed themselves upon a hill which had enough plant cover to keep them fairly secure. What's more, the dreaded longbowmen were so distributed as to guard all the approaches.

Approaching the hill came John II at the head of his feudal mob. What anyone with an ounce of brains would have done would have been to surround the hill and wait. Within a couple of days, the English would have had to come down and fight at a disadvantage, or stay where they were and be starved into surrender.

This did not suit the chivalrous John, to whom the only decent way of fighting was to charge directly forward to the sound of trumpets. Nor had he learned the lesson of Crécy that you don't simply charge at thousands of waiting longbowmen unless you can in some way neutralize or overpower them. Instead he had the dim idea that the Battle of Crécy had shown it was better to fight on foot than on horseback — so he dismounted his knights and sent them slogging forward.

A fully armed knight trying to advance on foot is clumsy and ungainly, sacrificing the limited mobility the horse gives him, and gaining only in being a smaller target than horse and man together. Painfully, the knights moved forward and the longbowmen found their mark. It was Crécy again, and yet some of the knights managed to reach the Black Prince's line.

Despite a slaughter, the French might have finally overwhelmed the greatly outnumbered forces of the Black Prince had they managed another push. At the crisis, however, the French forces sheered off in panic and the Black Prince sent his forces forward to counterattack.

To give John credit, he fought like a demon personally. At his side was Philip, the youngest of his four sons, fourteen years old at the time. While his father slashed away with his battle-ax, Philip acted as lookout against the now swarming enemy, crying out, "Look to the right, father; now to the left." As a result, the boy was known as "Philip the Bold" for the rest of his life.

In the end, 2500 French knights lay dead and another 2500 were captured; worse even than at Crécy. It was worse for the English, too, however, for the Black Prince had lost about 2000 in killed and wounded.

This new battle confirmed the belief, on both sides, in the apparent invincibility of the English. Its worst aspect, as far as French prestige and French pride was concerned, was the fate of King John. Had John merely been killed, it would have been all to the good, actually, for the Dauphin, Charles, who was far more capable than his father, would have simply carried on as the new king. John, however, was taken prisoner (and his young son Philip with him).

For King John himself, this was no calamity. The Black

Prince went out of his way to treat John as king, even though the official English position was that he was merely John of Valois and a usurper. The Black Prince did this for two reasons. For one thing, it redounded more greatly to his credit to have captured a King of France, rather than a Count of Valois. For another, to have the king in captivity would wreck French morale, so it was important that the French be made to see, in every way possible, that John was actually a captive king.

John was treated with royal consideration, therefore. He was taken first to Bordeaux and then to England, where he lived a life of careless ease. The other members of the French aristocracy who were captured were treated with similar gallantry and "chivalry." What was a lost battle to them?

The Black Prince behaved here as a model of chivalry, but only to knights. The lower orders and the peasantry, who had not caused the war, and who fought only because they were forced to by their masters, were treated with the utmost barbarity. The Black Prince, who could kneel to his royal captive, could also order the massacre of unarmed prisoners, provided they were not noble.

To be sure, the knightly captives had to raise huge ransoms for their freedom, but these ransoms were gouged out of the peasants and townsmen whom they controlled. Naturally, the greatest ransom was assigned to John, and the Kingdom of France, groaning under its chaotic troubles, now had to bleed itself white to ransom its carefree king, who was living luxuriously in England after a battle which the royal stupidity had lost.

THE WISE DAUPHIN

France was falling apart. The eighteen-year-old Dauphin, now ruling as regent for his captured father, seemed to have nothing going for him. He had been at the Battle of Poitiers, but along with two of his brothers had fled the field (probably by orders of his father who did not want to see the whole royal family captured). This gave him the reputation of a coward and runaway, and his slight build and sickly constitution certainly did not give him the appearance of a warrior.

What's more, he came back to a Paris which had had enough of its inept nobility. The Estates-General, which had tried to press for fiscal reform with John II the year before and which had been beaten down by the necessities of war, would wait no longer. Nothing could be worse than the disastrous battles fought by the stupid nobility.

Paris was virtually in the hands of the middle class therefore, and Etienne Marcel, the leader of the merchants, had more power — in Paris, at least — than the Dauphin. Marcel fortified and armed the capital and put it in readiness for a siege. Strongly, he pressed the Dauphin for reforms, for dismissing the old councilors who had brought disaster, for new powers to the middle class, for new systems of taxation.

The Dauphin, a shrewd young man, realized the desirability of reform, but did not wish to place himself in the hands of the overbearing Marcel, either. He did his best to temporize, while from his far captivity in England, King John took time out from his gay social life to send proclamations forbidding the Estates-General to meet, and declaring anything they accomplished to be without force.

Certainly, the royal pronouncements carried little weight at this time. Worse yet, Charles the Bad escaped from prison and formed an alliance with Marcel. (Not that Charles was interested in either the people or reform, but he would work with anyone if that suited his ambitions.)

The Dauphin had to give in. In March, 1357, he agreed to a far-reaching program of reform that limited his own powers considerably. But giving in was not giving up.

The Dauphin fell back on his wits. As it happened, he was

just the reverse of his father, with brains in his head and not in his biceps. (He was eventually to be known as "Charles the Wise.") He was an excellent public speaker and he was not ashamed to address himself to the people of Paris. In a series of speeches he began to win them over to himself by making capital of the suspicions many felt concerning the motives of Charles the Bad. It did not escape the notice of many Parisians that Charles the Bad had brought troops of his own into Paris and that these troops included English mercenaries.

But then, in 1358, a new disaster befell France.

Its chivalry had been decimated by successive battles, its people slaughtered by the Black Death; but everything had fallen worst and hardest on the peasants. The peasants were leaderless, uneducated, unarmed, powerless. All despised them, pillaged them, stole from them, killed them. The nobility taxed them and told them it was their duty to pay; the clergy tithed them and told them it was the will of God that they suffer; the merchants held themselves aloof; the soldiers found them fair game.

And now they were being crushed and tortured to provide the ransoms needed by the nobles who had been captured at the Battle of Poitiers and who were sitting it out in easeful captivity. It meant the lot of the peasant had simply passed the bounds of the possible.

In 1358, bands of them seized clubs and scythes, and began to attack the houses of the nobility, crying "Death to gentlemen!" It was enough for them if someone they captured had uncallused hands. That was sufficient cause for death. Since the common name for a peasant in France was "Jacques Bonhomme" ("Goodman Jack"), this rebellion was called a "Jacquerie."

Throughout history there have been peasant rebellions which have followed always the same course. Blindly, the peasants sacked and destroyed, and when members of the "upper classes" fell into their hands, they killed ruthlessly and cruelly, for never in their lives had they been taught gentleness and mercy by those now in their power.

Eventually, the organized power of the state would be brought against the peasants and then the rebels would, of course, be defeated. Visited upon them, then, would be the full vengeance of the angered upper classes. For every one of themselves that had fallen, dozens of peasants would pay the price in horrors that equaled and surpassed any the peasants had inflicted.

The Jacquerie caused a reaction in favor of the nobility and the alliance between Charles the Bad and Etienne Marcel foundered. Charles the Bad, who enjoyed killing peasants anyway, led the fight against the Jacquerie, while Marcel, seeing in them possible supporters of his fight for government by the middle class, tried to treat with them.

What with the shock of the Jacquerie, the discomfort at the alliance with Charles the Bad, the smooth persuasions of the Dauphin, this attempt on Marcel's part to talk to revolting peasants lost him his support. On July 31, 1358, this merchant who was trying to establish a nineteenth-century government (complete with a representative parliament and a businesslike tax policy) on a fourteenth-century France, was struck down and killed in the course of a riot.

And yet though France seemed buried in woes, the worst of all was still King John. In England, John signed a treaty that handed away virtually all of northern France in return for his freedom. The southern shores of the Channel, he agreed, were to be English.

This agreement represented such total surrender that when the terms were presented in Paris, the Dauphin Charles managed to overcome his loyalty to his father and refused to sign it. On May 19, 1359, the Estates-General supported him. If such a treaty was the only way in which King John could get out of captivity, then he could rot in England (though the Estates-General was careful not to put it in those words).

King Edward decided, then, that it was time to teach the French another lesson, since the Battles of Crécy and of Poitiers had not pounded sufficient sense into their heads. On October 28, 1359, he landed a proud and glittering army at Calais and made for Reims, at whose cathedral the kings of France were, by tradition, crowned. Edward intended to be crowned there as King of France.

But now two things turned against him. For one thing, the weather did. It rained almost constantly and it was a bedraggled army indeed that finally found itself at Reims on November 30. Second, Edward was, for the first time, fighting an intelligent enemy. The Dauphin Charles had no intention of obliging Edward with a pitched battle. He had seen to it that Reims was well-provisioned and in good shape and now he was willing to let the English army sit before its walls till it froze.

Edward did sit before Reims for weeks, and the weather got worse and worse. The citizens of Reims sat tight and there was no French army on the horizon to offer battle and be slaughtered. At last, in chagrin and anticlimax, Edward had to march his men away. He spent a winter raiding and pillaging the countryside, losing men to disease, and finding himself increasingly beset by a hostile populace. And still there were no great victories to boast of.

Now the English felt the disadvantage of winning great victories. If they went to France and won *no* great victories, that alone would be a terrible defeat for them.

As the winter drew to an end, Edward marched to Paris itself in March of 1360 and settled down to a siege. Surely, that would force the Dauphin to grant him the battle he desperately wanted. Edward did everything he could to force it, too. He flaunted himself at the walls, sent men riding forward to challenge any Frenchman to single battle and to do so as insultingly as possible.

The French knights may have chafed, but the Dauphin Charles sat tight. Until the French learned to fight after the

English fashion, he was not going to make a move. It might be
unchivalrous; it might be considered cowardly; but he intended
to bear the shame rather than destroy the nation. He refused
to allow one man outside the walls of Paris. Let the English sit
there.

Charles knew what he was doing, too. The English army was
reduced in numbers as the result of the previous winter's campaigning and was in want of provisions besides. It was not
equipped to withstand a really bad spell of weather and the
only thing the English could hope for was that the French
would fight, without real hope of victory, or that they would
surrender — and Charles would allow neither.

Then, on April 14, 1360, the day after Easter Sunday (and a
day long to be known to the English as "Black Monday"), a
tremendous hailstorm struck the English camp. The fierce wind
and unseasonable cold, the hail and the darkness not only
ruined the besieging army, but filled them with a superstitious
fear that God Himself had turned against them.

The siege was lifted, for Edward III's will had broken. He
had had enough and wanted only to go home. Though he may
not have known it at the time, he was never to fight again.

Two weeks after Black Monday, peace negotiations between
England and France began at Bretigny (bray-tee-nyy'), fifteen
miles south of Paris. Edward III did not claim the crown and
the kingdom, he did not even claim the entire Angevin Empire;
he let himself be beaten down to the return of Aquitaine alone,
the land of his great-great-great-grandmother Eleanor; plus
some enlargement of the English foothold in the Calais region.

Had France been in a position to hold out, Edward would
have had to settle for even less, but France was weary to death.
Defeat, plague and insurrection had made it necessary for it to
accept peace at any terms short of outright national death. The
Dauphin therefore gave in and handed over Aquitaine to England — though without any intention of considering that cession
in any way final.

At that, the Dauphin's treaty was not as bad as King John's had been. England owned considerable tracts in the southwest anyway, and Aquitaine was relatively far from its home base; relatively hard to defend; relatively hard to use as a springboard against the rest of France. In comparison, to have handed over large tracts of northern France just across the channel from England itself would have given the English a base that might have been enough to kill France.

It is notable that representatives of the ceded provinces protested vigorously against the move. National feelings were continuing to grow stronger.

THE SHREWD GENERAL

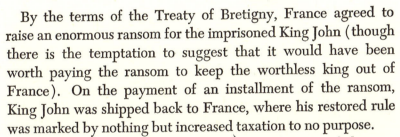

By the terms of the Treaty of Bretigny, France agreed to raise an enormous ransom for the imprisoned King John (though there is the temptation to suggest that it would have been worth paying the ransom to keep the worthless king out of France). On the payment of an installment of the ransom, King John was shipped back to France, where his restored rule was marked by nothing but increased taxation to no purpose.

Behind him, as hostage for payment of the rest of the ransom, John had left his second son, Louis of Anjou. This son escaped from the English in 1362, and King John, in a fit of chivalry, declared that his honor was impugned and voluntarily returned to his luxurious imprisonment in England — where he was more comfortable than on the throne, anyway. In England, in 1364, he died at the age of forty-four, more as a result of overeating than anything else, after a reign of fourteen years, during which he showed himself more oblivious of the responsibilities of his position than any French king had up to his time.

During his brief return to France, indeed, he did something

that eventually brought more harm to France than any other deed in his entire feckless reign.

Toward the end of 1361, Philip, Duke of Burgundy (a grandson of Eudes IV, whose feud with Robert of Artois had helped start the ruinous Hundred Years' War), died, leaving no direct descendants. The ineffable Charles the Bad at once claimed the duchy, but lands without heirs normally passed to the king and King John hastened to make Burgundy part of the royal domain. This, in itself, was excellent, for the duke had ruled over sections of east-central France which were fertile and prosperous. Placed firmly under the direct rule of the crown, it would have gone far toward balancing the loss of Aquitaine.

King John, however, having gained the duchy, promptly handed it over as an appanage to his youngest son, Philip the Bold, the one who had fought at his side at the Battle of Poitiers, and who had shared imprisonment with him in England. As a result, Burgundy was to enter a period of cultural and military glory, but France was to be wounded nearly to death.

When King John died, the Dauphin succeeded as Charles V "the Wise." He had need of all his wisdom and he used it. He abandoned chivalry; he abandoned the expensive luxury of feasting and tournaments, all the useless panoply of nonsense that could be conducted only upon the prostrate and starving bodies of French peasants.

By modern standards, in fact, Charles V might more nearly have deserved sainthood than had his great-great-great-grandfather Louis IX. Charles was as gentle, chaste and devout as Louis was and yet he found room for tolerance, too. He labored to decrease the power of the Inquisition and even (an unheard-of attitude) intervened on occasion to prevent Jews from being needlessly mistreated.

Despite his enlightened attitude, he was careful not to alienate the clergy, whose support he badly needed. He added to the religious flavor of the coronation still further, and had himself anointed with oil supposedly sent down by heaven at the time of the conversion of Clovis, founder of the Frankish realm, eight centuries before. In return he expected the clergy to absolve him of the sin of breaking the oath with which he swore to observe the Treaty of Bretigny, for that oath he intended to break.

As befitted his sobriquet of "the Wise" he was interested in learning and patronized philosophers and scientists. He collected over 900 books (an enormous number for that pre-printing age) and established the first royal library in France.

In particular, he patronized Nicolas Oresme (oh-ram'), a churchman at Rouen. He had Oresme translate several of Aristotle's books from Latin to French, something which further helped fix Francien as the national language. Oresme also wrote a book on economic theory in which he strongly urged the absolute inviolability of the coinage, as the best way to encourage trade and prosperity. Charles V tried to adhere to Oresme's theories and to avoid the debasement of the coinage which had been so disastrous a habit of his father's.

But everything he did was with an eye to the continuing English threat. He needed strength. In addition to reorganizing the financial structure of the kingdom, he rebuilt the French navy, restored and strengthened the army, fortified Paris (and beautified its public buildings, too). He also labored to keep the Estates-General powerless; not because he did not see the advisability of the reforms urged by the middle class; but because he recognized in it a source of divisiveness and partisanship which he felt the nation could not afford in the face of the external threat.

Most important of all, he discovered an instrument in the form of Bertrand Du Guesclin (dyoo-geh-klan'), a minor noble of Brittany. Du Guesclin was a fighting man, rough-hewn, ugly, unlearned and shrewd. He had shown his mettle in the battles of the civil war in Brittany between two claimants to the ducal throne and had done well even against the English, fighting against them with admirable skill and fortitude. He was already middle-aged, for he was about forty years old when Charles V came to the throne.

One of Charles' first acts as king was to consolidate his power in Normandy and subdue those parts that were still under the control of Charles the Bad of Navarre. Charles the Bad still depended on English support and was maneuvering to prevent the royal coronation, for he continued to dream of the crown.

The royal forces were put under Du Guesclin who, about sixty miles west of Paris, inflicted a signal defeat on the forces of Charles the Bad and broke his power. The news reached Reims two days later, on May 18, 1364, just as Charles V was undergoing the coronation ceremonies, and it was taken as a good omen.

After the battle, Du Guesclin returned to Brittany to fight for his duke against the English. There, fortune turned the other way. The duke was killed and Du Guesclin captured. Charles V, who knew he could not spare the rough Breton, promptly ransomed him for 40,000 gold francs.

Charles V had another task waiting for Du Guesclin.

Charles the Bad, unable to maintain himself in the north of France, had returned to his own lands in Navarre and there was seeking new allies. In particular, he made overtures to the Kingdom of Castile, which lay west of Navarre and which made up part of what we now call Spain. It was then ruled by Pedro, a king known to historians (and to his own people) as "Pedro the Cruel."

Charles the Bad hoped for good results in this endeavor since Pedro was at odds with France. France, it seems, had previously attempted to establish an alliance with Castile in order to force the English in southwestern France to fight on both sides of the Pyrenees and thus face a two-front war. To cement the alliance, a marriage was arranged in 1353 between Pedro the Cruel and Blanche of Bourbon, a princess of the Capetian royal house.

The young Castilian king was, however, desperately in love with a local beauty, Maria de Padilla, and having gone through the form of marriage felt that that was enough. He abandoned his wife the next day, had her imprisoned, and when, eight years later and still imprisoned, she died, the rumor at once made the rounds that she had been poisoned at her husband's orders.

But Pedro had an older half-brother, Henry of Trastamara, who could not really lay claim to the throne because he was of illegitimate birth. Henry, however, aspired to the throne anyway and, after several unsuccessful attempts in this direction, left for France in 1356, hoping he could find allies there. Pedro's mistreatment of a French princess had alienated the French nobility and created strong sympathy for Henry's claims. It was only the troubles with England that kept France from taking strong action.

But then, in 1366, with the situation stabilized in the north, Charles V decided that the old grievance with Pedro, combined with the suspicion that Pedro would now ally himself with Charles the Bad, made it necessary to send Bertrand du Guesclin south. The expedition would serve two purposes. If it succeeded and if Henry of Trastamara were placed on the Castilian throne, his help against the English in Aquitaine would be certain, and could be enormously helpful. And then, win or lose, the expedition would serve to draw off bands of soldier-brigands (so-called "Free Companies") who were ready to fight for anyone for pay and who occupied themselves between engagements by looting and torturing peasants.

Du Guesclin gathered together 30,000 of these brigands and, with Henry of Trastamara in tow, marched southward, detouring by way of Avignon. Through all France's troubles since the accession of Philip VI, the French victory over the papacy was still maintained. Urban V was now Pope, the sixth to have Avignon for his seat. Du Guesclin respectfully asked the Pope for a large sum of money, and the Pope, noting that 30,000 brigands of the worst sort were surrounding the city, did not think it wise to refuse. Du Guesclin then proceeded to the Pyrenees and beyond.

Pedro the Cruel, recognizing himself to be in serious trouble, did the inevitable thing. He called for the help of Edward the Black Prince, who had been put by his father into the position of ruler over Aquitaine. The Black Prince, whose rule was incompetent, and who took greater joy in the simplicities of battle than in the complexities of peace, answered the call gleefully.

Thus the war between England and France was renewed, quite unofficially, on Spanish soil. The two armies, with Castilian contingents on both sides, met at Nájera (nah'hay-rah), 190 miles north of Toledo, the Castilian capital, on April 3, 1367. Once again the English longbowmen performed vigorously and were especially effective against the Castilians who had not encountered them before. The French knights, more heavily armed than ever, were relatively untouched by the arrows and fought valiantly and well, but the Castilian rout was decisive.

It was a French defeat and Du Guesclin was taken prisoner and had to be expensively ransomed once more. However, the Free Companies were virtually wiped out, something not entirely unfortunate for France, and Henry of Trastamara escaped from the scene of the lost battle, living to fight another day.

The victory was an expensive one for the Black Prince, too. He had spent a great deal of money which he would have to get back by extortion from his already disaffected Aquitainian subjects. He received very little in the way of gratitude from Pedro the Cruel, with whom he soon quarreled and whom he then abandoned. Besides his health was ruined. The Black Prince fell sick in Spain and never really recovered.

Even as a military feat the victory was useless, for Henry soon returned, received new help from France and new reinforcements led by Du Guesclin. In a new battle on March 14, 1369, at Montiel (mone-tyel'), 100 miles southeast of Toledo, one in which the Black Prince was not involved, the decision was reversed. Henry of Trastamara won the victory and Pedro was taken prisoner. The brothers fought a hand-to-hand battle and Pedro was killed.

Henry of Trastamara reigned as Henry II for the next ten years and remained a firm and loyal ally of France. All future rulers of Spain over the next five and a half centuries were descended from him.

Charles V, with the alliance with Castile established, was ready to reopen the war in France itself. The Aquitainian nobility, increasingly restless under English exactions, had been appealing to Charles as the overlord. In feudal theory, the Black Prince was still vassal to the King of France and could be called to account. Charles ordered the Black Prince to appear before him. The Black Prince refused, of course, threatening to come, if he had to, with an army at his back.

This he couldn't do easily, and well Charles knew it, for the Black Prince's legacy of Spanish illness kept him from his horse.

The Black Prince's refusal, however, was used by Charles V to argue that the Treaty of Bretigny had been broken by the English and the war was renewed.

Edward III, maintaining, of course, that it was the French who broke the treaty, declared himself, once again, King of France and, once again, an English army landed at Calais. Edward III had now been on his throne forty years, however, and was rapidly sinking into senility. He did not lead the army in person. Instead he placed his fourth son, John, at its head. John had been born in Ghent in Flanders in 1340, just before the Battle of Sluys, and was sometimes called John of Ghent (or, in English distortion, John of Gaunt) in consequence.

There was thus a two-pronged invasion of France in 1369, by two sons of the English king. John of Gaunt pushed southwestward from Calais and the Black Prince pushed northeast-ward from Bordeaux. In the course of this offensive, the Black Prince performed his last military feat.

Limoges (lee-mozhe'), 110 miles northeast of Bordeaux, was an Aquitainian city that was nominally under English control. It had, however, openly declared its allegiance to France. Furious, the Black Prince had his men take the city in 1370, while he himself looked on from a litter, being too ill to travel in any other fashion. After the city was taken, the Black Prince venge-fully ordered the slaughter of its habitants. As terrorism usually does, it had the effect of further turning the populace against the terrorists.

The Black Prince could do no more. He lingered on in Bordeaux a few more years and then returned to England — his sickness never leaving.

His deeds and those of his father were immortalized by a French poet, Jean Froissart (frwah-sahr'), who was born in Flanders about 1337. He grew up while Flanders was in alliance with England during the early decades of the Hundred Years' War and he remained pro-English all his life.

Toward the end of his life, he wrote a history of his times, *Chronicles of France, England, Scotland and Spain,* dealing with events from 1325 to 1400, and with the Hundred Years' War in particular. It is considered the greatest piece of historical writing of the Middle Ages, but it is heavily slanted toward chivalry. It glorifies and idealizes the knightly battles, with the two Edwards, father and son, as the great heroes. There is virtually nothing about anything but that; only scant mention of the Black Death, for instance.

Despite Froissart's account, however, knightly heroism was not decisive, particularly against Charles V and Du Guesclin. The Black Prince's effort failed after the slaughter at Limoges and John of Gaunt got nowhere either.

Charles V had shattered precedent by making Du Guesclin the Constable of France, that is commander in chief of the

French forces, a post usually reserved for some great but incompetent nobleman. Under Du Guesclin, the French army
followed one cardinal rule: there were to be no great battles.
The French were going to fight a guerrilla war.

When John of Gaunt advanced, therefore, with deliberate
destruction, trying to lure the French army into battle, Du
Guesclin grimly faded from before him, only to come back in
flying raids at his flanks and at isolated bodies of men. John
lost half his army eventually and won no glory. In 1373, John
tried again, with precisely the same result.

And while English armies postured and paraded, Du Guesclin kept up a steady series of minor battles that nibbled away
at English-controlled territories. He specialized in night attacks
which the English indignantly denounced as "unknightly" but
which achieved their aim. The English-controlled territories
shrank steadily, district by district, castle by castle.

Du Guesclin's Spanish policy showed its worth when Castile's navy sailed with that of France to defeat the English at
sea a hundred miles north of Bordeaux. English control of the
seas vanished for a time and this cut Aquitaine off from England and aided Du Guesclin's policy tremendously.

In 1376, the Black Prince's lingering illness ended with his
death, and half a year later, in 1377, Edward III died, too.
Succeeding to the English throne was the Black Prince's young
son, the ten-year-old Richard II (who had been born in Bordeaux). In 1380, Du Guesclin died and so did Charles V. Succeeding to the French throne was the eleven-year-old Dauphin, who reigned as Charles VI.

By then, virtually all the English conquests in France, after
forty years of fighting, were gone. Patiently, Charles V and
Du Guesclin, in a guerrilla war in which there was not a single
major battle, had reversed the decisions of the Battles of Sluys,
Crécy and Poitiers. The mighty English effort had ended in
nothing after all.

The English foothold in the southwest and the northeast

was as small and precarious at the death of Edward III as it had been at his accession a half-century earlier. France was as large and as united (on the map) as she had been at the accession of Philip VI. With Dauphiné and Burgundy in Capetian hands and with Castile in alliance, she might seem even larger and more unified.

And yet the map does not tell the whole story. A generation of war, insurrection and plague had brought down her population, her wealth and her strength. Despite what the map would show, France had been reduced enormously from her position under Philip IV.

THE KING'S UNCLES

To France, the deaths of Charles V and Du Guesclin were a disaster, for their firmness and wisdom had been removed from the government. Worse, the new king, Charles VI, was but a boy. Worse yet, the new king had uncles interested only in the increase of their personal power.

There were three uncles to begin with: Louis of Anjou, John of Berri (beh-ree') and Philip the Bold of Burgundy.

Of these, Louis of Anjou was the oldest. He had once been hostage for his father, John II, and it was his escape from English imprisonment that had been John's excuse for return to gilded imprisonment. Louis of Anjou was, however, the least harmful of the uncles because his ambitions were fixed outside France. He was a great-great-grandson (through his grandmother) of Charles of Anjou, who had once briefly ruled Naples and Sicily. Because of this, Louis hankered for nothing less than the title of king. The reigning Queen of Naples, Joanna, was persuaded to adopt Louis of Anjou (her second cousin, once removed) as her successor, and when Joanna died in 1382, Louis went off to claim his kingdom. He died himself in 1384, however, with only the title of king, not having been able to establish the actuality.

As for John, Duke of Berri, he lived a life of luxury. He financed beautiful buildings and bought great works of art and patronized men of art and literature — all at the expense of his subjects, whom he taxed mercilessly. He did his best to expand his dukedom at the expense of the royal domain, and he also did his best to bring about peace with England (since only so could his own luxurious life be continued with security).

Philip the Bold of Burgundy, like John of Berri, was primarily interested in extending his personal holdings. In 1369, he had married Margaret of Flanders, the daughter of Louis of Male (mahl), the then-reigning count of the region. Louis of Male had succeeded his father when the latter died during the slaughter at the Battle of Crécy (he himself was present, aged sixteen, but had escaped alive) and he had no sons. Charles V, keenly aware of the importance of Flanders and of its continuing pro-English sentiments, had been certain that if something weren't done, Margaret would marry some English prince and Flanders would then be united with England politically as well as economically. To prevent that, he pushed through the marriage with Philip of Burgundy.

Charles was no fool, of course. He had no trouble in seeing that a union of Flanders and Burgundy would be nearly as pregnant with trouble as would a union of Flanders and England. It was only his intention to block the latter, not promote the former. He therefore forced Philip the Bold to swear an oath not to claim rule over Flanders through his marriage. Philip reflected that Charles was both older than he and rather sickly. He expected to survive his royal brother and so he swore to this readily.

After the death of Charles V, however, the extortionate tax policies of Louis of Anjou produced antitax riots all over

France, and particularly in Paris. Taking advantage of these disorders, the people of Flanders rebelled under the leadership of Philip Van Artevelde, son of the Jacob who had done so much to launch Edward III on his war against France a half-century before.

The younger Van Artevelde followed the tactics of his father, offering to recognize Richard II as King of France in return for military help. Young Richard, however, was no Edward and he made no move, especially since it was now England's turn to be undergoing a peasants' revolt.

Philip the Bold, son-in-law of Louis de Male, who had been waiting for over a decade for the death of his brother and his father-in-law, had no mind to see his inheritance go glimmering now. He brought a large French army into Flanders, and at Roosebeke (roh'suh-bay'kuh), seventy miles east of Courtrai, the French chivalry once again met the Flemish townsmen. On November 27, 1382, battle was joined. This time, the French army was larger and their attack more careful. After a hard fight, they killed Van Artevelde and overwhelmed the Flemings.

The French had not forgotten their shameful defeat at Courtrai. After killing the Flemish pikemen on the battlefield, they sought out the church where the golden spurs that had been the relics of that battle were hung. They then burned the church and killed those inhabitants of the town that had not had the foresight to flee. A savage and merciless repression was clamped down on Flanders by Philip the Bold and it was to be a long time before the lowlanders would dare assert themselves again.

The last Flemish holdouts were suppressed in 1384, but no sooner was Louis of Male secure in his position, when he died. It was now up to Philip the Bold to remember his oath not to claim the county, but it was an easy task for him to persuade his careless nephew, the sixteen-year-old Charles VI, to grant him the favor of taking Flanders.

To his rich and strong domains in east France, Philip thus added the wealthy towns of Flanders. Though only dukes, he and his descendants became the wealthiest lords in France, wealthier than the king. The time was to come when Burgundy-Flanders was to be the wealthiest and most cultured land in all Europe.

After that, disorders in Paris were brutally repressed also, and the kingdom was quiet. Preparations were made for a renewal of the war with England under what seemed favorable conditions, since the rule of Richard II was weak, and the English nobility were squabbling for power as avidly as the French nobility were. In 1386, France seemed even on the point of launching an invasion of England. Ships for the purpose were collected in the Channel ports — and then nothing came of it. At the last moment, presumably, the royal uncles of Berri and Burgundy decided there was nothing to be gained from major warfare.

It was obviously to the interest of the uncles to keep Charles VI a puppet-king and they did their best to involve him in a life of amusement and futile excitement so that he would be content to leave the business of government to them. His father, Charles V, knowing his own weak constitution, and foreseeing that he might be followed by a boy-king, had established fourteen as the age at which a king would be considered old enough to rule for himself. This was an attempt to cut any regency as short as possible. Yet Charles VI reached and passed his fourteenth birthday and made no move to take over the government.

It was not until Charles VI was nearly out of his teens that he began to chafe at being treated as a minor. On November 2, 1388, with but a month to go before his twentieth birthday, he declared he would take over the government. The uncles argued smoothly against this, but Charles was firm and it was clear that public opinion was in his favor.

Naturally, all that was wrong with the kingdom was blamed

on the rapacious policies of the uncles and it was hoped that Charles VI's personal rule would mark a turn for the better. Indeed, a new truce was signed with England, in which the English were forced to evacuate more of their footholds.

Charles VI continued, however, to be interested only in amusements. He was irresponsible, luxurious and carefree, but at least he restored the running of the government to the councilors of his wise father, so there was a chance that eventually the gay son might be persuaded to take his task more seriously.

Unfortunately, the continual round of pleasures seems to have weakened the king's constitution. In April, 1392, there were discussions in process concerning the possibility of a full-fledged peace treaty between England and France, when negotiations were thrown into disarray through a royal illness. Charles VI developed a fever which was high enough to produce convulsions and, presumably, to cause brain damage.

The king apparently recovered, and later that year, he insisted on leading an expedition into Brittany to punish an attempted assassination of the Constable of France. It was an extraordinarily hot summer and he fell ill with fever on the way. Again he recovered, and against everyone's advice he started out again.

On August 5, 1392 (the story goes), a man all in white suddenly appeared out of the forest. He dashed toward the column of marching men, seized the king's bridle and cried, "Stop, noble king, go no further; you are betrayed."

The startled king managed to continue onward, despite the warning, when the page who carried the royal lance let it drop, accidentally, so that it hit a shield resoundingly.

That was it; the king drew his sword in terror and began to lunge at those about him. He was held down only with difficulty, and it was clear that he had gone mad. From then on, the madness never left him for long. He had been known as "Charles the Well-Beloved" (who does not love a child-monarch?), but he is known in history, now, as "Charles the Mad."

8

TO THE BOTTOM

CIVIL WAR

All that Charles V had regained for France now trembled at the lip of an abyss, and once again France was struck by unlooked-for disaster.

If Charles VI had gone clearly and permanently mad, things might not have been so bad; a strong and enduring regency might have been established. That, however, was not the way it was. For the rest of a long reign that was to continue for thirty years more, the king was to alternate between madness and sanity, each period lasting an average of half a year or so. And whenever he was sane he tried to rule.

The result was no continuity in government; no security in decision-making. There was almost total anarchy and the nobility moved in like vultures.

Philip the Bold took over control of the government at once, and held on at intervals. Now that he was ruling Flanders, he was more than ever interested in full peace with England in order to secure the wavering loyalty of his new subjects. The English king, Richard II, struggling with his own nobility, was just as anxious for peace. In 1396, a marriage was arranged between Richard II (then a widower) and Isabella, a young daughter of Charles VI. Though a full peace could not be negotiated, the truce that then existed was extended for an additional twenty-eight years.

So much was to the good. Philip might want peace for his own selfish purposes, but whatever the motivation the result would be a blessing to France. However, Philip also made free with the royal treasury, a policy which brought him into contact with King Charles' younger brother, Louis of Orleans. Louis had been a favorite of the king during the latter's short period of personal rule (and also a favorite of the queen, Isabella of Bavaria) and he felt he had first claim on the treasury.

Both men were enormously ambitious, and between the uncle of the king and the brother of the king, there began a rivalry that was to become a blood feud, then a civil war, and was to ruin France.

Louis of Orleans had married the daughter of the Duke of Milan and he had the dream of building a kingdom for himself in Italy (the will-o'-the-wisp dream that had started with Charles of Anjou). For this, he needed money with which to hire soldiers, and it bothered him that Philip of Burgundy was dipping his hands into the till.

As for Philip, he also needed money badly. For one thing, he was a patron of the arts, was munificent to poets and painters, indulged in great building projects, and appreciated fine jewelry. His court at Dijon was magnificent — and fearfully expensive. Furthermore, he was having (of all things) crusading problems.

The French had lost their last footholds in the Holy Land a century before, in 1291, and the west had more or less reconciled itself to the permanent loss of Jerusalem. But now new and closer dangers had arisen.

Not long after the last Crusaders had left the Holy Land, a new group of Turks, the Ottoman Turks, began a steady expansion. At about the time of the Battle of Crécy, these Turks, having established a small kingdom in northwestern Asia Minor, crossed over the Hellespont to the European side in response to the call of one of two battling Byzantine factions. For the first time, Turks had appeared in Europe (and they were never to leave).

Over the next half-century, Ottoman Turkish power spread inexorably. In 1389, they defeated the Serbs at the Battle of Kossovo (kaw'suh-voh) and took over almost the entire Balkan peninsula, while in Asia they had spread over almost all of Asia Minor. The Byzantine Empire was reduced to little more than the city of Constantinople and a few outlying districts, so a wild call for help winged westward.

The Turkish boundary in Europe now abutted that of the Kingdom of Hungary, which was under the rule of Sigismund, (sij'is-mund) whose wife, Maria, was descended from Charles of Anjou. Sigismund also called for help and, in 1396, the Pope preached a crusade just as in old times. (At this time, there were two Popes, one in Rome and one in Avignon — the continuing weakness of France had at last allowed a movement for a return to Rome to take place and succeed — but both Popes called for the crusade.)

The Turkish frontier was now about 600 miles from Burgundy. There were Turkish outposts at points closer to Paris than to Jerusalem. The French answered the call.

Leading the western knights was a twenty-five-year-old Frenchman, John of Nevers, the son of Philip the Bold. He gathered a sumptuous group of knights, for which his father had to find the money.

The knights met the Hungarian army at Budapest on the Danube, and with great gaiety proceeded to march downstream.

They eventually reached a Turkish outpost at Vidin (vih'din) which they took by storm. The whole campaign seemed a holiday and they marched another hundred miles to Nicopolis (nih-kop'oh-lis), on what is now the north-central border of Bulgaria.

There, on September 28, 1396, the French chivalry sighted the advance troops of the Turks. Sigismund of Hungary, who understood the Turks somewhat, suggested that he deal with the advance troops with his own forces while the western knights kept themselves in reserve for the main Turkish army when it appeared. The knights hooted this down. They had learned nothing, after all. Chivalry demanded that they press onward and mow down everything in their path. Straight forward was what they wanted — as at Courtrai, Crécy and Poitiers.

Straight forward they went, smashing the Turkish troops, scattering them — and scattering themselves in pursuit. Then, tired and disorganized, they suddenly and unexpectedly found themselves face to face with the formidable host of the Turkish sultan, Bajazet (baj'uh-zet'). He had had to lift the siege of Constantinople to march northward and was in no good mood in consequence. The tide of battle turned and quickly became another massacre of French chivalry.

Very few of the knights were saved but among those few was John of Nevers. In order to bring him home, Philip the Bold had to squeeze 200,000 gold ducats out of his subjects and out of the French treasury. John of Nevers, for his behavior in this battle, was forever after called "Jean Sans-Peur," that is "John the Fearless," though a fairer estimate of the value of fearlessness under the conditions of the Battle of Nicopolis might have awarded him the name of "John the Stupid."

In 1404, Philip the Bold died, and John the Fearless succeeded as Duke of Burgundy. In Philip's last years, however, Louis of Orleans had gained complete control of Queen Isabella (the rumor spread that the handsome Louis supplied the love that the mad king could not) and, through her, of the periodically mad Charles VI. He was therefore dominant in the government.

This fact John the Fearless resented, since he believed that, having succeeded to the lands of his father, he should also succeed to his father's power over the royal treasury.

Had there been a strong external threat, the quarreling princes might have been forced to make up their differences somehow, but, as it happened, France was at the moment perfectly free to commit suicide. Richard II of England had been deposed and killed by a cousin, who reigned as Henry IV, and the new English king had his hands full with rebellious lords. England was out of the game and France could indulge itself in civil war if it wished. (How Charles the Bad would have loved to fish in such troubled waters, but he had died in 1387.)

The quarrel between Orleans and Burgundy deepened, and both sides began to gather arms and jockey for allies and for position. If Louis of Orleans controlled the queen, John of Burgundy controlled the Dauphin Louis who had married John's daughter. If Louis of Orleans now controlled the government and the treasury, his luxurious life gave rise to cries of waste and graft, and John began to pose as a fiscal reformer and to back the middle class.

The one remaining uncle of the king, John of Berri, saw that matters were heading for open civil war, and he tried to prevent that. On November 20, 1407, he managed to bring John of Burgundy and Louis of Orleans together in a kind of summit meeting. He had them dine together and promise friendship.

Undoubtedly, neither one was serious in his protestations, but John the Fearless was quicker in his planning. On November 23, 1407, Louis of Orleans was returning from the king's palace to his own mansion with a few retainers. The hour was early enough so that the shops ought to be open and their lights ought to supply a flicker in the streets that would make it easier to spot assailants and be ready for them. Somehow, though, the shops were closed and the streets were dark. Louis must have been growing uneasy over this but, if so, it was too late. At a certain point along the route, he and his men were suddenly set upon and Louis was hacked to pieces.

John the Fearless boldly admitted he had hired the assassins and said he had killed Louis for his luxury and tyranny, and to save the people of France from unjust taxation. The merchants of Paris were delighted at talk such as that and John became their hero. The nobility on the other hand turned against John and rallied round Charles, the thirteen-year-old son of Louis, who had now succeeded to the title of Duke of Orleans.

Among the most forceful of those who aligned themselves with Charles of Orleans against John the Fearless was Bernard VII, Count of Armagnac (ahr-muh-nyak′), a district in southern France about fifty miles west of Toulouse. In 1410, Charles of Orleans married Bernard's daughter, and his faction came to be called the Armagnacs. After that, it was Armagnacs versus Burgundians in open warfare. (It was in the course of this fighting, in 1414, that the harquebus, the distant ancestor of the modern rifle and the first portable gunpowder weapon, came into use.)

The Armagnacs were strong with the nobility, in the south and southeast particularly, and were hawkish against England. The Burgundians were strong with the middle class and the intellectuals, in the north and northeast particularly, and favored an accommodation with England.

For some years after the assassination of Louis of Orleans, John the Fearless remained in control of Paris. There he encouraged the middle class under the leadership of a butcher named Simon Caboche (kuh-boshe′). In May, 1413, the "Cabochian Ordinances" were proclaimed, whereby the government was to be conducted by three regularly constituted councils and where a number of other reforms, designed to end arbitrary rule, were instituted. Once again, there was a motion toward representative government and away from autocracy, as under Marcel a half-century before.

Caboche's followers were too wild and strident, however, and John, who had no real interest in reform, found them uncomfortable allies. The more settled townspeople were frightened, and there was a reaction in favor of the Armagnacs. In August, Charles of Orleans marched his forces into Paris to the cheering of the populace. John the Fearless did not carry fearlessness to the point of failing to leave hurriedly for Flanders and safety.

The Armagnacs were the party of medieval chivalry and they tore up the Cabochian reform at once and settled back into the old ways.

DISASTER AGAINST ALL ODDS

John the Fearless could not resist the fatal weakness of other French nobles of the period. Like Robert of Artois and Charles the Bad, he did not hesitate to react to personal defeat by calling in the national enemy. He asked for English help — and got a great deal more of it than he expected.

The English king, Henry IV, had been unable to act freely in the course of his troubled reign. He had to deal with several rebellions and he had been able to do no more in the way of taking advantage of the French civil war than to send some archers now and then.

In 1413, however, just half a year before John the Fearless was driven out of Paris, Henry IV died. John's appeal, therefore, reached the old king's young and vigorous son, who now ruled as Henry V. England was momentarily quiet, the rebels were beaten. Young Henry V wanted to keep it that way, so he felt the need of some glorious foreign adventure to drown internal divisions. By supplying victories for the nation to celebrate, he might make the English forget that his father had usurped the throne.

Since France was drowned in its wretched civil war and since the Burgundian faction would rather fight with the English than against them, it seemed a good time to initiate a new invasion and to return matters to the days of Edward III. Henry V raised a force of six thousand armed men and twenty-four thousand longbowmen and took them across the Channel to Normandy, as Edward III had done, seventy years before.

Henry V's forces landed at Harfleur (hahr-fleur′) on August 14, 1415. The move to Harfleur, rather than to English base at Calais, was a good strategic stroke. Harfleur, at the mouth of the Seine River, was at the time the most important Channel port in the hands of France. If Henry could take it, he would have complete control of the Channel and from then on could invade France and supply his forces at will.

He placed Harfleur under siege and for five weeks maintained that siege without interference from the French. He used cannon at Harfleur. These were still of only limited effectiveness, but they presented a large advance over the primitive "bombards" at Crécy.

French inaction during the siege was partly the result of their adherence to the tactics of Du Guesclin, which insisted that the English never be offered a major battle. For another, the Armagnacs had just consolidated their hold on Paris, and John the Fearless, off in Flanders, would surely return if the Armagnacs moved down the Seine River.

Though the French response gave all the appearance of poltroonery and caused the proud knights to chafe, it was militarily sound, and it was the proper way to destroy Henry. On September 22, 1415, Harfleur surrendered, but by that time at least half of Henry's army had withered away through desertion and through death in battle and by disease. There were not wanting those who advised him now to be satisfied with the city he had captured and to return to England.

This Henry could not do. To return with a bedraggled remnant of his army, with but one siege and one city to show for the effort, would be virtual defeat, especially since the French might retake the city as soon as he left. He would have to have something better to show.

With that in mind, apparently, he decided to hasten to Calais, there to refit and refurbish his army, possibly reinforce it, too, and accomplish some greater feat before returning. He counted on the French not to interfere with his march, since they were showing themselves so hesitant in meeting him in battle.

Leaving men behind to hold Harfleur, he struck off along the coast toward Calais on October 8, 1415. His army, now made up of only 15,000 men, set forth on its 125-mile journey, along the route taken by Edward III when he was marching to safety in Flanders seventy years before. Edward's march had included no thought of battle but had ended with Crécy. Henry's march included no thought of battle, either.

Henry was well aware of the weakness of his situation. He gave the orders that there was to be no looting, for he dared not rouse the ire of the populace. The peasants and townsmen of France could scarcely defeat the veteran English army but even one-sided skirmishing would lead to death and delay and Henry could afford no further attrition of the army.

Nevertheless, attrition was what he had. The weather was, and remained, miserable, raining nearly constantly and turning raw and chilly at night. Dysentery and diarrhea afflicted and weakened the army. Nevertheless, so quickly did Henry move his army that in three days they had traveled fifty miles and had reached the vicinity of Dieppe (dyep). They were nearly halfway to their goal. Two days later, they reached Abbeville, near the mouth of the Somme River. Sixty miles beyond, due north, lay Calais and safety.

The French, however, were still following a rational plan, if an inglorious one. They were fading away before the English and letting the rigors of the march complete what the siege at Harfleur had begun. When the English reached the Somme, they found the bridges broken down. Henry had expected that, but he also hoped to use the ford which Edward III had used under similar circumstances.

The French were prepared for that, too. When the English reached the river, the French were waiting on the other side. If the English wanted to wade across, they would have to fight warm, dry Frenchmen as they climbed the opposite bank, wet and shivering.

That was impossible. The increasingly anxious Henry had to find another way of crossing and he began a march upstream to find it. This was the very worst part of the entire campaign. The food supplies gave out, yet the English army tried to be as circumspect as possible in seizing supplies. They no longer had an assured goal, since they did not know where a ford might be found and each day of march upstream took them farther and farther from Calais, leaving them weaker and weaker.

What's more, the English could be certain that the French on the other side of the river were keeping a sharp eye on them. The French moved upstream, too, keeping pace with Henry, but making no attempt to cross the river themselves. The French were content (at least so far) to let the river flow between the armies and to wait for the English invaders to sicken and die.

By October 18, the English had reached Nesle (nel), over fifty miles upstream from Abbeville, and it was only then that they found a peasant willing to point out a ford that could be reached across a marsh. There was no time to search for anything better. The army dismantled some houses in the vicinity and used the wood to make a rough flooring over which they could cross the marsh. That night, they quietly crossed the Somme.

The French army was caught napping. Apparently, they did not know of the ford or, if they knew of it, thought it impractical. In either case, while the English were crossing, the French were elsewhere. Had they been on the spot and had they waited till the English were half over and then attacked, that would undoubtedly have been the end of Henry and his army.

But it didn't happen. The English were on the right bank of the Somme River at last and the army was intact. Yet they were now over ninety miles south of Calais, and Henry had only about 10,000 men left who were fit to fight. (Eight thousand of them were longbowmen, however.) Between him and Calais lay an untouched, unwearied French army, at least three times as large. Certainly anyone who at this moment had considered Henry's situation would not have given a finger-snap for his chances of coming out alive.

And if the French had kept their heads and had continued their cautious policy of avoiding battle, but had taken to small harassing actions instead, as Henry's fading army hastened northward, the English would have been destroyed. The French commander, Charles D'Albret (dal-bray'), was a disciple of Du Guesclin and attempted to do that, in fact.

Unfortunately for the French, the rational strategy continued to be an inglorious one and the French knights were horrified at D'Albret's tactics. As Henry marched northward, they pleaded with him to force a battle. The French were, after all, medieval knights, heavily armored, riding huge horses, and carrying thick lances. They faced a moth-eaten huddle of greatly outnumbered infantrymen and archers.

The odds seemed so heavily in favor of the French that for them to avoid battle was surely an unbearable disgrace.

D'Albret found no arguments against them. It had been sixty

years since the great Battle of Poitiers, longer still since Courtrai and Crécy, and those battles had not happened to the
present French knights but to their grandfathers and great-
grandfathers. As for Nicopolis, that had happened at the other
end of the world.

So the lessons of four great defeats for heedless French
knights were forgotten, and the French army once again made
preparations to stop an English army that only wanted to reach
safety. They had in this way stopped Edward III at Crécy and
now, under almost the same circumstances, they stopped Henry
V near the town of Agincourt (aj'in-kawrt). To the French,
the town is Azincourt (a-zan-koor'). This was thirty-five miles
south of Calais and only twenty miles northeast of the ill-
omened Crécy.

The English found the large French army in their path on
October 24. A battle was inevitable and if the French fought
it rationally, they still couldn't help but win. Henry V's only
chance was to hope that the French knights would fight in their
usual undisciplined tournament fashion, something that had
already cost them four great defeats in the fourteenth century.
Assuming they would do so, he took advantage of the ground
in masterly fashion.

In the first place, he drew his pitifully small army across a
front no more than a thousand yards wide, with either flank
blocked off by dense woods. Only so many Frenchmen could
be squeezed into those thousand yards, so that the English
faced an actual front line little more numerous than themselves.
Henry had his men at arms (barely a thousand in number) in
the center, but at either side were the formidable groups of
longbowmen, eight thousand of them, ready to strike (despite
the discomfort of rampant diarrhea), and with hard, sharpened
stakes driven into the ground before them, points upward, in
case the charging horse should somehow reach them.

Henry's practiced eye noted also that the continual rains,
which had made his march such a nightmare, had turned the

freshly plowed ground into a quagmire bad enough for men as heavily armed as the French dismounted fighters, and even worse for those heavily armed men who remained on their horses. The French chivalry had steadily strengthened their armor in the hope of making themselves safe from arrows, but they succeeded only in making themselves ever less mobile.

The English army waited apprehensively through the night for the inevitable battle the next day, but Henry seems to have been confidently counting on the French to defeat themselves and, according to legend, proudly denied needing reinforcements, when one of his officers wished that the army was ten thousand men more numerous.

The French army, confident of victory, spent a euphoric night, however, with its leaders (so the legend goes) laying wagers on the number of prisoners they would take.

Came the morning of October 25, 1415.

The French knighthood, some on horses, some on foot, lined up in the mud opposite the waiting English band. They didn't have to do a thing, really. The knights needed only to wait outside of bowshot — and keep on waiting. Had they done so, Henry and his army would have had to stay there and fall apart or come out in a desperate attack and be cut down.

The French knights could not bring themselves to do so. At the signal, they charged — or tried to charge. Mired in the mud, they could barely slog forward, and the line became ragged at once, laboring forward in utter disorder.

When they were within bowshot, a confused melee of men and horses were so crowded together as to have barely room to move. Henry gave the signal in his turn and eight thousand yard-long arrows went hissing through the air and landed among the thick ranks of the enemy. It was impossible to miss with those arrows. Horses reared, men cried out in agony, and the French confusion was worse confounded.

French knights who, in the turmoil, slipped and fell in the deep mud, could not rise again. Some even suffocated in the

mud, held helplessly down by their heavy armor. And when
the French were thoroughly helpless, Henry ordered his footmen and archers forward with ax and sword. It was a slaugh-
terhouse, in which the French dying stopped only when the
English arms grew weary of rising and falling.

Of the five great battles that France's medieval chivalry had
lost against more disciplined enemies since 1300, the Battle of
Agincourt was by far the most disastrous. The number of
French dead was put at 10,000, as high as the entire English
army, and at least 1000 knights were captured and held for
ransom. The English, on the other hand, reported their own
losses to be just over 100 (though it may have been ten times
as much in actuality).

There have been few battles in history in which a small army
so catastrophically defeated an enemy that far outweighed them
not only in men but, apparently, in equipment as well.

COLLAPSE

With the battle over, it seems to some, in hindsight, that
Henry might have exploited his victory, pursued the French
remnants and marched triumphantly on Paris. A more coldly
rational view makes it seem that Henry could do no such thing.
His army, despite the great victory, was sick and exhausted and
could do no more. Henry had to bring it to safety quickly, so
he marched on to Calais, reaching it on October 29, four days
after Agincourt and three weeks to the day after having left
Harfleur.

In a strictly material sense, the Battle of Agincourt had
gained Henry nothing. His men were still few and sick. He had
still lost most of the army he had taken to France, with but a
single port city to show for it.

And yet, few victories have had so great a moral effect. The battle and, even more, the circumstances under which it had been fought, gave the English a feeling of superhumanity that they never entirely lost from that day forward. It seemed to them more than ever that English soldiers were somehow capable of defeating ten times their own number, through some kind of racial superiority. This belief, based on Crécy and Agincourt, and held to in the face of any amount of subsequent evidence to the contrary, was to be an important moral factor in the conversion of tiny England into the vast British Empire of the early twentieth century.

For France, the results were equally enormous but in reverse. Crécy and Poitiers had been bad enough, but Agincourt sent them into a state of absolute shock. Charles of Orleans, the titular leader of the Armagnac party, had been taken prisoner; other important leaders were dead; and France was left in utter confusion and humiliation. It was hard to see that the French defeats were due to lack of discipline, and the inability to understand the importance of the longbow. For a while the French, too, accepted the superhumanity of the English — or perhaps their supermonstrosity.

The English army remained in Calais till November 17, resting, and then returned to England to receive a hysterical acclamation. Henry V entered London on November 23, having been away from England for three and a half months.

As for the French, despite the incredible disaster that had befallen them, they continued the civil war. John the Fearless had not taken part at all in the action that had ended with Agincourt and so he was spared any part of the disgrace (unless it be considered a disgrace to let your country be defeated without moving to help it). If he had acted quickly, he might have taken over Paris and gained complete control of the shattered country.

But John the Fearless was not nearly as fearless as his name proclaimed him to be. He hesitated, and it was Bernard of

Armagnac, the father-in-law of the captured Charles of Orleans, who acted first. Bernard filled Paris with his troops and took control of the mad king.

For two years, the Armagnacs controlled Paris, while John the Fearless kept it under intermittent siege. John managed, in the process, to seize the queen and to declare her regent of the country, ruling in place of her mad husband (but with John himself in real control, of course).

Meanwhile, the two oldest sons of Charles VI died, and the third son, the namesake of his father, became the new Dauphin. When young Charles became Dauphin in 1417, he was only fourteen years old, physically weak and temperamentally lethargic. He was the puppet of those who controlled him.

So there it was — the Burgundians had the queen, and the Armagnacs had the new Dauphin, and the two factions continued to divide the country in their implacable hostility. And while they did so, Henry V could plan his next moves undisturbed. He strengthened his fleet and used it to clear the Channel of French and their allies, the Genoese. With the Channel firmly under English control for the first time since the days of Edward III, he could count on longer and more secure actions on the Continent.

He also made an alliance with Sigismund, the German Emperor. This served to cut France off from possible outside help and also greatly increased Henry's own prestige.

Finally, on July 23, 1417, nearly two years after his first invasion, Henry launched his second. It was now to be more than the capture of a single city; Henry systematically began to conquer Normandy, the ancestral home of the English royal family.

In June of 1418, he placed Rouen under siege — the city that had once been the Norman capital of William the Conqueror. The siege was to last months, but Henry had no reason to fear French interference. For the French, there was still the disastrous civil war.

The Parisians were restive under the control of Bernard and his Armagnac troops. They were entirely on the side of John the Fearless, who had constantly supported the townsmen against the feudal reaction of the Armagnacs. Furthermore, it was the Armagnacs who had been defeated at Agincourt and who had brought disgrace to France. This fact, too, made for effective propaganda with the populace.

So Paris rose in rebellion against the Armagnac chiefs even while Rouen was being placed under siege. Throughout May and June, the riots grew worse, and on July 12, 1418, there came the climax. Every Armagnac the Parisians could find was killed, including Bernard himself.

On July 14, John the Fearless entered the capital to the acclaim of the populace. The queen was with him and in the capital was the mad king who was now also under his control. If John could have taken the Dauphin as well, the whole apparatus of government would have been in his hand.

As it was, though, a few of the Armagnac party had escaped the massacre and had managed to leave Paris in the midst of the disturbances, taking the Dauphin Charles with them. They retired to Bourges (boorzh), 120 miles south of Paris, where the Dauphin, poor specimen though he was, remained the sole hope of the Armagnac party and of those Frenchmen who were anti-English and who rallied around the national cause.

Henry V, ignoring the ebb and flow in Paris, maintained his siege of Rouen. John the Fearless could do no more to interfere than the Armagnacs had done, and in January, 1419, the scarecrow remnants of the city's population had to give up. Henry then began to lead his army upstream toward Paris itself.

Now, only now, did the two French factions, come to feel that soon there might be no France to quarrel over. On July 11, 1419, the Armagnacs and Burgundians reluctantly signed a truce, presumably so that their united forces could begin to resist the formidable Henry.

By then, though, the English were almost at the capital, taking Pontoise (pone-twahz'), only twenty miles downstream. Despite the truce, John the Fearless (not fearless at all, really) quailed before the dread victor of Agincourt. Taking the queen and the mad king with him, he abandoned Paris without a fight, scuttling for Troyes (trwah), about eighty miles southeast of Paris.

The Armagnacs were sure that this was a Burgundian betrayal; that John the Fearless had merely put the Armagnacs off their guard with a faithless truce and had then abandoned the capital by arrangement with the English.

The outraged Armagnacs asked for another meeting, which took place at Montereau (mone-troh'), about midway between Paris and Troyes. At this meeting, the Armagnacs had the upper hand. The abandonment of Paris had placed John the Fearless in a bad light and a show of strength on the part of the Armagnacs might have united the French behind the Dauphin. Unfortunately for France, the Armagnac party overreacted. On September 10, 1419, John the Fearless was struck down by one of the Armagnac faction and assassinated. He was served as he himself had served Louis of Orleans a dozen years before.

That made the continued truce between Armagnacs and Burgundians impossible. The reaction to the assassination was to strengthen the Burgundian cause and weaken that of the Armagnacs.

Succeeding to the Duchy of Burgundy was John's twenty-three-year-old son, Philip, who came to be known as "Philip the Good." Resentment at his father's death led him (rather reluctantly) to throw himself into the arms of the English. He reached an alliance with Henry V and agreed to recognize his claim to the throne of France.

The next step was to prepare a treaty of peace between France (as represented by Philip of Burgundy, who controlled the king and queen) and England. All of France north of the Loire River was to be ceded to England, except, of course, for those areas ruled by Philip. Charles VI was to remain king of France, while he lived, as a gesture of legitimacy, but the king's one surviving son, the Dauphin Charles, was declared illegitimate. To make this plausible, Henry forced Queen Isabella, the Dauphin's own mother, to swear to the illegitimacy and, indeed, since the boy was born ten years after the beginning of his father's fit of madness, it is not at all impossible that he was illegitimate in actual fact.

Whether he was illegitimate or not, however, his mother's declaration offered a legal reason to exclude him from the throne.

The next step was simple. Charles VI was induced to adopt Henry V as his son and to declare him the heir to the throne. Furthermore, just in case this would not be considered enough, Henry V was to marry Charles VI's nineteen-year-old daughter, Catherine. (She was also born after the oncoming of Charles' madness, but no one dared raise any question as to *her* legitimacy.) With such a marriage, if Henry had a son, that son would be the grandson of Charles VI and it was to be hoped the French would accept him.

The Treaty of Troyes was signed on May 20, 1420, and on June 2, Henry married Catherine. On December 6, Henry V entered Paris in triumph, and on December 6, 1421, Catherine (who was then in England) bore a son to Henry. The son, who Henry confidently expected would some day reign over the united kingdoms of England and France, was likewise named Henry.

AT THE POINT OF DEATH

It seemed that Henry V had the touch of endless victory. When his son was born, he was still only thirty-four years old, and in six years of battling in France, he had all but conquered the country, never losing a battle.

And indeed, France seemed at the point of death. Trade dwindled, prices rose, poverty deepened. France, militarily humiliated and disgraced, was becoming an economic desert. Even the University of Paris was dwindling in these hard times, when English soldiers arrogantly held Paris in their grip, and France, it seemed, would lose even its intellectual leadership.

And yet, though English supremacy seemed complete and unchallenged, it was actually a tenuous thing. The English were far fewer than the French, and England could force its will on the larger country only as long as two factors remained true — over both of which they had no real control.

First, the English would remain supreme only as long as the French insisted on fighting after the medieval-tournament fashion. But would they? Agincourt was the beginning of wisdom for them. It had taken a century and a quarter, but they were beginning to learn that a tournament was not a battle — not anymore.

Second, the English would remain supreme only as long as the French civil war kept the English fighting only half of France, with the occasional help of the other half. If ever the civil war ceased, then, at that very moment, England would be in deep trouble.

And even though, while Henry V lived, the French had not yet learned to fight properly and had not ended the civil war, they somehow still resisted.

The French Dauphin in Bourges, branded with illegitimacy though he was, feeble and passive, an utter nonentity, nevertheless represented France, and somehow that meant something. There remained castles for the English to subdue and men for the English to kill despite the Treaty of Troyes, despite Henry's marriage with Catherine, despite the occupation of the capital.

When Henry was not there in person, there were even English defeats. After his marriage, Henry took his bride back to England with him, and, while he was out of France, Henry's brother, Thomas of Clarence, thought he would try to gain a little glory of his own. There seemed no reason to fear the French since a few English could defeat any number of Frenchmen; hadn't Agincourt proved that? On March 23, 1421, Thomas led a party of three thousand English deep into Anjou, and there at Baugé (boh-zhay), 150 miles southwest of Paris, allowed himself to be ambushed by a superior force of Frenchmen. He was defeated and killed.

It wasn't much of a defeat, but Henry well knew it was the mystique of victory that kept the French subdued and he had to hasten back to France for the third time, leaving his pregnant wife at Windsor Castle near London.

In France, he had to present both the English and French with another victory and so he laid siege to the town of Meaux (moh), fifteen miles east of Paris. It was a hard siege that continued into the gathering winter of 1421 (and was still going on when the news reached him that a son had been born to him in England). After seven months he took the city, to be sure, and his list of victories remained unspoiled, but this victory was no true victory. It had cost him his army and, worse still, his health.

He caught dysentery during the siege and his condition grew steadily worse. He was able to greet his wife and see his infant son for the first time when they came to Paris in the spring of 1422, but life was ebbing. On August 31, 1422, England's hero-king, still only thirty-five years old, died. He never survived to gain the throne of France that would have been his at the death of Charles VI, for mad King Charles managed to live on for seven weeks more.

Charles VI died on October 21, 1422, having reigned for forty-two years, much of it in madness, through a most disastrous period in the history of France. Henry V's infant son, only nine months old at the time of his father's death, had been proclaimed King Henry VI, and now with Charles VI's death, he was also proclaimed as King of France, and was called Henry II by the French count.

The infant's grandmother Isabella, Charles VI's queen, recognized King Henry VI as King of France. So did Philip the Good of Burgundy. So did the University of Paris, the representatives of the northern provinces and of Guienne, the city of Paris itself, and so on.

Naturally, he could not rule in his own name, but he had uncles. Controlling the English territories in France was John, Duke of Bedford, a younger brother of Henry V. Another uncle, Bedford's younger brother, Humphrey, Duke of Gloucester, controlled England.

At Bourges, the Dauphin Charles was proclaimed King Charles VII of France and in November, 1422, was crowned in Poitiers. That did not help him much, for it was in Reims that the traditional crowning of the French king took place. Without a coronation at Reims, no one could be truly King of France, and Reims was in the hands of the English.

The English, who lacked the proper feel for French custom, did not bother to crown their baby-king at Reims, confidently leaving that for when he would come to his majority (something which proved to be a mistake). They sneered at Charles VII as "King of Bourges" and never granted him any title higher than Dauphin.

Bedford was almost as able a general as Henry V himself and while he lived England's cause continued to prosper.

At Cravant (kra-vahnt'), ninety miles southeast of Paris and on the borders of Burgundian territory, a small force of English and Burgundians overcame a somewhat larger French force on July 21, 1423.

Of more significance was a battle at Verneuil (vair-noy'uh), sixty miles west of Paris, a year later. Fought on August 17, 1424, this was another battle after the Crécy-Agincourt fashion, and the last. English archers, protecting the army's baggage,

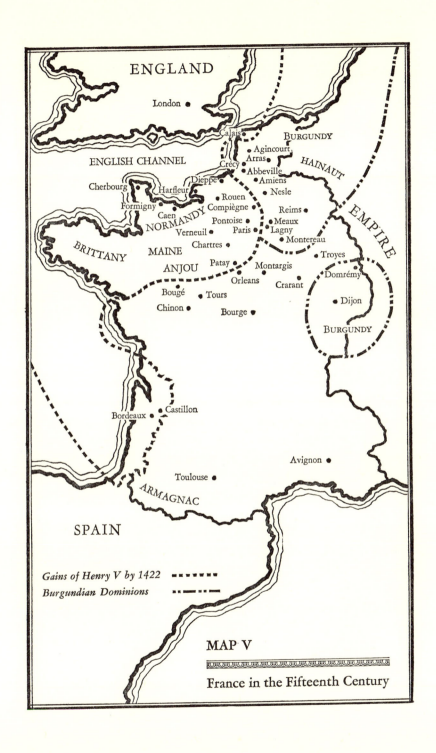

ENGLAND

London •

ENGLISH CHANNEL

Calais

BURGUNDY

HAINAUT

Agincourt
Crécy • Arras
Abbeville
Dieppe • Amiens
Cherbourg • Harfleur • Nesle
Formigny Rouen
Caen Compiègne Reims •
NORMANDY Pontoise Meaux
Verneuil • Paris • Lagny
Chartres • Montereau

EMPIRE

BRITTANY

MAINE
ANJOU Patay Montargis Troyes •
Orleans Crarant Domrémy
Bougé • Tours • Dijon
Chinon • Bourge •

BURGUNDY

Bordeaux • Castillon

Avignon •

SPAIN

Toulouse •

ARMAGNAC

Gains of Henry V by 1422   ▪ ▪ ▪ ▪ ▪
Burgundian Dominions   ▪—▪—▪—

MAP V

France in the Fifteenth Century

were attacked by a considerably larger force of French knights. The archers won again, and handily, but this time the French did not try a straightforward charge. They actually attempted an outflanking maneuver. They were defeated — but they were learning.

Bedford tried also to bind the conquered French territory to England by enlightened policies. He reformed legal procedures, tried to work through French administrative bodies and French appointees, founded a university at Caen and in all ways tried to show that the united kingdoms of France and England would be a case of partnership, not conquest.

There was no way, though, in which Bedford could force the English soldiers to be as enlightened as he himself was. Blinded by Agincourt, the English had only contempt for the French and their depredations generated a smoldering hatred that Bedford could not allay. Indeed, the more abysmal the defeats under which France labored, the higher surged the feeling of nationalism. All Frenchmen could feel a bond in their common fear and hatred of the English.

Bedford's greatest and most immediate plague, however, was the behavior of his foolish brother, Humphrey of Gloucester.

It seems there was a Flemish heiress, Jacqueline of Hainaut, whose properties were of interest to Philip the Good of Burgundy, for they were needed to round out his own Flemish dominions. He therefore married the lady to a sickly relative of his, planning to control the land in this way.

Jacqueline did not relish the marriage. She therefore had it annulled by Pope Benedict XIII (who ruled in Avignon and whose papal status was not recognized in much of the west), then escaped to England and proposed marriage to Humphrey. No one but an Englishman, and a very highly titled Englishman, could protect her and her dominions, she rightly felt, from Philip the Good.

It would seem, though, that Humphrey of Gloucester must have realized that if he married Jacqueline this would be a mortal affront to Philip the Good. It would also seem that Humphrey must have known that Philip's alliance with England was absolutely essential to the national policy and that on that alone rested the hope of success in France.

Nevertheless, Humphrey, eager for rich lands in Flanders, married Jacqueline, and the spectacle was presented to the world of an English prince beginning what amounted to a private war against England's essential ally. We can only suppose that Humphrey, who had been at Agincourt but who was not fighting the French these days, was a victim of what we might call the "Agincourt-psychosis." He really thought that the English needed no allies and no help; that they could win battles by innate superiority alone.

John of Bedford, however, who was actually fighting the French, knew better. He had to work like a demon to bring Humphrey to heel and to soothe Philip's feelings. In the end, he managed to work it out. Humphrey's marriage was declared void in 1428 and he married someone else (his mistress, in fact). Philip was mollified, after winning substantial concessions at the expense of English holdings.

Enormous, if not easily visible, damage was done, however. Bedford's hardworking attempts to keep Philip of Burgundy in line emphasized to Philip just how important he was to the English. It naturally made him less ready to help without a heavy price. Furthermore, he had experienced what he could only consider to be English perfidy. His affection for the English, never based on anything stronger than political expediency, cooled further.

Philip recognized the growing force of French nationalism and he did not intend to accompany the English to defeat. As long as the English won their battles, he would be with them, but not a moment longer. Once the English began to lose (if they ever did) he would be ready to dodge out of the way.

And that meant that even a single important English defeat might bring about the end of the French civil war and, almost inevitably, the wreckage of the whole English conquest — and Bedford knew that.

His only choice was to continue and strengthen the aura of victory that had surrounded the English ever since Agincourt. With the regions north of the Loire River firmly in his hands, he had no choice but to extend the English sway southward. Even while he was laboring to heal the quarrel with Burgundy, he began the southward thrust.

9

RECOVERY

MIRACLE AT ORLEANS?

Bedford's target was Orleans, seventy miles south of Paris, and at the northernmost bend of the Loire River. Orleans was the northernmost bastion of the French nationalists in the south and the largest city still holding allegiance to Charles VII. If it fell, it was doubtful whether Charles VII would be able to hold the south in line thereafter, and whether any organized resistance to the English would remain possible.

The English began their campaign southward in 1427 by placing the town of Montargis (mon-tahr-zhee′), forty miles east of Orleans, under siege.

Charles VII recognized the danger and was desperate enough to organize an attempt to break the siege. The French had not dared interfere with an English siege since Henry V had first landed in France a dozen years before. Yet now a French force was marching cautiously toward a confrontation with the English.

The relief army was under the command of John, Count of Dunois (dyoo-nwah'). He was an illegitimate son of that Louis of Orleans who was assassinated by John the Fearless, in the act that started the civil war. He was therefore a half-brother of Charles of Orleans, who had been captured at Agincourt, and a first cousin of Charles VII. He is sometimes called the "Bastard of Orleans."

He was only twenty-four years old at the time and he was the greatest of the new leaders who were arising on the French nationalist side at this time. There were others, so that Charles VII, so poor a creature in his own right, was to receive, in the future, the name of "Charles the Well-Served."

Under the Bastard of Orleans, the French relief columns were handled so well that the English were forced to draw back, and the besieged townsmen, encouraged, sallied forth to join their relievers. Under the double attack, the English withdrawal became a full retreat and a thousand to fifteen hundred of them were killed or captured.

It was not a decisive victory for the French by any means and only a small English force was involved. It did not stop Bedford's offensive. However, any victory of the French over the English, under any circumstances, was a much-needed boost to French morale. The Bastard was the hero of the day.

In 1428, six thousand English reinforcements under Thomas, Earl of Salisbury, landed in Calais and marched southward to join the four thousand veterans Bedford had earmarked for the offensive. On October 12, 1428, these men, with Salisbury in command, began to establish siege lines about Orleans.

With Salisbury was John Talbot, a fire-eating English warrior, whom the English in after-years idolized for his fighting qualities (if not for his brains). Talbot fought in Wales and Ireland during Henry V's first expedition to France and was not at

Agincourt (undoubtedly to his everlasting regret). He went to France in 1419 and was the fighting mainstay of the English forces there after the death of Henry V. He was the victor of some forty skirmishes and battles and, indeed, was so uniformly victorious that he seemed invincible.

Despite the array of English spears and bows about their walls, and despite the presence of Talbot ("the English Achilles" he was called), the inhabitants of Orleans girded themselves for the siege, burning their suburbs to deny the protection of houses to the besieging forces. Their were few actual soldiers in the town, but the townsmen themselves manned the walls, and all were under the leadership of the very man who had once defended Harfleur resolutely against Henry V (and had been imprisoned for thirteen years for his pains).

The English drew up artillery as part of their weaponry. The design of cannon had improved to the point where they could now form a major part of the attack. They were still not strong enough to batter down city walls, but they could be used with considerable effect against soldiers.

The English, however, were never present at Orleans in sufficient numbers to draw the net entirely around the city. They could not stretch their forces thin enough and it remained always possible for reinforcements and supplies to slip into the city. This was the essential flaw in the English offensive.

Cannon were brought into the city and on October 27, 1428, just two weeks after the siege began, a cannon from within the city fired a ball that struck the Earl of Salisbury in the face, wounding him hideously. He was carried downstream and died on November 3. (Legend has it that the cannon was fired by the gunner's young son, while the gunner was eating lunch.)

The day after the wounding, the Bastard of Orleans, at the head of several hundred fighting men, managed to make his way into the city. Other French soldiers followed, little by little.

English morale was shaken by Salisbury's death, but the com-

mand was taken over by William de la Pole, Earl of Suffolk,
and he immediately set the English troops to work building a
chain of fortified posts about the city.

Grimly, the English held to their siege for month after month,
and slowly the situation within the town deteriorated. But the
besieging forces suffered too. Both sides were in dire need of
supplies as the winter progressed and the French began to make
strenuous efforts to get supplies into the town and to prevent
supplies from reaching the English.

On February 12, 1429, when the siege was completing its
fourth month, a column of French tried to intercept a wagon
train being sent to the English from Paris. This included many
barrels of dry herrings, for it was the Lenten season and fish
was in high demand. The supply train was under the command
of Sir John Fastolfe, who had fought well at Agincourt and in
Normandy.

As soon as Fastolfe was aware of the oncoming French, he
took vigorous measures for the defense. He drew his wagons
into a line that served as an impromptu fortification. From behind the shelter of those wagons, he placed his English longbowmen at one flank, and Parisian crossbowmen (the Parisians
were still hotly pro-Burgundian and anti-Armagnac) on the
other.

The French fought well, but there was little they could do
against the wagon-protected bowmen, and the English won
again. Burst barrels strewed herring all over the field so that the
action is known as the "Battle of the Herrings."

The French relieving forces were particularly disheartened
at this repulse because it seemed one more in an endless string
of victories won in the field by the English. There seemed no
use in fighting at all, so what was left of those forces marched
hastily away. No other forces were sent with any intention of
battle. Orleans was left to its fate and after two more months
had passed, it seemed that Orleans must fall and that the Bas-

tard, whatever his resolution and ability, would simply have to surrender.

And then a very strange thing happened, one of the strangest in history, and something that would have been derided as incredible if it had appeared in a work of fiction.

A peasant girl appeared on the scene.

Her name was Jeanne Darc and she was born about 1412 at the village of Domrémy (dome-ruh-mee'), at the eastern borders of France, 160 miles east of Paris. After the Treaty of Troyes, Domrémy lay in that part of France which had been handed over to the overlordship of the English king.

Jeanne Darc, or Joan Darc in English, is never known by that name. Her last name has been misspelled as d'Arc, as though she were of the nobility, so that in English she is invariably known as Joan of Arc, although there is no place called Arc from which she came or over which she had some claim.

In her teens she was experiencing visions, hearing voices and imagining herself called on to save France. In 1429, these visions and voices finally drove her to action. Charles VII had still not been crowned at Reims, though six full years had passed since the death of his father. What's more, the siege of Orleans might end in another English victory and that might defeat him forever. It seemed to Joan that her mission had to start at once, that she had to relieve the siege and crown Charles.

In January, 1429, Joan left for Vaucouleurs (voh-koo-leur'), twelve miles north of Domrémy, where there was a fortified outpost that still held out for Charles VII. Its captain was sufficiently impressed by her (or perhaps sufficiently eager to get rid of her) to send her on to Charles VII with an escort of six men. Charles VII was then at Chinon (shee-nohn'), ninety miles southwest of Orleans and 270 miles from Domrémy. Joan had to cross English-controlled territory to reach Chinon, and so she dressed in man's costume to avoid the kind of trouble a young girl might have if encountered by soldiers. She arrived at Chinon on February 24, 1429, two weeks after the Battle of the Herrings had ended French attempts to do anything active about the siege of Orleans.

It was a superstitious age. When a girl announced herself as a miraculous maid sent by God, she might be taken for exactly that; or as a dangerous witch sent by the Devil for the ensnarement of men. It was not easy to tell which. Charles VII actually received Joan and she was then questioned by learned theologians for three weeks in order to determine whether she was of divine or diabolical inspiration.

It may well be that some of the worldly men around Charles were not really concerned with which she was, and perhaps didn't believe she could be either. They might have been trying to decide whether she would be accepted by the soldiers as a miracle maid or not. If the French and (even more) the English could be made to believe that God was fighting on the side of the French, that could have an important effect on morale on either side.

The decision arrived at was (theologically) that Joan was sent by God and (practical-politically) that this attitude would carry conviction. She was therefore sent to Orleans with an escort of about 3000 soldiers under John, Duke of Alençon (ah-lahn-sone'), who had led the French forces at the lost Battle of Verneuil and had been in captivity for a while as a result. On April 29, 1429, Joan and her escort slipped into the city.

It is important to understand that by now the defending force within the city was quite substantial and, indeed, they outnumbered the thin line of besieging English. What kept the French from emerging to do battle was not the lack of means, but the lack of will. The French were simply unable to believe they could win. What's more, the English had suffered considerably in the course of a half-year siege and all that kept them to their task was that they were simply unable to believe they could lose.

It was only a matter of morale that kept the situation in being, against the military sense of it all. Once the news arrived that a miraculous maid was coming to the aid of the French, the situation with respect to morale changed suddenly and dramatically and what followed was almost inevitable. While few events in history have seemed so miraculous as what Joan of Arc accomplished, it is not really as miraculous as it seemed.

Very likely, the Bastard of Orleans counted on Joan's effect on the morale on both sides, and, within a week of her arrival, he launched an attack, on May 4, on the fortified posts set up by the English at the eastern approaches of the city. He did not even bother telling her about it. On learning of the fighting, however, Joan hastened to the eastern walls. The French soldiers, heartened at her appearance, fought the more savagely and the English fell back.

The first sign of French victory set in motion a vicious cycle for the English. If the French advanced more than was their wont, it was a sign that Joan was heaven-sent or hell-sent but, in either case, of miraculous help to the French and not something mere men could fight against. The English were all the readier to retreat further, and to accept that further retreat as further evidence.

When Joan was struck by an arrow, the English cheered, but it was a superficial wound and, when she appeared on the battlements again, it was easy to believe that she was invulnerable. And the English fell back still more readily.

By May 8, the English had abandoned the siege, leaving their strongpoints, their artillery, their dead and wounded. They made all haste to get out of the reach of Joan's influence.

Orleans was the Stalingrad of the Hundred Years' War. The siege of Orleans had been the high point of the English advance into France. The myth of English invincibility was broken, the hot glare of Agincourt dimmed; and from here on in, there could be only recession for the English forces.

CHARLES IS CROWNED

Joan, having brought about the relief of Orleans, wanted to press on immediately to the coronation of Charles at Reims. But the French generals were not quite ready for that.

So far there had been the mere lifting of a siege and that was not enough. A siege had been lifted at Montargis two years before and that, in itself, had not stopped the English offensive, merely delayed it. More must be done; the English must be pursued and defeated. The English had never been defeated in the field in a major battle in the entire course of the Hundred Years' War (that had already lasted nearly a century). If the French could win a victory in the field, then, and only then, could they risk the march to Reims.

But was it safe to try for that victory? The French generals must have understood that if the French army was checked, even in a minor way, the glamour would rub off Joan at once and her influence might vanish altogether. The English might then advance a second time, place Orleans under a second siege and this time, with the disappointment of Joan in mind, the city would surely fall at once.

It was a hard decision, but it was not until over a month had passed after the raising of the siege that the French set off in pursuit. It was not till June 28, 1429, that the two forces met at Patay (puh-tay'), fifteen miles northwest of Orleans. (So near were the English even eight weeks after the siege had been lifted.)

The English army, under the command of Talbot and of Fastolfe, were caught by surprise. It had never occurred to them that a French army might come seeking them. They did not have time to entrench themselves behind the usual line of pointed stakes.

Fastolfe, viewing the situation calmly, pointed out that the English troops were outnumbered. This, in itself, might not be decisive, but the English were also disheartened and could not be counted on to fight their best. Fastolfe therefore recommended a further retreat, thus avoiding battle. The army could then wait for reinforcements and a better occasion.

Talbot, however, would hear of no retreat. It was now the turn of the English to follow dreams instead of reality, for to Talbot it seemed that a few Englishmen could forever defeat any number of Frenchmen in the style of Agincourt.

While Fastolfe and Talbot were arguing, the French, heartened by Joan's presence, attacked, and, although Talbot fought with reckless heroism, all fell out as Fastolfe had known it would. The French won and 2000 dead strewed the battlefield at the conclusion of the day. Fastolfe managed to withdraw the surviving remnant of the English, but Talbot was taken prisoner.

In later English mythology dealing with the Hundred Years' War, Talbot's reputation was saved by making Fastolfe out to have been a coward, whose defection caused the lost battle. This was sheer libel, and the reputation of a brave and sensible general was sacrificed to safeguard that of a rash fool. The libel was made eternal by its use in Shakespeare's play, *Henry VI, Part One*. Shakespeare furthermore used a form of Fastolfe's name, "Sir John Falstaff," for the immortal fat man of his plays *Henry IV, Part One* and *Henry IV, Part Two*.

The Battle of Patay was a fitting climax for the lifting of the siege of Orleans. This first victory of the French over the English in the field in a century of fighting changed everything.

The French could *now* follow up their advantage by moving northward. Surely, the French populace, heartened and made proud by victory, would rise against the English on all sides.

But where should the French move now? From the strictly

military standpoint, the natural objective would have seemed to be Paris, but Joan of Arc insisted on Reims and she was undoubtedly right. There was an overwhelming psychological advantage to having Charles VII made king with all the religious panoply that, in tradition, had been part of the coronation at Reims for a thousand years.

It was Reims, then. A sizable French army was gathered at Gien (zhyen), a town on the Loire River, forty miles upstream from Orleans. On June 29, 1429, it set forth on the nearly two-hundred-mile journey northeastward to Reims, through countryside that, in theory, was largely under the control of English and Burgundians.

The French leaders were right. On all sides, delirious Frenchmen hailed the first victorious and confident French army they had ever seen. With Joan of Arc marching in the lead, France underwent a kind of religious upheaval. Many joined the army as though they were going on a pilgrimage or on a crusade. What's more, garrisons within the cities they encountered had no heart to fight. Even the English, badly mauled and more badly dispirited, made no move to interfere.

On July 10, the French army reached Troyes, seventy miles south of Reims; Troyes, where the disgraceful peace treaty with Henry V had been signed nine years before. The town was thought to be heart and soul with Philip of Burgundy, but when the French army demanded its surrender, threatening assault otherwise, it gave in at once. A few days later, Châlons (shah-lone'), twenty-five miles southeast of Reims, gave in just as easily. And with each such easy victory, the aura of the miraculous heightened, and made the next victory all the more certain, all the easier.

On July 16, 1429, Charles VII and Joan of Arc rode into Reims at the head of the army. There was no fight. And on July 17, 1429, Charles VII was crowned at Reims, in full traditional style, with Joan nearby. When the coronation was over, Joan knelt to him. She had up to this point never addressed him as anything more than the Dauphin, but now, with deepest respect, she hailed him as her king.

In whatever way one rationalized the amazing events of the preceding two and a half months (no more than that!), the lifting of the siege of Orleans, the defeat of the English in the field at Patay, the holiday march through a supposedly hostile countryside, the coronation at Reims — to all Frenchmen the only explanation was that of the miraculous. Charles VII was a true king, though his mother swore him ten times a bastard. The English must lose. God was fighting on the side of France. Who could doubt it?

Worse than the French enthusiasm, from the English standpoint, was the chill that now fell over their relations with Burgundy. Philip the Good was no fool and he recognized a turning point when it was as explosively dramatic as this one was. He waited, now, only for some opportune moment to switch sides with maximum benefit to himself.

And worst of all, from the English standpoint, was that the English themselves began to despair of victory. Yet even while the clouds turned black in France, the English lords in England itself were dividing into various factions that quarreled for power over the boy-king.

The slow swing of the balance-pans seemed to be bringing about a healing of disunion in France and, simultaneously, a tearing of civil war in England. The wisdom of hindsight tells us that the English ought now to have made peace, asking for no more than their ancestral Normandy and various key points along the Channel coast. There might have been a fighting chance that by keeping their sights low they might gain a permanent foothold on the Continent.

Unfortunately for themselves, the English could not break the spell of Agincourt. They kept on fighting for a dream of total victory that receded and receded. And since they would accept nothing less than total victory, they in the end had to accept total defeat.

Of course, the coronation at Reims did not signalize that English defeat at once. Indeed, as long as the Duke of Bedford remained alive, the English side of the war continued to be fought with skill and determination. In the aftermath of Patay, the English pulled back from some of their forward positions, but, with less territory to defend, they could concentrate the more effectively.

From the standpoint of the French, the coronation ought to be followed by some great move to keep the fires of enthusiasm burning. And now, surely, that meant Paris.

Joan favored an immediate move on Paris, but some of the king's more conservative advisers did not. Much had been gained by daring, but daring can shade over little by little into rashness. Rashness can quickly lose all that daring has gained, to be sure, so caution became popular and Joan found herself increasingly isolated.

For over a month, the French army marched through the territory between Reims and Paris, fighting some skirmishes, taking some places, but it was not till the end of August that Joan could force an actual move against Paris. By that time, however, the English had received needed reinforcements and had organized their defenses. The still anti-Armagnac, pro-Burgundian Parisians manned the walls.

The French attack was carried out halfheartedly on September 8, by a leadership unwilling to risk a major defeat, and when the first assaults were beaten off, a retreat was ordered on September 9.

It was not a major defeat, but it was bad enough. Joan had led the attack and yet the French had not won. They had instead had to retreat as in the old days. Worse yet, Joan had received a wound in the thigh. It shook the faith in her divine mission and gave rise to the thought that her inspiration involved only the coronation of the king and nothing further. Increasingly, the French leaders in the government and the army were unwilling to follow "miracles" beyond the point of diminishing returns. Increasingly, they grew tired of Joan and her strenuous demand for action and more action.

The French retired beyond the Loire again, and Joan, perforce, had to go along with them, so the winter was relatively quiet for her.

Meanwhile, it was time for Philip of Burgundy to move. The hold of the English on the territories east of Paris had been broken, but that of the French was still tenuous. These territories, bordering his own realm, were a virtual no man's land. Why might he not take them for himself? They would be of the utmost value to him, for with them he could unite his east-central-France dominion and his lands in Flanders and the Low Countries. Such a union would give him a compact realm and make of Burgundy a major power. Limitless horizons opened before his dazzled eyes.

He began a cautious encroachment into the territories and by March, 1430, he advanced so far as to threaten siege to the key town of Compiègne (kome-pyen'yuh), fifty miles northeast of Paris. In April, Joan determined to save the area and dashed toward Compiègne with a small escort. She had varying success, nerving some towns to resist the Burgundian forces, while others closed their gates against her.

When a Burgundian army finally began to place its ring about Compiègne, Joan hastened to enter the city so that she might repeat her miraculous deliverance of Orleans just a year before. On May 23, 1430, she led two sorties against the Burgundians and then the miracles ran out. She was unhorsed and captured, and her remarkable thirteen-month military career was over.

For over half a year she remained in Burgundian hands, to the frustration of the English. For them, imprisonment wasn't enough; she might escape, and that very escape might be made to prove further evidence for the divinity of her mission. And if she had to be imprisoned, it was not in Burgundian hands that the English wanted her. England no longer dared trust Philip of Burgundy very far, and they were not sure that he would not use Joan against the English if he thought he could get away with it.

What the English wanted was to have Joan in their own hands. They wanted her examined and declared a witch by the highest possible ecclesiastical authorities. They then wanted her punished as a witch — by death. The hope was that such an ecclesiastical trial, followed by capital punishment, would be accepted as proof that Joan was inspired by the Devil; that the victories won by the French over the past year would then not be counted against the English, so to speak; and that English morale would rise again, and French fall, to the positions held before the coming of Joan.

English pressure on the Burgundians therefore mounted steadily, and on January 3, 1431, Philip finally sold her to the English for 10,000 francs. She was placed in the charge of Richard, Earl of Warwick, and her trial began almost at once in the city of Rouen, the capital of Normandy, and the heart of the English dominions in France.

For nearly five months, Joan was questioned and cross-questioned in a maze of theological crosscurrents. She held her own remarkably well, but the only choice she really had was life imprisonment as a recanted heretic, or the stake as a heretic who would not recant. In other words, she must either admit she was a witch or else be declared one. Since she would by no means admit she was a witch, it finally came to the stake, something for which the English had been waiting more or less impatiently.

On May 30, 1431, just a year after her capture, and two years after the relief of Orleans, she was burned alive in the public square of Rouen, maintaining the divine nature of her mission to the end.

Yet though she was proclaimed a witch by the English, and though she died at the stake, those who burned her won nothing by it. Indeed, they lost. The flames did not convince the French; rather they kindled the fires of patriotism the higher in their hearts. Was it reasonable to suppose that Frenchmen would believe (as the English clearly thought they should) that only by the help of the Devil could a French army defeat an English one?

The French, rather, were more than ever convinced that Joan's mission had been a holy one and that she was a saint. That she died condemned made no difference. Many saints had died condemned. Jesus himself had died condemned. Indeed, the burning of Joan actually lowered the morale of the English, rather than of the French. Many Englishmen were burdened with the uneasy feeling that they had burned a saint.

And, to be sure, the time was to come when Joan would be rehabiliated and officially made a saint. She lives in history as the savior of France and her name has become a very byword for anyone leading a fight for national salvation. The exact date of her birth is uncertain, but on the day of her death she had certainly not reached her twenty-first birthday, and perhaps not her twentieth. No person, of either sex, who died a teen-ager, or very little more, ever had so crucial an effect on history or so impressed both contemporary and later times.

But her sainthood lay in the future. What of the year between her capture and her death, when she was merely a girl facing torture and death? To their everlasting disgrace, Charles VII and those about him made no move to attempt to rescue her, to offer to ransom her, or even merely to appeal to her captors for mercy. Considering what she had done for Charles and for France, it seems unbelievable that this could happen and yet it did.

Perhaps Charles and his advisers were a little worried that she might indeed be a witch or, failing that, that she was, in any case, just a low-born girl. Probably they were actually glad to see her go. She had been impossible to handle and had refused to be guided. Things were a great deal easier without her.

It is quite fair to say that the French leaders were as guilty of Joan's burning as the English were, and more disgracefully so.

PHILIP IS CONVINCED

The English followed up what they desperately hoped would be a reversal of the psychological battle by now crowning their own king, Henry VI, as king of France. The ceremony took place on December 17, 1431, and proved in several ways a fiasco.

Henry VI was still only ten years old, a frightened boy of no great intelligence who had been beaten, as a matter of course, by his tutors, in the belief that this would knock understanding into his head. It merely helped make him addle-pated and for the rest of his long reign he was to be a feeble puppet in the hands of whoever could seize control of him. (He was to be troubled in later life with periods of outright madness after the fashion of his French grandfather, Charles VI.) The lad was no symbol of English strength, therefore, and impressed no one.

Second, the English had missed their chance. They had not crowned Henry in Reims when they might have, and now it was too late, for Reims was no longer under English control. The coronation took place in Paris, and to the French people generally such a ceremony meant precisely nothing. It had been Charles VII who had been crowned in Reims, and therefore only he who could be considered king in the eyes of God.

Finally, the English made the mistake of making the coronation into a purely English affair, cutting French participation to a minimum and omitting such frills as an ostentatious reduction of taxes, liberation of prisoners or distribution of money. As a result, the coronation brought about a dramatic decline of the Parisian loyalty to the English cause.

The failure of the English attempt to reverse the effect of the meteoric career of Joan of Arc had its effect on the shrewd mind of Philip the Good of Burgundy. Undoubtedly, he watched closely in order to observe the effect of the trial and execution of Joan and of the coronation of the English boy-king. He saw clearly that the revolution which had been brought about by Joan was *not* being reversed. He saw that although Charles VII, in the absence of Joan, had relapsed into passivity beyond the Loire once more, the French armies were continuing and extending their new aggressive attitude.

The Bastard of Orleans, for instance, by no means lost his ability to fight just because Joan was no longer with him. In 1432, he was nibbling at the outskirts of Paris, taking Lagny (lah-nyee′), only fifteen miles to the east. He was at the approaches to Normandy, too, taking Chartres, fifty miles southwest of Paris. And if the French had awakened and were no longer paralyzed with dread of the English, there was the fact that the French population was some seven times that of the English.

Philip judged all this and decided that English defeat in an extended war was certain. He suggested to the English that they attempt to reach an accommodation with the French and salvage what they could. When, still Agincourt-dazzled, they refused, he was convinced at last that he had no choice but to go his own way. He began independent negotiations with Charles VII.

These negotiations dragged on for years, since Burgundy's price for peace was high. During those years, the English might have dragged Philip back to his earlier allegiance rather easily by some signal victory or by some unmistakable show of strength. This they could not offer — rather the reverse. The situation in England was rapidly degenerating into a civil war and English morale in France dipped dangerously. Bedford himself, even with his hands full in France, had to hasten back to England to impose a compromise peace on the battling factions.

Then in Normandy, the very heart of the English power on the continent, there was a serious rebellion in 1434. This showed plainly that the hearts of Frenchmen everywhere were turning to the national cause. The fact that the English suppressed the rebellion was less important than the fact that the rebellion had taken place at all.

The negotiations between Philip and Charles entered their final phase in Arras (ahr-rahs'), a city in Burgundian territory a hundred miles north of Paris. English representatives arrived, but could not accept the terms that were clearly being settled upon by both French factions. They left in frustration.

The Duke of Bedford did not live to see the final end of the Anglo-Burgundian alliance. On September 15, 1435, he died at the age of forty-six. He was the only English leader who placed the cause of the war in France above personal ambition. With his death, the English armies in France became the pawn of ambitious politicians at home.

Five days after his death, on September 20, Burgundy and France made their peace at the Treaty of Arras, and the civil war that had begun with the assassination of Louis of Orleans a quarter century before was ended. It had been this civil war which had given Henry V and the English their great chance and it was the close of the civil war that meant a final end to any possibility of their carrying on in their project for French conquests.

By the Treaty of Arras, Charles VII had to make great concessions to Philip the Good. He had to recognize Philip as an independent sovereign, so that no French king could later claim the right to deprive him or his descendants of their title and realm; the Duke of Burgundy was to be no man's vassal. Second, the extent of the Burgundian land was markedly increased. Its boundaries were extended to include the lands it had recently conquered. Burgundy even expanded to take in and include certain fortified cities on the Somme River that brought its boundary to within eighty miles of Paris. The Somme fortresses, to be sure, could be bought back by France for a large sum of money, but that was only theory. Philip had no intention of selling them unless France were backed by superior force as well as by gold. Finally, Charles VII had to apologize for the assassination of Philip's father, John the Fearless, and to promise to punish the murderers.

In return for all this, Philip had to do nothing positive. He merely agreed to recognize Charles VII as king of France and to make no further war on him. The Treaty of Arras was one-sided indeed, but even so it was something Charles and the French desperately needed, and its worth was demonstrated almost at once.

Paris, which had been held by the combined forces of England and Burgundy, could not be held by the English alone. The English locked themselves into fortified posts and then, seeing clearly that they would be starved out, abandoned the city and moved downstream to Rouen. On April 13, 1436, after sixteen years of English occupation and half a year after the Treaty of Arras, Paris declared for Charles VII.

In November, 1437, Charles VII made his formal entrance and Paris was French again. (It was not yet the capital, however. Charles VII never trusted the city from which he had been ejected in his boyhood and persisted in residing in various palaces on the Loire. It was nearly a century before Paris became the definite home of the French court once more.)

The English still retained Normandy and Guienne, and there at least they were as yet unassailable — or at least safe from the exhausted strength of France. On the other hand, they were by no means capable of launching a large-scale offensive.

Both sides, reduced to unimportant skirmishing, entered a period of marking time, which France used constructively in a painful reform and reorganization, while England slipped steadily further into the chaos of civil war.

10

VICTORY

THE CHANGING SCENE

To begin with, Charles VII had to reorganize the finances of the kingdom. It was not only that the ravages of the long war had produced financial chaos. It had also undone the work of Philip IV with regard to the papacy and had raised once again the danger of French money being made to flow into Italy in uncontrollable quantities.

As long as the Popes ruled in Avignon they remained under the control of France. Safe in the southeast, the Popes remained French puppets through all the disasters under Philip VI and John II, in the northeast and southwest. During those reigns, the Popes continued to appoint a majority of French cardinals and these continued to elect French Popes.

But then, in 1378, toward the end of the reign of Charles V, the seventh Avignonese Pope, Gregory XI, was visiting Rome. He had every intention of returning to Avignon, but happened to die before he could do so. The Roman mob forced those cardinals who were in Rome at the time to elect an Italian Pope who would agree to stay in Rome. The new Pope ruled in Rome as Urban VI. Back in Avignon, however, other cardinals denounced the Roman election as illegal and chose a Pope of their own who would agree to stay in Avignon and who ruled as Clement VII.

Thus began the "Great Schism," which lasted for four decades, and during which the papacy became a political football. There were two Popes during the entire period, and each used against the other all the greatest fulminations of the Church without (to the puzzlement of the faithful) any damage done to either side.

The various nations lined up according to strictly political considerations. France backed Avignon, of course, and so did her allies, Scotland and the Spanish kingdoms. Since England and Burgundy were at war with France, they backed Rome, and so on.

During the course of the Great Schism, the Avignonese papacy grew steadily weaker, in line with the gathering chaos in France during the catastrophic reign of Charles VI.

The prestige of the papacy suffered enormously during the Great Schism. Indeed a movement arose that favored making the papacy a kind of limited monarchy, giving superior power to a council of churchmen. For a while, this "conciliar movement" was powerful and it was one such council, the Council of Constance (on what is now the northern border of Switzerland) that finally brought an end to the schism.

In 1417, with France prostrated by the shock of the Battle of Agincourt, the papacy at Avignon was weak indeed and the opportunity was not to be missed. The churchmen at the Council of Constance declared councils to be superior in decision-making power to the Pope, then elected a new Pope, Martin V, who was to rule in Rome and whom all were directed to accept.

Europe, weary of the schism, did accept him, and although the last Avignonese Pope, Benedict XIII, continued to call himself Pope till his death in 1423, hardly anyone else did. Nor could France do a thing to help him. With his death, all traces of the century-and-a-quarter Avignonese interlude were erased.

Martin V tried to end the conciliar movement, even though he had been the beneficiary of it, but for another generation the Church continued to be beset by antipapal sentiment.

In 1431, a Council met at Basel in Switzerland and this attempted to establish, once and for all, the supremacy of a council over a Pope. The council called for reforms that involved the decentralization of the Church organization, assigning less power to the Pope and more to the various national sections of the Church.

This movement was ultimately defeated because of the obstinate resistance of Pope Eugene IV, who had succeeded Martin V in 1431. While the struggle was continuing, however, Charles VII seized his chance.

On July 7, 1438, Charles issued the "Pragmatic Sanction" of Bourges (a term used to signify a basic law governing some important segment of the governmental structure), which adopted the edicts of the Council of Basel. By those edicts, he, and those of his lords who had on their territories bishops and abbots, could themselves approve appointees to those positions without having to consult the Pope.

This meant that the French portion of the Catholic Church would, in this and other respects, be independent of the papal power to a considerable extent. This point of view (called "Gallicanism") had had its beginnings with Philip IV and now, after the long and dreadful interval of the war with England, was being reasserted.

Gallicanism meant a further intensification of the steadily growing feeling of nationalism in France, since even the Church would, in France, owe a practical allegiance to the king and to the secular establishment.

Furthermore, where the power was, there the pocketbook would be, too. As long as the papacy held the gift of Church office, money would flow to Rome; when it was the State that held it, money would flow to the king. Furthermore, with an autonomous Church hierarchy in France, it was that much easier for Charles to pass rules that limited payments of all kinds to Rome and conserved scarce money for the rebuilding and reorganization of the nation.

To handle the money, Charles VII made use of a merchant of Bourges named Jacques Coeur (kawr). He was the first of the financiers in the modern tradition, one who applied systematic organization to the money resources of a kingdom, centralizing its control under the king. He had made himself rich through trade with the east and now he produced, through this eastern trade, a steady commercial expansion of France.

Charles furthermore undertook to reform the army. France, as in the early days of Charles V, was overrun by independent bands of mercenary soldiers. These were now called "écorcheurs," meaning "flayers" because they stripped those they caught of everything, and flayed their skin when they had nothing else. Charles now forced these into an army controlled by himself, forbidding all private armies. He saw to it that the new standing army was paid regularly out of government funds, thus discouraging the habit of allowing unpaid soldiers to support themselves at the expense of the countryside.

One aspect of military improvement was crucial. Charles supported two brothers, Jean and Gaspard Bureau (byoo-roh'), who reorganized the artillery. They improved the design of cannon and made better the quality of gunpowder. Having thus increased the efficiency of the weapons, they oversaw the production of more of them, and placed them under the control of specialists. What's more, army commanders were forced to treat the guns and gunners with decent respect, regardless of the fact that the gunners were generally commoners.

Charles VII's armies became the first to make an able and systematic use of artillery, and this marked the final end of the medieval fashion of making war. The heavy plate armor of the knight lost the last vestige of its usefulness.

City walls, which, unlike personal armor, were impervious to longbows, also began to fall before the new artillery. The Bureaus had their first chance to show this in 1439, when the French laid siege to Meaux. That town had been the scene of Henry V's last victorious operation seventeen years before. The walls which had resisted Henry V for such long, bitter months could not stand against the colossal battering of the cannon and Meaux fell quickly. Indeed, the sieges in the final decade of the Hundred Years' War were all brief affairs compared to the long sieges in the days of the English ascendancy.

Charles VII did another thing which was to become characteristic of his successors. He took a mistress. This is not to say that the kings before him had not engaged in extramarital amours; it was a common enough habit of all men. Charles, however, did it openly, was faithful to the mistress he chose (a beautiful girl named Agnes Sorel) for her entire short life, and gave her a semi-official position in the court. For the six years between 1444 and 1450, when she died while still in her late twenties, she was the uncrowned French queen.

Charles' reforms were not carried through without opposition. Everything he did tended to concentrate power under the king. Many of the great nobles, used to being a law unto themselves during the decades of French misery, resented the movement that seemed to be reducing them to mere servants of the Crown.

They looked for a leader behind which they could unite and found one in the teen-age Dauphin, Louis.

Louis had been born in 1423, not long after Henry V's death, and had spent his formative years living through the very low point of French history. He was ugly and withdrawn. His father was not fond of him and the dislike was cordially returned. When the nobles approached the young man in 1440 and held out the prospect of an increased role in the government for him, he agreed to lead them, at least nominally.

The insurrection was called the "Praguerie." This was a reference to the city of Prague, in Bohemia, which was then a notorious center of rebellion. There the followers of John Huss, a religious reformer who had been burned at the stake in 1415, were still fighting desperately against the German Empire.

The nobles tried to win over the general population by calling for peace with England and lower taxation. The townsmen and the peasants, however, remembered too well the miseries of being ruled by a quarrelsome and generally incompetent aristocracy and clung to the king and to a strongly centralized government as the one chance at efficiency and prosperity. Arthur de Richemont (reesh-monte'), who led Charles VII's army as Constable, methodically reduced the strong points of the insurrectionists and, before the year was out, the Praguerie was crushed.

Charles VII used his victory with moderation. He was determined not to exacerbate a civil war to the advantage of the English. To have punished the recalcitrant nobles harshly would have pushed many into the arms of the English. He therefore forgave them and made it clear that he preferred their cooperation to their enmity. They responded appropriately and the brief civil war was at an end.

As for the Dauphin, Louis, he was forgiven, too, and was placed in charge of his titular province, Dauphiné, east of the mid course of the Rhone River. This had the advantage of keeping him away from the court and from further temptation. As it happened, the young Dauphin proved an able and honest administrator and, under him, Dauphiné did well.

Even so, the Praguerie slowed the pace of Charles' reforms. He had to go a little easier if he were to keep the nobility in good humor. And while the king's attention was on his own subjects, the English strengthened their hold on Normandy and even resumed the offensive, inching forward in the direction of Paris.

It looked as though the war would have to be resumed, but Charles still delayed for a few years — till he was ready.

THE LAST BATTLES

The period of near quiet that fell in France after the French recapture of Paris in 1437 was a time of trauma within England. Factionalism remained supreme and amidst the unending struggles for control over the weak Henry VI there were quarrels between the hawks and the doves; those who would still pursue the mirage of military victory in France, and those who would keep Normandy and Guienne and accept peace.

The leading hawk was the English king's uncle, Humphrey of Gloucester, who could not forget he had fought at the Battle of Agincourt. He himself had done much to ruin the English cause by his senseless near war with Philip of Burgundy, but he patronized learning and cultivated popularity with the people. (He was known as "Good Duke Humphrey.")

Nevertheless, he was a poor politician and his influence waned. In connection with the war he sustained a major defeat over the matter of Charles of Orleans.

Charles of Orleans, like Humphrey of Gloucester, was a still-living symbol of the Battle of Agincourt. Charles had been among the French leaders, had been taken prisoner on the battlefield, and had ever since been living a captive in England. The conditions of his English imprisonment were as light as those which had been inflicted on his great-grandfather John II, and, during its quarter-century duration, he engaged himself in the writing of love poetry of much merit, some of it in

English. Indeed, he is considered by many to be the last of the medieval troubadours, and his luster in the history of literature more than makes up for his failure as a military leader.

Those English leaders who opposed Gloucester began to push for the release of the man defeated at Agincourt as a reasonable gesture of conciliation with France. Philip of Burgundy, somewhat uncomfortable at having switched sides, and therefore willing to see peace come, negotiated the release. King Charles, for his part, agreed to pay the enormous ransom set by the English as his contribution to the de-escalation of the war.

In November, 1440, Charles of Orleans returned to France. He had no chance of regaining his one-time political preeminence, since the disgrace of Agincourt clung too closely. Very likely this did not bother him; he had long left politics behind. He retired to a peaceful life of ease and literary patronage. He continued to write poetry, and to his court at Blois the greatest French poets flocked. He married again, lived with his wife happily, and had a son by her when he himself was over seventy years old — a son, moreover, who was someday to become King of France. The loser of the Battle of Agincourt had far more reason to congratulate himself on his life than the victor had.

The value of the release of Charles of Orleans as a gesture to peace was neutralized by the Praguerie, which gave the English hawks new heart. For a moment Humphrey of Gloucester's prestige rose, but then the insurrection of the French nobility faded out and the struggle between hawks and doves began again.

The new struggle centered about the still-young Henry VI of England. He was in the early twenties now, and it was clear that he would never really rule, but always remain the weak puppet of some strong minister. Nevertheless, he was of an age to marry and the nature of the marriage might influence the future course of relations with France.

Humphrey of Gloucester wanted King Henry to marry the

daughter of John IV of Armagnac, the strongest nobleman in southern France. John of Armagnac had participated in the Praguerie and, though he had capitulated, he might easily be persuaded to rise against the king again. Once his daughter became the English queen, he might agree to play the role of a new Burgundy and give England another chance at total victory.

Charles VII was not blind to this possibility. The royal army (with the young Dauphin among its leaders) ranged over the south, and in 1443 effectively disposed of Armagnac's strength. From this blow, Humphrey of Gloucester never recovered and his influence on events was nil thereafter.

Leading the party of the doves in England was now William, Earl of Suffolk. He had led the English forces who had been forced to retreat from Orleans after Joan of Arc's arrival, but he had fought valiantly before that time and after, and he felt that it was enough.

In 1443, he came to France to arrange a truce, something he felt England badly needed if it was to deal with its problems at home. It would help make such a truce palatable to the English if Suffolk could bring home a highly titled and beautiful young princess to be the English queen. And there seemed a possibility at hand.

René of Anjou was a member of the House of Valois. He was the great-grandson of King John II of France, and was second cousin of the reigning King Charles VII. His grandfather, his father and his older brother (each named Louis) had claimed the crown of Naples and fought for it, but not one had actually succeeded in establishing himself as king in fact. When René's older brother, Louis III, died in 1434, René inherited the title, and called himself King of Naples. He never sat on the throne and, in actual fact, had neither power nor income. Nevertheless, he could call himself king and he was of "the blood royal." That gave him an exalted social status.

René had, as it happened, a young daughter, Margaret of

Anjou, who was thirteen years old when Suffolk came to France. Surely, she would be just right. The French seemed to think so, too.

A truce was signed on May 28, 1444, for two years with, of course, options for renewals, and the marriage took place the following April in the city of Tours (toor) on the Loire, about seventy miles downstream from Orleans. Margaret of Anjou, now fifteen, became Queen of England.

As usual, in compromise settlements, neither side was really pleased. England's possession of Guienne, Normandy, Calais and a few other places was confirmed, which could scarcely please France. On the other hand, England undertook to return to French domination the county of Maine, lying just to the south of Normandy, since this was part of the hereditary domains (in theory) of René of Anjou, King Henry's new father-in-law. The hawkish party in England did their best to treat this as a shameful surrender, but, in 1447, Humphrey of Gloucester was assassinated and his tongue, at least, was stilled.

Even so, no English government, however dovelike its sentiments, dared actually give up Maine. The cession had been made on paper but the English found excuse after excuse to avoid actually leaving the province. Nor did Charles press them unduly. As long as the English remained in possession, the truce could be declared broken whenever it suited the French to do so.

In 1448, France was ready. Its army was reorganized, its batteries of artillery ready. Since England still hadn't given up Maine, Charles declared the truce broken, and sent his army westward to occupy Maine and invade Normandy.

At the time, the English in Normandy were under the leadership of the incompetent Edmund, Duke of Somerset. The French swept all before them, taking Rouen and Harfleur in 1449, cities it had cost Henry V much to capture thirty years before. (Talbot was again captured at this point and was kept in prison for a year before being ransomed.)

Somerset fell back to Caen, sixty miles west of Rouen, and was there besieged.

The English stirred themselves to a last effort in the north. In March, 1450, a new English army landed on the Norman coast, one larger than either Edward III or Henry V had ever taken to France. The French reacted quickly, and on April 15, 1450, the English and French armies met at the village of Formigny (fawr-mee-nyee'), on the Norman coast, twenty-five miles west of Caen.

Alas for England, the days of Agincourt were over. The English were not facing a huge and disorderly mob, but an army no larger than their own and better organized. The English still had their archers as the backbone of their forces and still fought defensively, expecting the French to charge into range of the arrows.

The French did not do so. Instead they brought up the efficient cannon of the brothers Bureau. The cannon had a longer range than the longbow and it was now the English who were galled by long-distance missiles at which they could not strike back; and missiles far worse than arrows.

For a while the battle held even, despite this, but when French reinforcements arrived on the scene, the English broke. They tried to retreat, but the retreat turned into a rout, and two thirds of the English army remained dead on the battlefield.

Suffolk's policy of peace had thus broken down and ended in defeat and disgrace for England. He did not long survive. He was first banished and then, on May 1, 1450, even as he tried to leave the country, was cut down by assassins. That, however, did not end the tale of British defeats. Caen fell to the French on July 6, and the port of Cherbourg on August 12. That was England's last foothold in the region and all of Normandy was lost to the English forever.

Charles VII entered into Rouen triumphantly in 1450, not long after the Battle of Formigny, and in that city, on the site where Joan of Arc had been burned nineteen years before, he ordered a reinvestigation of the case. (After all, he could scarcely allow it to be said that he had been crowned with the help of a convicted witch who had been burned for her sorceries.)

It was quite clear that Charles expected Joan's sentence to be revoked, as on the earlier occasion the English had expected her to be convicted. And of course, the tribunal sitting in judgment met the political necessities on this occasion as on the former.

Joan's conviction was reversed and she was declared no witch, though there was no way of unburning her, to be sure.

With the north taken, the French armies, secure in their use of artillery, turned to the southwest. There they faced Guienne and its capital city of Bordeaux, a region which had been English not merely for thirty years but for nearly three hundred, and which had grown so used to being under the kings of England that they scarcely felt French.

There, too, however, the French made steady progress, and there, too, the English made a last effort. They still had Talbot, the last of the captains dating from the days, a generation before, when it seemed that the English were unbeatable and could plow, at will, through uncounted numbers of French. Talbot was nearly seventy years old now, but he was still the same fighting fool he always was — all bravery and little discretion.

When, on June 5, 1451, Bordeaux opened its gates to the French, Talbot was sent with an army to Guienne. The population at once joined its accustomed rulers, and, in October, Talbot was able to retake Bordeaux and recover a considerable portion of Guienne. That meant that eventually he would have to face a reinforced French army that was sent into the province.

The French army reached the English outpost at Castillon (kas-tee-ohn'), thirty miles east of Bordeaux, and Talbot hastened to its relief. But Talbot was Talbot; it was the English turn to be headlong fools. Talbot plunged into furious battle on July 17, 1453, without waiting for artillery support. The French, on the other hand, placed their artillery behind a strong defensive line, as they had done at Formigny.

It was no longer the French who were lured into arrow range; it was the English who were drawn into cannonball range. A strong English column was diven by Talbot into a mad charge against the French lines and they were mowed down by the artillery. Talbot was killed, the English army was destroyed and the reign of the longbow was over. It had been master of the battlefield for a century.

All of Guienne was quickly retaken, Bordeaux falling to France for a second and last time on October 19, 1453. The Battle of Castillon was the last battle of any consequence in the Hundred Years' War. In fact, the long struggle with England, which had begun in the time of Louis VII of France and Henry II of England, was over and the victory was to France.

The only land on French territory retained by the English was Calais and the region immediately about it. Even that would undoubtedly have fallen to the French were it not for the fact that it was on the doorstep of the dominions of Philip of Burgundy and he preferred to have the English there just in case.

Actually, the Hundred Years' War didn't end legally. There was never a peace treaty. Despite everything, no English government could bring itself to make peace with France and admit that Crécy and Poitiers, and, even Agincourt had come to nothing; that Edward III and the Black Prince and Henry V had fought to no purpose. All the English would sign was a truce and that was all the French got. And with the English still at Calais and still in control of the Channel, France had to live on for some decades waiting to see if once again the English would yet invade.

But a serious invasion of consequence never came and if we

look back on the time from our own vantage point, we can mark
the Battle of Castillon as the end of the Hundred Years' War in
fact, if not in law.

THE END OF AN ERA

The Battle of Castillon and the end of the Hundred Years'
War marked the end of an era for England and France and was
part of a larger complex of events that marked the close of an
era for Europe and the whole world.

In itself, the Hundred Years' War ended forever the time of
medieval warfare and initiated the modern gunpowder age in
which artillery was supreme — something that was to continue
down to the mid-twentieth century.

It also raised national feeling in both France and England to
such a pitch as to destroy forever in western Europe the last
vestiges of the international community of "Christendom." The
new nationalism was to make its mark felt also in other parts of
western Europe, notably in Spain, Portugal, Scotland and the
Scandinavian countries. Only in Germany and Italy were the
forces of medieval fragmentation to retain a hold, with ill consequences that were to make themselves felt into the mid-
nineteenth century.

As though to emphasize the passing of the old, there came,
on May 30, 1453, just six weeks before the Battle of Castillon,
the final and permanent fall of the city of Constantinople to the
Ottoman Turks. The long history of the Byzantine Empire was
over, along with the last vestige of an independent culture that
stretched back continuously to Augustus, the first Roman Emperor, fifteen centuries before, and even to the Trojan War,
twenty-six centuries before.

Militarily, the fall of Constantinople was a negligible factor.

It had long been surrounded and helpless in the Turkish grip. The psychological effect of the event, however, was enormous. It seemed to make visible the vanishing of the past and to symbolize the vast change that had taken place.

Nor was it a matter of political and military change alone. The Hundred Years' War and the Black Death, in particular, had wiped out the economic basis of feudalism and therefore the whole structure of the medieval way of life. The armored knight was now a museum piece, while the low-born pikeman at close quarters and the low-born gunner at long distance were kings of the battlefield. Castles had become useless relics of the past and only the king could afford the enormously expensive artillery train that made effective war possible. This meant that the day of the centralized absolute monarchy was at hand and the aristocracy was to change gradually from a group of brawling rebels and fighters into a collection of social parasites.

The drop in population had made labor so valuable that serfs could and did win new privileges. Serfdom ended and the era of the free peasant (not much better off in some ways) began.

Beyond the political, military and economic aspects of society, great changes were taking place in man's intellectual life. Even while the Hundred Years' War was going on, Italy had been in cultural ferment. As the power of the papacy declined, a new burst of art and literature had come into being, one which no longer drew its inspiration from the Bible and the writings of the Church Fathers and was no longer primarily concerned with the relationship of man to God. The new culture sprang, instead, from the rediscovered classics of the ancient pagan world, and it dealt with the relationship of man and man. This rebirth of an interest in man for his own sake ("humanism") came to be called the "Renaissance" — the French word for "rebirth."

It was the men of the Renaissance who, aware of the fact that the spirit of the ancient world (pagan, daring and free)

seemed to be reborn, came to call the long interlude between
the fall of the ancient culture and its rediscovery, the "Middle
Ages."

For over a century, this new move in culture was confined
largely to Italy. Europe beyond the Alps remained backward
in that respect. The medieval universities and, in particular,
the University of Paris remained bastions of conservatism and
actively resisted the Renaissance influence.

Nevertheless, once the Hundred Years' War was over and
France recovered its strength (which took another generation),
it began an attempt at military expansion. France's armies invaded Italy in 1494 and brought back the Renaissance with
them and, through France, the Renaissance spread rapidly elsewhere.

This greater breadth of human experience and daring in the
cultural field was matched by the more literal expansion in
the geographic sense. During the course of the Hundred Years'
War, the small nation of Portugal, with no Mediterranean coast
and with only an Atlantic shore, undertook a steady program of
exploration out into the Atlantic and down along the African
shore. By the time of the Battle of Castillon, Portuguese navi-
gators had passed the westernmost bulge of Africa and were
heading farther south. At the end of 1487, the southernmost tip
of Africa had been reached.

In 1479, the Iberian peninsula (except for Portugal) was
united into the nation of Spain, and, in 1492, united Spain destroyed the last Moslem kingdom in the south. In that same
year, the Spanish rulers sponsored Christopher Columbus on
his journey which ended with the discovery of the American
continents, and, in 1497, the Portuguese explorer Vasco da
Gama rounded Africa and reached India.

Europe had in this way burst out of its medieval isolation.
It was no longer hemmed in by the superior force of Arabs,
Turks and Mongols. The Turks, to be sure, threatened Europe
for another generation or so, but Europe had bypassed them

all, exposed the whole planet, and laid the groundwork for the Europeanization of the world.

In still another way, a new age was dawning. In 1454, the year after the close of the Hundred Years' War and the fall of Constantinople, the German inventor Johann Gutenberg devised a system for printing with movable metal type.

With a speed impressive for the time, the invention spread. The number of books increased enormously, thanks to the use of printing, the development of new inks and, most important of all, perhaps, the existence of paper.

Paper was a Chinese invention originally, as, probably, were many other medieval innovations such as the mariner's compass, gunpowder and windmills. Paper could be made out of textile rags, or even out of wood. Entering Europe by way of the Moslem world and Spain as early as the twelfth century, it was superior to the papyrus of the ancients, which had been made from a relatively rare reed. It was also enormously cheaper than the almost prohibitively expensive parchment which was made from animal skins and was almost the only decent writing surface of the early Middle Ages.

With many books available, the push toward literacy strengthened, and the ability to read and write spread wider and wider beyond the priesthood and the merchants. With printing also, newly discovered information could be more quickly transmitted from person to person so that there was a more effective and interactive intellectual community that transcended localities and even nations.

Since new ideas traveled more rapidly and extensively, it was increasingly difficult for upholders of old ways to suppress change. Heresies and radical innovations had been kept under control throughout the Middle Ages, but with printing the hostile idea escaped and could not be caught. It was by use of the printing press that Martin Luther established the "Reformation" in the early sixteenth century, and permanently fragmented western Christianity.

And it was only with printing that one could speak of a growing scientific community, as opposed to individual scientists. It was printing, therefore, that laid the groundwork for the birth of modern science in the mid-sixteenth century.

All these changes put together make for one of the great watersheds of human history — the changeover from the medieval age to the modern age. Sometimes an attempt is made to mark the changeover with a single event — the fall of Constantinople or the discovery of America being the two most often cited. That, however, is not the way history works.

The modern age began early in some respects; the medieval lingered long in other respects. The French king Philip IV was modern in some ways in the thirteenth century. The Austrian Emperor Francis Joseph I was medieval in some ways in the nineteenth century.

However, much of the changeover, perhaps even most of it, can be squeezed into a half-year period from 1450 to 1500. In 1450, western Europe was still largely medieval. In 1500, western Europe was largely modern.

And so it is convenient to end this book at the watershed, with the close of the Hundred Years' War in 1453. The book, dealing with French history from Hugh Capet to Charles VII, covers the five centuries of medieval France and describes how this period served to shape the France we know today.

FORECAST

The history of France certainly did not end with the close of the Hundred Years' War. Indeed, the most was yet to come.

The end of the war did not mean the end of national danger. Burgundy was still independent and a greater threat to exhausted France than ever. It took an additional quarter-century, and the shrewd guidance of Charles VII's son, the Dauphin Louis (who was to reign as Louis XI), to put an end to that threat.

With France truly unified, it could launch itself on foreign adventures and fight for generations against a new enemy — against a united realm that included the German Empire and Spain.

Then, when it emerged triumphant from that struggle, France found itself the strongest military power in the world and, for a while in the first decade of the nineteenth century, it even seemed that it was to overshadow and absorb all of Europe. Only its old enemy, England (enlarged to the nation of Great Britain), stood intransigently in its way, and the decision came after the conclusion of a new Hundred Years' War between the two nations.

But that dramatic story will be dealt with in other books of this series.

987 Death of Louis V, the last Carolingian king of France; election of Hugh Capet

992 Death of Charles of Lorraine; end of the Carolingian line

996 Death of Hugh Capet; succession of his son, Robert II

1031 Death of Robert II; succession of his son, Henry I

1035 Death of Robert of Normandy; succession of his illegitimate minor son, William

1060 Death of Henry I; succession of his minor son, Philip I

1066 William of Normandy conquers England; becomes William I (the Conqueror) of England

1071 Turks defeat Byzantines at the Battle of Manzikert

1087 Death of William I of England; succeeded by his older son, Robert Curthose in Normandy; by his younger son, William II in England

1096 Pope Urban II initiates First Crusade at Clermont

1099 Crusaders take Jerusalem

1100 Death of William II of England; succession of his son, Henry I, who eventually takes over Normandy as well

1108 Death of Philip I; succession of his son, Louis VI

1119 Henry I of England defeats Louis VI and William Clito (son of Robert Curthose) at Battle of Les Andelys

1124 Emperor Henry V fails in invasion of France

1128 Matilda of England marries Geoffrey of Anjou, foundation of Angevin (Plantagenet) line; Death of William Clito

1134 Death of Robert Curthose

1135 Death of Henry I of England; disputed succession between his daughter Matilda and her cousin, Stephen of Blois

1137 Death of Louis VI; succession of his son, Louis VII, who has just married Eleanor of Aquitaine

1141 Matilda of England driven out of England to Normandy

1144 Moslems retake Edessa in Holy Land

1146 Bernard of Clairvaux preaches new crusade

1147 Louis VII leaves on Second Crusade

1149   Louis VII returns to France after crusading fiasco

1151   Death of Geoffrey of Anjou; succession of his son, Henry, in Anjou and Normandy; death of Suger

1152   Eleanor of Aquitaine divorces Louis VII and marries Henry of Normandy

1154   Death of Stephen of Blois; Henry of Normandy succeeds as Henry II of England, founding Angevin Empire

1160   University of Paris in existence

1170   Assassination of Thomas Becket; Peter Waldo founds Waldensian movement in southern France

1180   Death of Louis VII; succession of his son, Philip II

1187   Saladin retakes Jerusalem from the Crusaders

1189   Death of Henry II of England; succession of his son, Richard I

1190   Philip II and Richard I of England set off on Third Crusade

1191   Crusaders take Acre; Philip II returns to France

1192   Richard I of England leaves Holy Land; captured and imprisoned in Germany

1194   Richard I of England ransomed, returns to west

1198   Richard I builds Château Gaillard; Innocent III elected Pope

1199   Death of Richard I of England; succession of his brother, John

1203   John of England captures and does away with his nephew, Arthur of Brittany

1204   Philip II takes Château Gaillard; death of Eleanor of Aquitaine; Fourth Crusaders take Constantinople

1205   Philip II takes Rouen; end of Angevin Empire

1208   Start of Albigensian (Waldensian) Crusade

1209   Simon de Montfort takes Beziers

1212   Children's Crusade

1213   Simon de Montfort defeats Albigensians at the Battle of Muret

1214   Philip II defeats England and the German Empire at the Battle of Bouvines

1215   John of England signs the Magna Carta

1216   Louis, son of Philip II, invades England, occupies London; John of England dies; succession of his son, Henry III

1217   Louis defeated, leaves England

1218   Fifth Crusade

1223   Death of Philip II; succession of his son, Louis VIII

1226   Death of Louis VIII; succession of his minor son, Louis IX, with Blanche of Castile as regent

1227   Death of Genghis Khan, the Mongol leader, after his conquest of most of Asia; succession of his son, Ogdai Khan

1228 Sixth Crusade under Emperor Frederick II

1229 Jerusalem restored to Crusader control by negotiation

1233 Inquisition founded

1234 Louis IX begins rule in his own name

1240 Mongols invade Europe, reach Germany

1241 Mongols, undefeated, leave western Europe forever at news of death of Ogdai Khan

1244 Moslems retake Jerusalem second time

1248 Louis IX leaves on Seventh Crusade

1249 Louis IX takes Damietta on the mouth of the Nile River

1250 Moslems defeat Louis IX at Battle of Mansura; later take him prisoner; death of Emperor Frederick II

1252 Death of Blanche of Castile

1254 Louis IX back in France

1258 Louis IX signs peace treaty with Henry III of England

1260 Baybars of Egypt defeats Mongols

1261 Byzantines under Michael VIII retake Constantinople

1265 Charles of Anjou, younger brother of Louis IX, leaves to establish kingdom in south Italy

1266 Charles of Anjou defeats Manfred, son of Emperor Frederick II, at Battle of Benevento

1268 Charles of Anjou defeats Conradin, grandson of Emperor Frederick II, at Battle of Tagliacozzo

1270 Louis IX leaves on Eighth Crusade; dies at Tunis; succession of his son, Philip III

1272 Death of Henry III of England; succession of his son, Edward I

1282 Sicilian Vespers

1285 Death of Philip III; succession of his son, Philip IV; death of Charles of Anjou

1291 Moslems take Acre, last Crusader holding in Holy Land

1294 Boniface VIII elected Pope

1296 Boniface VIII issues bull, "Clericis laicos"

1300 Boniface VIII declares Jubilee year

1302, May 18 Flemish massacre of French at Bruges

July 11 Flemish pikemen defeat French knights at the Battle of Courtrai

November Boniface VIII issues bull "Unam sanctum"

1303 Boniface VIII manhandled by men acting on orders of Philip IV; dies soon after

1305 Clement V elected Pope; establishes seat at Avignon; beginning of the "Babylonian Captivity of the Papacy"

1307   Philip IV arrests Templars; Edward I of England dies; succession of his son, Edward II

1314, March 19   Jacques de Molay, last head of the Templars, burned at the stake
April 20   Death of Pope Clement V
October 29   Death of Philip IV; succession of his son, Louis X

1316   Death of Louis X; posthumous succession of his new-born son, John I, who quickly dies and is succeeded by his uncle, Philip V

1322   Death of Philip V; succession of his brother, Charles IV

1324   First use of cannon in warfare, at Ghent

1327   Deposition of Edward II of England; succession of his minor son, Edward III

1328   Death of Charles IV, end of direct Capetian line; succession of his cousin, Philip VI of Valois; Philip VI defeats Flemish pikemen at the Battle of Cassel

1330   Edward III of England begins personal rule

1334   Robert of Artois goes to England to stir up war

1337, May   Philip VI declares English possessions in Guienne forfeit
October   Edward III of England declares himself King of France; beginning of the Hundred Years' War

1340   Edward III destroys French Fleet in the naval Battle of Sluys

1346, July 12   Edward III lands in Normandy
August 26   Edward III defeats French at the Battle of Crécy

1347   Edward III takes Calais; Black Death enters western Europe from Crimea

1349   Philip VI buys Dauphiné; his son becomes first Dauphin

1350   Death of Philip VI; succession of his son, John II

1351   Black Death subsides

1353   Pedro the Cruel of Castile marries Blanche of Bourbon

1355   Estates-General meets in Paris; Etienne Marcel leader of the middle class

1356   Black Prince Edward defeats French at the Battle of Poitiers; takes John II prisoner

1358   Peasant rising (Jacquerie) in France; Marcel murdered

1359   Edward III of England lands in Calais; lays unsuccessful siege to Rouen

1360   Edward III lays siege to Paris; army badly damaged on "Black Monday," April 14; Treaty of Bretigny signed, awarding Aquitaine to England

1361   Philip the Bold, son of John II, becomes Duke of Burgundy

1364   Death of John II; succession of his son, Charles V; Bertrand du Guesclin destroys power of the French rebel, Charles the Bad of Navarre

1367 Black Prince Edward defeats the French at the Battle of Nájera

1369 Du Guesclin defeats Pedro of Castile at the Battle of Montiel

1370 Black Prince Edward takes Limoges

1376 Death of Black Prince Edward

1377 Death of Edward III of England; succession of his grandson, Richard II

1378 Death of Pope Gregory XI in Rome; start of Great Schism

1380 Death of Du Guesclin; death of Charles V; succession of his minor son, Charles VI, with the new king's uncles in control

1382 Philip the Bold of Burgundy defeats Flemish pikemen at the Battle of Roosebeke

1384 Philip the Bold of Burgundy succeeds as Count of Flanders; Burgundy and Flanders united in a rich domain

1387 Death of Charles the Bad of Navarre

1388 Charles VI begins personal rule

1389 Ottoman Turks defeat Serbs at the Battle of Kossovo; take over the Balkans

1392 Charles VI goes mad

1396 Turks defeat French knights under John of

Nevers (son of Philip the Bold of Burgundy) at the Battle of Nicopolis

1399 Deposition of Richard II of England; succession of his cousin, Henry IV

1404 Death of Philip the Bold of Burgundy; succession of his son, John of Nevers (John the Fearless)

1407 Assassination of Louis of Orleans at the instigation of John the Fearless; beginning of the civil war between Armagnacs and Burgundians

1413 Charles of Orleans, son of Louis of Orleans, wins control of Paris from John the Fearless; death of Henry IV of England, succession of his son, Henry V

1415, August 14 Henry V of England invades France at Harfleur
September 22 Henry V takes Harfleur
October 25 Henry V defeats French at the Battle of Agincourt
November 23 Henry V returns triumphantly to London

1417 Henry V of England launches second invasion of France; Council of Constance ends Great Schism

1418 Parisians massacre Armagnacs and John the Fearless takes over Paris

1419 Henry V of England takes Rouen; assassination of

John the Fearless of Burgundy; succession of his son, Philip the Good

1420, May 20   Treaty of Troyes; England given all France north of the Loire River

June 2   Henry V of England marries Catherine, daughter of Charles VI

December 6   Henry V enters Paris

1421   French defeat and kill Thomas of Clarence, younger brother of Henry V at the Battle of Baugé

1422, August 31   Death of Henry V of England; succession of his infant son, Henry VI

October 21   Death of Charles VI; succession of his son, Charles VII

1423   John, Duke of Bedford, uncle of Henry VI of England, defeats French at the Battle of Cravant; death of Benedict XIII, last Avignonese claimant to the papacy

1424   John of Bedford defeats French at the Battle of Verneuil

1427   Bastard of Orleans forces English to lift siege of Montargis

1428   English begin siege of Orleans

1429, January   Joan of Arc leaves Domrémy on her mission

February 12   English defeat French at the Battle of the Herrings

February 24   Joan arrives at court of Charles VII

April 28   Joan and escort enter Orleans

May 8   English forced to lift siege of Orleans

June 28   French with Joan defeat English at the Battle of Patay; Talbot taken prisoner

June 29   Charles VII sets forth for Reims

July 17   Charles VII with Joan at side crowned at Reims

September 9   French assault on Paris, with Joan, fails

1430   Joan taken at Compiègne by Burgundians

1431, January 3   English buy Joan from Burgundians

May 30   Joan burned alive in Rouen

December 17   Henry VI of England crowned King of France in Paris

1435, September 15   Death of John, Duke of Bedford

September 20   Treaty of Arras signed between Charles VII and Philip the Good of Burgundy; end of French civil war

1437   French take Paris

1438   Pragmatic Sanction of Bourges

1439   French take Meaux, using new artillery for the first time

1440   The Praguerie rises against Charles VII and fails

1444   Truce of Tours; England

retains Normandy; Henry VI of England to marry Margaret of Anjou
1449 French retake Rouen; Charles VII has Joan's conviction reversed
1450, April 15 French defeat English at the Battle of Formigny
July 6 French take Caen
August 12 French take Cherbourg; English lose all of Normandy
1453, May 30 Turks take Constantinople; end of the Byzantine Empire
July 17 French defeat English at the Battle of Castillon; end of the Hundred Years' War
1454 Printing invented by Johann Gutenberg

INDEX

The Capetian Kings of the Direct Line

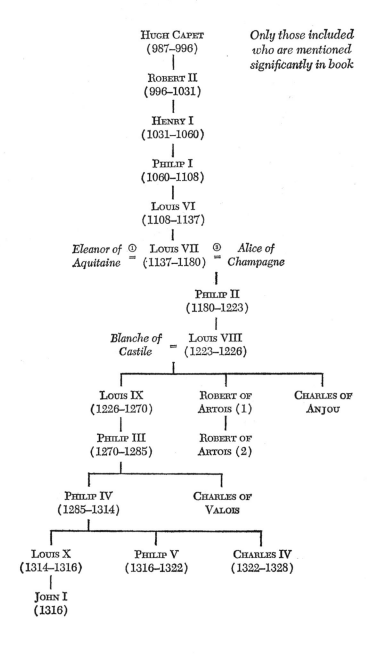

HUGH CAPET
(987–996)

Only those included who are mentioned significantly in book

ROBERT II
(996–1031)

HENRY I
(1031–1060)

PHILIP I
(1060–1108)

LOUIS VI
(1108–1137)

Eleanor of Aquitaine ① = LOUIS VII (1137–1180) ⑤ = *Alice of Champagne*

PHILIP II
(1180–1223)

Blanche of Castile = LOUIS VIII (1223–1226)

LOUIS IX
(1226–1270)

ROBERT OF ARTOIS (1)

CHARLES OF ANJOU

PHILIP III
(1270–1285)

ROBERT OF ARTOIS (2)

PHILIP IV
(1285–1314)

CHARLES OF VALOIS

LOUIS X
(1314–1316)

PHILIP V
(1316–1322)

CHARLES IV
(1322–1328)

JOHN I
(1316)

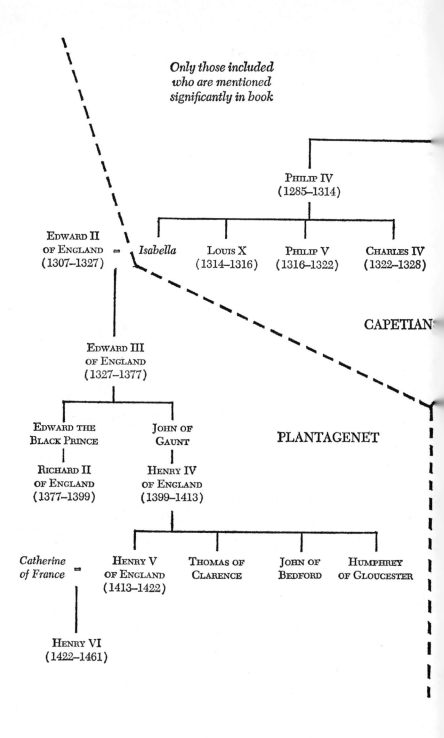

*Only those included
who are mentioned
significantly in book*

PHILIP IV
(1285–1314)

EDWARD II
OF ENGLAND   *Isabella*   LOUIS X   PHILIP V   CHARLES IV
(1307–1327)   (1314–1316)   (1316–1322)   (1322–1328)

CAPETIAN

EDWARD III
OF ENGLAND
(1327–1377)

EDWARD THE   JOHN OF   PLANTAGENET
BLACK PRINCE   GAUNT

RICHARD II   HENRY IV
OF ENGLAND   OF ENGLAND
(1377–1399)   (1399–1413)

Catherine   HENRY V   THOMAS OF   JOHN OF   HUMPHREY
of France   OF ENGLAND   CLARENCE   BEDFORD   OF GLOUCESTER
                 (1413–1422)

HENRY VI
(1422–1461)

The Valois and the Plantagenets

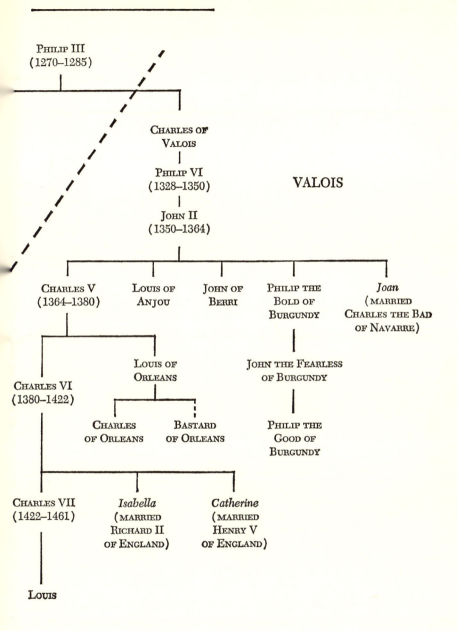

PHILIP III
(1270–1285)

CHARLES OF
VALOIS

PHILIP VI
(1328–1350)

JOHN II
(1350–1364)

VALOIS

CHARLES V
(1364–1380)

LOUIS OF
ANJOU

JOHN OF
BERRI

PHILIP THE
BOLD OF
BURGUNDY

Joan
(MARRIED
CHARLES THE BAD
OF NAVARRE)

LOUIS OF
ORLEANS

JOHN THE FEARLESS
OF BURGUNDY

CHARLES VI
(1380–1422)

CHARLES
OF ORLEANS

BASTARD
OF ORLEANS

PHILIP THE
GOOD OF
BURGUNDY

CHARLES VII
(1422–1461)

Isabella
(MARRIED
RICHARD II
OF ENGLAND)

Catherine
(MARRIED
HENRY V
OF ENGLAND)

LOUIS